Christianity and Catastrophe
in South Sudan

STUDIES IN WORLD CHRISTIANITY

The Nagel Institute for the Study of World Christianity
Calvin College

Joel A. Carpenter
Series Editor

OTHER BOOKS IN THE SERIES

Missionary Christianity and Local Religion
Arun W. Jones

The Rise of Pentecostalism in Modern El Salvador
Timothy H. Wadkins

Global Christianity and the Black Atlantic
Andrew E. Barnes

The Making of Korean Christianity
Sung-Deuk Oak

Converts to Civil Society
Lida V. Nedilsky

Evangelical Christian Baptists of Georgia
Malkhaz Songulashvili

China, Christianity, and the Question of Culture
YANG Huilin

The Evangelical Movement in Ethiopia
Tibebe Eshete

Christianity and Catastrophe in South Sudan

Civil War, Migration, and the
Rise of Dinka Anglicanism

Jesse A. Zink

BAYLOR UNIVERSITY PRESS

© 2018 by Baylor University Press
Waco, Texas 76798

All Rights Reserved. No part of this publication may be reproduced, stored in a retrieval system, or transmitted, in any form or by any means, electronic, mechanical, photocopying, recording, or otherwise, without the prior permission in writing of Baylor University Press.

Cover design by Aaron Cobbs
Cover photographs: (Top) Christian community worshipping in a cattle camp, c. 1994. Collection of Marc Nikkel. Used by permission of Durham University Library. (Bottom) Dinka woman (2014) by Tom McShane, www.tommcshanephotography.com.

Chapter 4 is a revised version of Jesse Zink, "Lost Boys, Found Church: Dinka Refugees and Religious Change in Sudan's Second Civil War," *Journal of Ecclesiastical History* 68, no. 2 (2017): 340–60. Used by permission of Cambridge University Press.

Chapter 5 is a revised version of Jesse Zink, "Women and Religion in Sudan's Civil War: Singing through Conflict," *Studies in World Christianity* 23, no. 1 (2017): 67–83. Used by permission of Edinburgh University Press.

Map 1.1, Mission spheres during the Condominium era, is from Robert O. Collins, *Land beyond the Rivers* (New Haven: Yale University Press, 1971), 294, and is used by permission.

This book has been cataloged by the Library of Congress with ISBN 978-1-4813-0822-9.

Printed in the United States of America on acid-free paper with a minimum of 30 percent post-consumer waste recycled content.

Series Foreword

It used to be that those of us from the global North who study world Christianity had to work hard to make the case for its relevance. Why should thoughtful people learn more about Christianity in places far away from Europe and North America? The Christian religion, many have heard by now, has more than 60 percent of its adherents living outside of Europe and North America. It has become a hugely multicultural faith, expressed in more languages than any other religion. Even so, the implications of this major new reality have not sunk in. Studies of world Christianity might seem to be just another obscure specialty niche for which the academy is infamous, rather like an "ethnic foods" corner in an American grocery store.

Yet the entire social marketplace, both in North America and in Europe, is rapidly changing. The world is undergoing the greatest transregional migration in its history, as people from Africa, Asia, Latin America, and the Pacific region become the neighbors down the street, across Europe and North America. The majority of these new immigrants are Christians. Within the United States, one now can find virtually every form of Christianity from around the world. Here in Grand Rapids, Michigan, where I live and work, we have Sudanese Anglicans, Adventists from the Dominican Republic, Vietnamese Catholics, Burmese Baptists, Mexican Pentecostals, and Lebanese Orthodox Christians—to name a few of the Christian traditions and movements now present.

Christian leaders and institutions struggle to catch up with these new realities. The selection of a Latin American pope in 2013 was in some respects the culmination of decades of readjustment in the Roman Catholic Church. Here in Grand Rapids, the receptionist for the Catholic bishop answers the telephone first in Spanish. The worldwide Anglican communion is being fractured over controversies concerning sexual morality and biblical authority. Other churches in worldwide fellowships and alliances are treading more carefully as new leaders come forward and challenge northern assumptions, both liberal and conservative.

Until very recently, however, the academic and intellectual world has paid little heed to this seismic shift in Christianity's location, vitality, and expression. Too often, as scholars try to catch up to these changes, says the renowned historian Andrew Walls, they are still operating with "pre-Columbian maps" of these realities.

This series is designed to respond to that problem by making available some of the coordinates needed for a new intellectual cartography. Broad-scope narratives about world Christianity are being published, and they help to revise the more massive misconceptions. Yet much of the most exciting work in this field is going on closer to the action. Dozens of dissertations and journal articles are appearing every year, but their stories are too good and their implications are too important to be reserved for specialists only. So we offer this series to make some of the most interesting and seminal studies more accessible, both to academics and to the thoughtful general reader. World Christianity is fascinating for its own sake, but it also helps to deepen our understanding of how faith and life interact in more familiar settings.

So we are eager for you to read, ponder, and enjoy these Baylor Studies in World Christianity. There are many new things to learn, and many old things to see in a new light.

Joel A. Carpenter
Series Editor

To all the peoples of South Sudan,
that they may know peace.

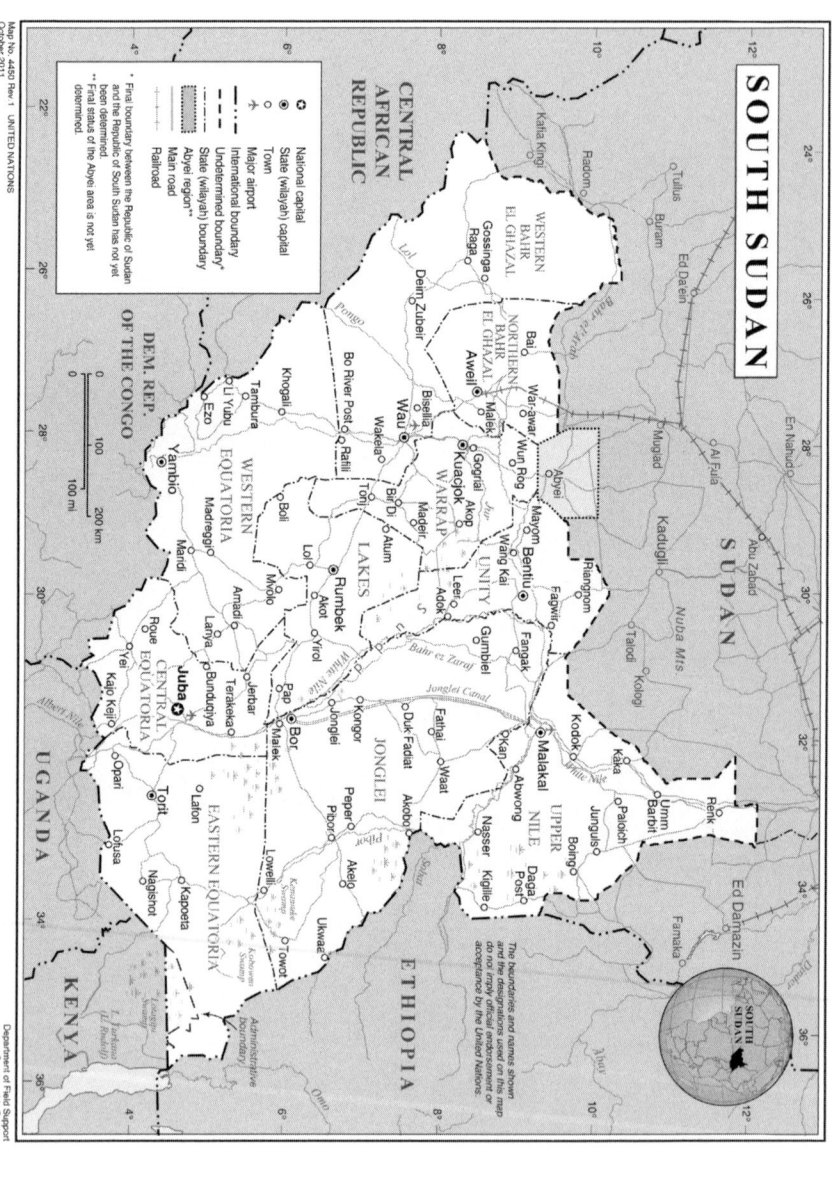

Map 1
The Republic of South Sudan at independence, July 2011

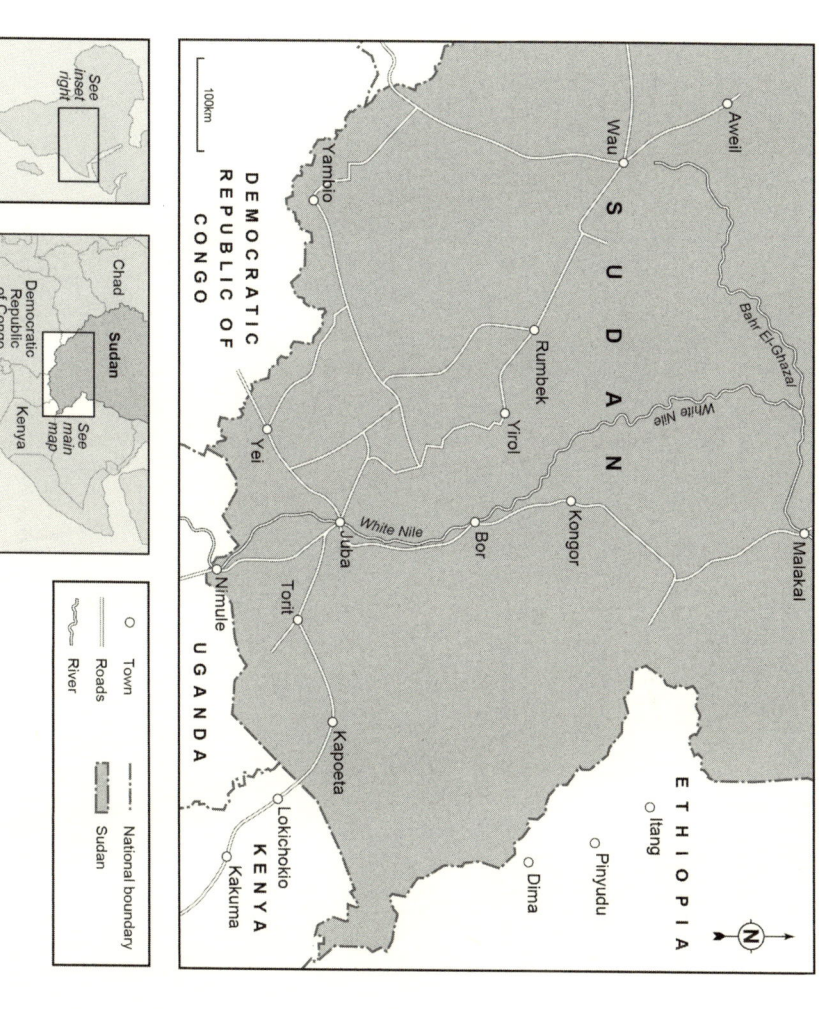

Map 2
Primary area of focus of book

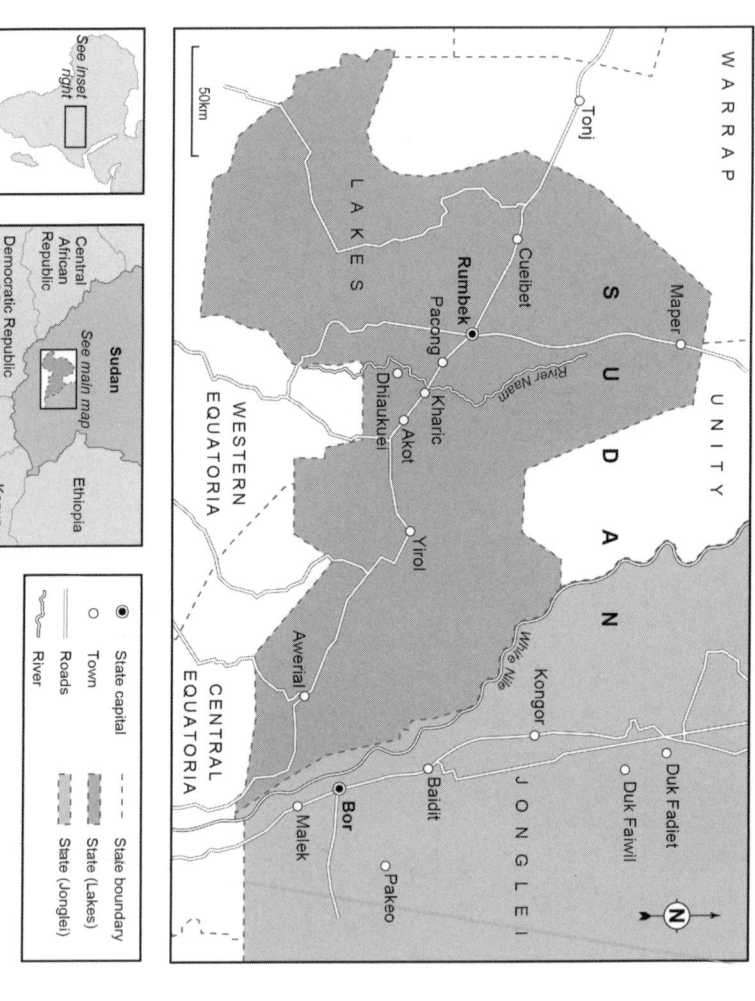

Map 3
Dinka communities on east and west banks of the White Nile

Contents

Dinka Orthography, Names, and Vocabulary	xiii
Abbreviations	xvii
List of Images and Maps	xix
Preface	xxiii

	Introduction *Religion and Civil War in Sub-Saharan Africa*	1
1	Religious Encounter in the Anglo-Egyptian Condominium	11
2	A Scattered Church *Independence, Civil War, and Migration*	35
3	Like a Rain Which Comes Suddenly *Grassroots Religious Change in Sudan's "Liberated Areas"*	59
4	Lost Boys, Found Church *Displacement and Conversion in Ethiopia and Kenya*	97
5	Singing through Civil War *Women's Leadership and Theological Reflection in a Growing Church*	133
6	Prophets of Judgment and Change *Isaiah, Archibald Shaw, and the Evolution of Nilotic Prophecy*	163

7	Prophet and Place *Continuity and Change in Dinka Anglicanism*	187
Conclusion *Christianity and Catastrophe*		217
Appendix: A Note on Methodology and Sources		227
Bibliography		231
Index		249

Dinka Orthography, Names, and Vocabulary

The language of the Dinka people is known as *Thɔngjieng* (*Thuɔŋjäŋ*). One linguist divides it into four dialects: Rek, Agar, Bor, and Padang.[1] The Summer Institute of Linguistics' *Ethnologue* divides Rek to produce five dialects: Northeastern (Padang), Northwestern (Rek), South Central (Agar), Southeastern (Bor), and Southwestern (Rek).[2] The lack of agreement is a reflection of the language's diversity and lack of standardization. There is no standard orthography, and writing conventions vary. There are some 78 different vowel sounds.[3] This book is concerned primarily with the Bor and Agar dialect groups, though the vocabulary used is widely understood across all dialects. In the list below, I have included the Dinka words used in this book, spelled in both English transcription and the Dinka alphabet. In the text of the book, I have generally retained breathing marks for vowels but used the English transcription of some Dinka letters for ease of reading. Thus "ŋ" is rendered as "ng." The letter "c" is frequently pronounced as "ch." As I have spelled names in accordance with how individuals spell them, this means that the name Acol Deng, for instance, is spelled as Achol Deng. I have retained the Dinka

---

[1] Job Malou, *Dinka Vowel System* (Dallas: Summer Institute of Linguistics, 1988), 1.
[2] "Dinka," *The Ethnologue*, http://www.ethnologue.com/language/din.
[3] Malou, *Dinka Vowel System*, ix.

vowels "ɛ" and "ɔ" The former is pronounced like the "e" in "let" and the latter like the "aw" sound in "saw."

Dinka names are patronymic. Thus Akurdit Ngong Akurdit refers to a man given the name Akurdit, who was the son of Ngong and the grandson of Akurdit. At Christian baptism, many Dinka took biblical names. Akurdit became Reuben Akurdit Ngong Akurdit. In a facsimile of Western naming practice, this is often shortened to Reuben Akurdit, though in practice he remains universally known as Akurdit. Such naming practices make subsequent references and alphabetization difficult. Initial references are to the full name. In subsequent references, I followed local custom in referring to people. Nathaniel Garang Anyieth becomes variously Garang, Garang Anyieth, or Bishop Nathaniel, while Benjamin Mangar Mamur becomes Mangar Mamur. In the bibliography and elsewhere, I have alphabetized according to the first Dinka name.

The following is a glossary of Dinka words and phrases used in this book. The spelling in Dinka characters, if applicable, appears in parentheses.

agayth: sub-group of *Jo Wo Liec*

aloong (*alooŋ*): a sub-group of *Jo Wo Liec* related to music

bëny bith: master of the fishing spear

Bung de Diɛt ke Duɔ̈ɔ̈r (*Buŋde Diɛt ke Duɔ̈ɔ̈r*): Book of Songs for Worship, a Dinka hymnal

gäm ë rou: second promise (in relation to baptismal preparation)

gäm ë tök: first promise (in relation to baptismal preparation)

jɔk (sing.), *jak* (pl.): local divinity

Jo Wo Liec (*Jɔl wɔ liec*): literally, "Turn back on us"; also a Dinka Anglican youth organization

jɔngrac (*jɔŋrac*): evil spirit

Jɔngdït Lajik (*Jɔŋdït Lajik*): Holy Spirit

jur (sing.), *juur* (pl.): those who are not Dinka, foreigners

lek: (good) news; the gospel

Lierpiɔu (or *Lirpiɔu*): name of a prominent *jɔk* among some Dinka on the east bank of the Nile River

luak: cattle byre

luang de guëër (*luaŋde guëër*): gathering byre (i.e., church)

luängic (*luäŋyic*): a sub-group of *Jo Wo Liec*

mën: central post that supports a *luak*

Muɔnyjieng or *Jieng* (*Muɔnyjiëŋ* or *Jiëŋ*): the Dinka people

Nhialic: God, the heavenly one

paweɛr: scattering (a kind of *riäk*)

ran ë Nhialic: person of divinity or a prophet

riäk: catastrophe, disaster

Thuɔngjieng (*Thuɔŋjäŋ*): the language of the Dinka people

tiet (*tiët*) (sing.), *tit* (pl.): ritual expert

toc (sing.), *toic* (*tuɔc*) (pl.): seasonal grazing land

Thiec Nhialic: literally, "Beseech God"; also a Dinka Anglican women's group

Tuk Yinhiɔl: literally, "Bow down"; also the "prayer warriors" of *Thiec Nhialic*

wut (sing.), *wuöt* (pl.): cattle camp; also a closely related kinship group

yath (sing.), *yiëth* (pl.): spirits

yang apar (*yaŋ apar*): a famine year (1986) where people ate *apar* plants

Abbreviations

ACOA	Anglican Communion Office Archive
BDD	*Bung de Diɛt ke Duɔ̈ɔ̈r*
BGC	Bishop Gwynne College
CCCWA	Cambridge Centre for Christianity Worldwide Archive, Cambridge, UK
CMS	Church Missionary Society (Anglican)
CMSA	Church Missionary Society Archive, Birmingham, UK
CPA	Comprehensive Peace Agreement
ECS	The Episcopal Church of the Sudan (Anglican)
GMSM	Gordon Memorial Sudan Mission (CMS)
JWL	Jo Wo Liec
NSCC	New Sudan Council of Churches
NSCCA	New Sudan Council of Churches Archive, Juba, South Sudan
SAD	Sudan Archive, Durham, UK
SAF	Sudan Armed Forces
SPLA	Sudan People's Liberation Army
SSNA	South Sudan National Archive, Juba, South Sudan
SUM	Sudan United Mission
UN	United Nations

UNHCR United Nations High Commissioner for Refugees
UNHCRA United Nations High Commissioner for Refugees Archive, Geneva, Switzerland
VFM Verona Fathers Mission (Roman Catholic)

List of Images and Maps

Map 1   The Republic of South Sudan at independence, July 2011. The United Nations, Department of Field Support, Geospatial Information Section. Used by permission.

Map 2   Primary area of focus of book. Prepared by Department of Geography, Cambridge University.

Map 3   Dinka communities on east and west banks of the White Nile. Prepared by Department of Geography, Cambridge University.

Figure 1.1   Dinka cattle camp, c. 1960. Cambridge University Library, Royal Commonwealth Society Collection, CMS/9/7/5. Used by permission.

Map 1.1   Mission spheres during the Condominium era. Robert O. Collins, *Land beyond the Rivers* (New Haven: Yale University Press, 1971), 294. Used by permission.

Figure 1.2   Roll call at Malek school, c. 1940s. Cambridge University Library, Royal Commonwealth Society Collection, CMS 30/23. Used by permission.

Figure 2.1   Church service at cattle camp on east bank of Nile River, c. 1950. Cambridge University Library, Royal Commonwealth Society Collection, CMS/9/1/17. Used by permission.

xx — List of Images and Maps

Figure 2.2   Bishop Daniel Deng Atong with the Rev. Kedhekiah Barac Mabior at the latter's ordination as deacon in Rumbek, Palm Sunday 1957. Cambridge University Library, Royal Commonwealth Society Collection, CMS/9/1/45. Used by permission.

Figure 3.1   Bishop Nathaniel Garang Anyieth, c. 1992. Collection of Nathaniel Garang Anyieth. Used by permission.

Figure 3.2   Reuben Maciir Makoi, c. 1994. Collection of Marc Nikkel. Used by permission of Durham University Library.

Figure 3.3   Church school in the west-bank community of Kharic, 1991. Collection of Marc Nikkel. Used by permission of Durham University Library.

Figure 3.4   Christian community worshipping in a west-bank cattle camp, c. 1994. Collection of Marc Nikkel. Used by permission of Durham University Library.

Figure 4.1   Dinka children in Pinyudu, c. 1988. Collection of Erik Gunnar Eriksson. Used by permission of Star of Hope® and the estate of Erik Gunnar Eriksson.

Figure 4.2   Teacher in a classroom in Itang Refugee Camp, December 1990. Collection of Timothy Biles. Used by permission.

Figure 4.3   The Rev. Peter Bol Arok with members of Christian community in Itang, 1990. Collection of Timothy Biles. Used by permission.

Figure 4.4   Zone 3 church in Kakuma Refugee Camp, c. 1994. Collection of Marc Nikkel. Used by permission of Durham University Library.

Figure 4.5   Ordination of Anglican clergy by Bishop Nathaniel Garang Anyieth at Adoor, Sudan, outside Aweil, April 1998. Collection of Marc Nikkel. Used by permission of Durham University Library.

Figure 4.6   Anglican clergy outside Aweil, c. April 1998. Collection of Marc Nikkel. Used by permission of Durham University Library.

Figure 5.1   Mary Achol Deng, April 2013. Collection of Jesse Zink.

Figure 5.2	Women in procession with crosses at Kakuma Refugee Camp, Kenya, c. 1996. Collection of Marc Nikkel. Used by permission of Durham University Library.
Figure 5.3	Youth "attacking" a *jɔk* with crosses, Kakuma Refugee Camp, Kenya, c. 1996. Collection of Marc Nikkel. Used by permission of Durham University Library.
Figure 7.1	Kon Ajith, Reuben Akurdit Ngong, and others outside church in Bor, September 1990. Collection of Reuben Akurdit Ngong. Used by permission.
Figure 7.2	Zion church at Pakeo, c. 1994. Collection of Marc Nikkel. Used by permission of Durham University Library.
Figure 7.3	Dhiaukuei Bible School, 1994. Collection of Marc Nikkel. Used by permission of Durham University Library.

Preface

On my second visit to South Sudan, I found myself with a group of mostly Dinka clergy debating what to do for dinner. We were in the town of Wau in western South Sudan, and the group had just spent the day organizing relief supplies to be sent to the disputed border region of Abyei. People were tired and there was a question about whether to take a taxi or walk to a local shop for dinner. "I'll walk," said one of the members of our group, a senior cleric in the region. "I walked from here"—he pointed to the ground—"to Ethiopia. Then I walked to Kenya." Almost as an afterthought, he added, "That's how I became a Christian." We walked to dinner that night.

That comment remained with me, and later I asked him to tell me more about it. The story he told was characteristic of the "Lost Boys" who are the subject of the fourth chapter of this book. When this priest was forced to leave his home village as a child, he was not a Christian and knew little of the faith. First in refugee camps in Ethiopia and then later in Kenya, he became a Christian, was educated, and returned to his home as a Christian evangelist where he was now involved in leadership in the church. It was one of many similar stories I heard during my early visits to South Sudan. I had originally traveled there as a theological student to learn more about the church and its ministry in the world's newest nation. But the more time I spent talking with people, the more I became interested in the church's recent history, the trauma it had experienced, and its resilience. In those conversations this book was born.

I conducted my research in South Sudan in what in retrospect appears to be a narrow window of hope about the future of the country. In July 2011, South Sudan declared its independence from Sudan. It was the culmination of a process outlined in the 2005 Comprehensive Peace Agreement and a decision endorsed overwhelmingly in a referendum of January 2011. I was in Juba, the capital, on 9 July 2011 as the country formally declared independence. A sign I saw that day at the independence celebrations said, "From today, our identity is southern and African, not Arabic and Islamic. We are not worse Arabs but better Africans." It was characteristic of the feelings that marked that day.

Yet in December 2013, shortly after my last research visit to the country, a split in the government led to violence in Juba that spread quickly across the country, often along ethnic lines. Various efforts to stem the fighting have largely proven ineffective. At the time of this writing, parts of the country continue to be consumed by violence, new streams of refugees have sought shelter in neighboring countries, and the world's newest nation is on the verge of becoming a failed state.

The Episcopal Church of South Sudan—the successor of the Episcopal Church of the Sudan that is the focus of this book—continues to play an outsized role in South Sudanese society. The recently retired archbishop, Daniel Deng Bul, was at various moments in his ministry asked to take part in peace and reconciliation efforts. More significantly, at the grassroots level bishops and priests continue to minister to displaced communities in similar ways to those documented in this book. The Diocese of Kajo Kaji, for instance, is now displaced and is working with refugees in northern Uganda in a way that is not dissimilar from the work of the Diocese of Bor described here. More worryingly, one also hears stories of the way interethnic divisions in society continue to affect the church. As the generation of church leadership described in this book retires, there is concern over divisions in the church at a time when the nation it serves is desperately in need of unity. This book cannot address all these issues. Its focus is historical. One of the most sobering parts of writing this book was to see the clear parallels between the events of previous civil wars and events taking place today. History is not so far in the past. Only by understanding what has come before will we—South Sudanese and all those who care about and support them—be able to see the path out of the current situation.

This book is a heavily revised and expanded version of a dissertation submitted to Cambridge University in 2015. My supervisor, David

Maxwell, was instrumental in channeling my interest in and enthusiasm for Christianity in southern Sudan into the dissertation and thence this book. His guidance, questions, and challenges improved my work immensely. The growing community of scholars in Cambridge dedicated to the study of African Christianity, especially Emma Wild-Wood and James Gardom, improved the quality of my work and made the period of my research especially fruitful. I am grateful to the examiners of my dissertation, Joel Cabrita and Kevin Ward, who gave pointed and encouraging feedback. Feedback from the Audrey Richards prize committee as well as anonymous reviewers further strengthened the work and gave me new questions to pursue. Several organizations funded my study and travel to South Sudan, including Emmanuel College, the Spalding Trust, the British Institute in Eastern Africa, the Faculty of History's Lightfoot Fund, and the Episcopal Church Foundation.

In South Sudan, I am indebted to the help and assistance of countless people who took an interest in me and my work and helped me along the way. To name them all would be impossible, but I note my particular thanks to Daniel Kon Malwal and John Jurkuc Wal, who both were exemplary translators. Samuel Galuak Marial and the students at Bishop Gwynne College were always welcoming and added depth and texture to this book. Hilary Garang Deng was a warm host when I visited him in Malakal. I can only hope I repaid this hospitality during his sabbatical term in Cambridge when his insights into the Sudanese church offered me new research avenues to pursue. Malith Kur helped answer some critical final questions in Montreal. Ben Stuchbery prepared the index.

The active community of people in the north Atlantic world who are connected to South Sudan have helped sharpen my interest in this subject, including Ellen Davis, Robin Denney, Sharon Hutchinson, and Andrew Wheeler. Over a dinner of chicken and chips in Juba one night, Jo Bailey Wells perhaps unknowingly planted the thought that became the seed of this book. Sam and Marvis Bergen were generous in their hospitality when I visited Reedley, California, to learn about Marc Nikkel. Joel Carpenter and the team at Baylor University Press encouraged me in the work, offered helpful feedback, and saw the book through to publication.

My wife, Debbie, helped keep me grounded and focused and constantly encouraged me in this work.

To all, my sincere thanks.

Introduction
Religion and Civil War in Sub-Saharan Africa

By June 1989, Bishop Nathaniel Garang Anyieth had been cut off from communication with friends, supporters, and other church leaders outside his region for nearly five years. Garang was the Anglican bishop of the Diocese of Bor, a vast area on the east bank of the Nile River in southern Sudan populated by a variety of sub-tribes of the Dinka people. In December 1985, one year after his consecration as bishop, he and a majority of the civilian population of the town of Bor had been forced to flee into Bor's rural hinterland in order to escape attacks by the Sudan Armed Forces. It was the early years of Sudan's second civil war. The army of the Khartoum-based government sought to control urban areas in southern Sudan like Bor. The rebel Sudan People's Liberation Army largely controlled the rural areas to which Garang and others fled. At that time, the diocese was a small collection of congregations located in the court centers and other small towns in the region, while the dominant religious expression in the rural areas was a set of beliefs and practices that had evolved among Dinka over generations.

Cut off by a war that would eventually result in the deaths of more than two million people and the displacement of hundreds of thousands more, Garang was unable to communicate with his superiors and international supporters. But in June 1989 Garang was able to get a letter to a friend. In it, he described what had taken place in the previous four years: "God is now moving among the Dinka people. There is great change when I came among them. . . . What is going on among the people here in our country is [a] mystery to them, and it is unknown to the world. One can burn his or her idol and come into the church or call Christians to burn it. You can see the cross everywhere. Many churches are being opened. Many new Christian songs are being composed in a great number, very very spiritual songs."[1] Dinka religious expression was changing rapidly, away from a religion of "idols" and towards Christianity. Nine months later, in a letter of appeal to Archbishop of Canterbury Robert Runcie, Garang wrote: "during this terrible time of seemingly uninterrupted suffering, God in His own plan is doing wonders in our country the Sudan. It is surprising to notice that there are more converts to Christianity now than any other time, particularly in the Southern Sudan, especially the Dinka Nationality."[2]

The changes that Nathaniel Garang described were one part of a movement of religious change the scale and rapidity of which have little parallel in the history of independent Africa. In the middle of civil war, in territory both within Sudan and among refugees who had been displaced across international borders, in communities led by women and men, young and old, educated and not, Dinka people on both the east and west banks of the Nile River repudiated the beliefs and practices of their traditional religion and turned in large numbers to Christianity, particularly the forms provided by the Episcopal Church of the Sudan, a denomination established by British missionaries and a member province of the Anglican Communion.

This book is the story of that religious change, tracing how an African people, the Dinka, once known by missionaries for their "resistance" to the gospel, turned to Christianity. It is a portrait of a church in crisis, shattered by the catastrophic impacts of civil war and at the same time encountering large numbers of potential converts and unsure how to respond. It is the account of how a mission church feebly planted by European missionaries became a grassroots indigenous movement that spoke clearly to the needs of its people at a time of immense trauma. It is the story of how a people, in the midst of violence, found in Christianity new answers and new resources to help them survive in a changed world.

* * *

Since the end of the colonial period in the 1950s and 1960s, many African countries have been formed and deformed by extended periods of

[1] Nathaniel Garang Anyieth, letter to Marc Nikkel, 30 June 1989 (NSCCA).
[2] Nathaniel Garang Anyieth, letter to Robert Runcie, 27 March 1990 (NSCCA).

conflict and civil war. Indeed, in many places, such as Mozambique, Angola, or Somalia, war became less an anomalous occurrence than a defining feature of a generation or more. Sudan fits this pattern. In 1955, months before formal independence, a mutiny in Torit in the far south sounded the first note in what became a lengthy civil war that spanned the 1960s and pitted a Khartoum-based government in the north against a rebel army in the south. After a decade of peace in the 1970s, a second civil war began in 1983 with an army mutiny in Bor, the seat of Nathaniel Garang's diocese. This second civil war was far more destructive than the first and ended only with the signing of a Comprehensive Peace Agreement in 2005. In addition to the millions who were killed, huge numbers of people were forced to leave their homes, whether to new settlements in southern Sudan, to a vast urban fringe around Khartoum, or across international borders to Ethiopia, Kenya, and Uganda.

African civil war has been studied from political, economic, and other perspectives. But the religious implications of civil war have rarely been considered.[3] On one level, this is a curious omission. Studies of Christian conversion during the colonial period have noted the ways in which religion changes and develops against the backdrop of turmoil in society, whether that backdrop be outbreaks of influenza or the bubonic plague or the chaos caused by the advent of colonialism.[4] Civil war is a new manifestation of past examples of social chaos. The prolonged civil war in southern Sudan made violence an ongoing social reality to which various communities adapted in different ways in different times, much as communities had in the past to other instances of social turmoil.[5] It should not be surprising that such social turmoil would have religious implications.

On another level, however, the silence on religion and civil war is less surprising. Most studies of African religious change are confined to the colonial period, whereas civil war as commonly understood is

[3] I am aware of a few works outside of the context of Africa that have linked religious change to civil war and societal crisis, from both academic and confessional perspectives. These include Virginia Garrard-Burnett, *Protestantism in Guatemala: Living in the New Jerusalem* (Austin: University of Texas Press, 1998), esp. 120–37, and Don Cormack, *Killing Fields, Living Fields: An Unfinished Portrait of the Cambodian Church—The Church That Would Not Die* (Crowborough, UK: OMF International, 1997).

[4] E.g., J. D. Y. Peel, *Religious Encounter and the Making of the Yoruba* (Bloomington: Indiana University Press, 2000), 47–87.

[5] Stephen C. Lubkemann, *Culture in Chaos: An Anthropology of the Social Condition in War* (Chicago: University of Chicago Press, 2008).

a feature of post-colonial African society. The difficulty of conducting research in a post-conflict setting poses further difficulties. The lengthy duration of many civil wars means that their impacts on society can be subtle, complex, and often contradictory. In the case of Sudan, war had an impact on gendered and generational relations, prompted new patterns of migration, and led people to ask new questions about their social existence and cosmological beliefs. Nor is the impact of war uniform. The effects of Sudan's civil wars were felt with varying degrees of severity in different parts of the country. Although Nathaniel Garang was cut off from contact for several years in the 1980s, at that time the impact of the war on his region was relatively weak. For all its destructiveness, there were aspects of social existence during the civil war that remained largely unaffected by warfare. The study of the impact of war must also be a study of areas where war's impact was weak.

The connection between religion and civil war may be a new field, but there is a long history of Africanist scholarship on religious change. One view connects religious change with the need people have to make meaning in a changing world. This intellectualist approach argues that religious change results from changes in society and the failure of existing religious understandings to come to terms with those changes. In an African context, this view has been most influentially articulated by the anthropologist Robin Horton.[6] Horton and others have argued that as social change came to sub-Saharan Africa, whether through trade, migration, or some other factor, more Africans would leave behind a religion centered on lesser spirits and turn toward a religious life that emphasized a single supreme being. A religion of lesser spirits is useful for social life in a local community—the "microcosm"—but as people become drawn toward a cosmopolitan "macrocosm" religious change is one natural result. While Horton's thesis has been the subject of sustained challenge, this "shattered microcosm" theory offers at least one central insight into religion: for Horton, religious change is explained by the need that people have to seek "explanation, prediction, and control of events in a new and unfamiliar situation."[7] Such power comes from

---

[6] Robin Horton, "African Conversion," *Africa* 41, no. 2 (1971); Horton, "On the Rationality of Conversion," *Africa* 45, no. 3 (1975).

[7] Horton, "African Conversion," 94. For critiques of Horton, see Humphrey J. Fisher, "Conversion Reconsidered: Some Historical Aspects of Religious Conversion in Black Africa," *Africa* 43, no. 1 (1973); Caroline Ifeka-Moller, "White Power: Social-Structural Factors in Conversion to Christianity in Eastern Nigeria,

several sources. Studies of Christian conversion have emphasized the ways in which converts prized the new resources it offered, whether literacy, biomedicine, military might, or some other factor.[8] To study religious change, therefore, is to study the resources that converts find in their new religion. This is only possible when the sorts of resources and tools that are considered valuable in the society are understood. Religious change is understood best in terms of criteria set by the converts.[9]

The resources of a religion are more than just material; they can include the narratives and ideas that shape a cosmology. Horton himself was largely dismissive of the content of religion, but others have argued persuasively that Christianity introduced "completely new concepts to the African religious repertory," such as a belief in life after death and an eschatological emphasis more generally.[10] Christianity is more than a tool to help people cope with a changing world; it involves a "cosmological revolution."[11] To study ideas means that religious change does not simply consist of a people's response to deficit, loss, and need, significant as these factors may be. There are aspects of Christianity that appeal to converts independent of the social situation in which they find themselves. In examining religious change, therefore, it is important to pay attention not simply to the process by which people convert but also to the form their new religion takes—the modes of worship, indigenous literatures, and forms of church they create in new circumstances.

Any instance of religious conversion, particularly one in the midst of a civil war, is too complex to be reduced to a single cause. Throughout this book there are two perspectives on religious change that mutually reinforce one another. The framework of the intellectualist approach connects the massive social disruption of civil war with the attendant religious change. But it takes a more careful study of the actual religious encounter and, in particular, the broad array of resources—spiritual,

---

1921–1966," *Canadian Journal of African Studies* 8, no. 1 (1974); Terence Ranger, "The Local and the Global in Southern African Religious History," in *Conversion to Christianity: Historical and Anthropological Perspectives on a Great Transformation*, ed. Robert W. Hefner (Berkeley: University of California Press, 1993), 65–98.

[8] Ifeka-Moller, "White Power," 61; J. D. Y. Peel, "The Christianization of African Society: Some Possible Models," in *Christianity in Independent Africa*, ed. Edward Fasholé-Luke et al. (London: Rex Collings, 1978), 446–47.

[9] Peel, "Christianization of African Society," 447.

[10] Richard Gray, *Black Christians and White Missionaries* (New Haven: Yale University Press, 1990), 67.

[11] Gray, *Black Christians*, 69.

moral, tangible—that are found in the new religion to explain why converts remain with their new religion and engage it deeply.

Any consideration of religious change needs to answer a deceptively simple question: what does religious change mean? How is it possible to know when people have changed their religion? European missionaries made religious change—conversion—the goal of their work, and many had a particular understanding of what this entailed. Anglican missionaries in southern Sudan demanded that Dinka entirely reject their existing social and religious order as well as practices such as polygamy, alcohol consumption, and dancing. Few Dinka were interested in fulfilling these strictures, and, as a result, missionaries came to believe they were having little success. They pinned their hope on the small handful of converts who made it through a rigorous and lengthy process to baptism. Yet even though the formal church was small, there was still a number of people who were affected by Christian ideas and discourse outside the church. When Dinka did begin to turn to official forms of Christianity in large numbers during the second civil war, they retained many aspects of their existing religious practices, including an emphasis on inspired religious leaders known as prophets and, in some instances, polygamy. To many missionaries of a previous generation this would have looked like an instance of insufficient religious change. Yet to the converts themselves it was an important moment of rupture and, indeed, conversion in their lives. What these perspectives demonstrate is that assessing religious change in another person is a difficult task. Thus, the most fruitful approach to understanding religious change and conversion is that of self-description. People who call themselves Christian and assert they have changed their religion are worthy of study as instances of religious change.

However conceived, the relationship of religious change and civil war raises several key themes to which this book will repeatedly return. The first is migration. The movement of people is by no means unusual in the history of sub-Saharan Africa. From freed slaves returning home to West Africa or migrant laborers seeking economic opportunity in the mines of southern Africa, movement has been a way in which Africans have responded to social change and sought new opportunities. By moving, these people shape and change society, including its religious life. Some freed slaves, such as Samuel Ajayi Crowther in Nigeria, returned home as Christian missionaries. Migrant laborers in South Africa sought new forms of religious expression and took them home with them, leading to the spread of early Pentecostal and Zionist churches across the country. Yet migration induced by war—often called displacement—is frequently placed in an analytically separate category.[12] The displaced are thought to lack agency, to have moved for reasons beyond their control, simply biding their time and waiting until they can return home. Yet in the case of southern Sudan, some Dinka used their time of displacement actively to respond to the war and prepare for the future. Displacement may have been a response to catastrophe, but it proved to be a generative period as well. The particular patterns of migration that were set in motion by the war and their similarities and differences with other forms of migration in African history are crucial to understanding the connection between religious change and civil war in southern Sudan.

The second theme is the immense social damage caused by warfare. War upends traditional means of production, calls generational relations into question, and forces a search for new means of survival. In the midst of these changes, people begin to look for new tools, resources, and opportunities. This pursuit of new models of living has impacts not only on how people survive but also on what they believe about the world around them. Warfare can cause people to question their beliefs about the nature of the world, the cosmos, and their place in it. This search for new resources of both a practical, this-worldly variety and a religious, other-worldly kind leads individuals and communities to consider new religious options.

A third and final theme concerns the nature of these new religious expressions. In the study of African religion, Christianity has often been used as a cipher for other concerns. Some studies of East African pastoralist peoples, including the Dinka, for instance, have sought to use their resistance to Christianity to make larger points about Marxism.[13] In the midst of such studies, it is easy to downplay the importance of religious piety and passion and the content of religious belief. Yet to spend even a little time with Christians in sub-Saharan Africa is to be convinced of the centrality of religious belief and practice to their lives. The actual content of religion is an important area of focus in its own right. That means it is important to look at what people believe and how this is expressed: the hymns they sing, the sermons they preach, and the actions

---

[12] Lubkemann, *Culture in Chaos*, 15–21.
[13] John W. Burton, "Christians, Colonists, and Conversion: A View from the Nilotic Sudan," *The Journal of Modern African Studies* 23, no. 2 (1985): 349–69.

they undertake in the name of their faith. Scholars who heed this passion and piety tend to focus on so-called independent churches or a newer generation of African-founded Pentecostal churches. Yet Christians of "mainline" or historic mission-founded denominations, such as Catholics, Methodists, or Anglicans, deserve this attention too. As a social and cultural history of the ways in which an Anglican mission became an African church, this book joins others in insisting that the study of mission-derived forms of Christianity is important in its own right and in challenging the historic divisions of African churches into mission and independent denominations.[14] At the level of popular religion, these distinctions begin to dissolve. Studying religion is particularly important in relation to South Sudan.[15] While there has been extensive study of the Sudans from political, security, economic, and other perspectives, it is only in recent years that the scholarly focus has shifted to its social history.[16] Yet such social life must surely be studied in order to understand the future directions of South Sudan.

These recurring themes—migration, the damage of war, and religious passion—provide the grounding for the arguments that are threaded throughout this book. First, the civil war created patterns of migration that led to a growing Dinka Christian movement, which was particularly strong among young people and women. Violence displaced urban residents to rural areas, rural residents to remote areas, and all kinds of people across international borders. Such movement scrambled traditional societal divisions and generated relationships between people who would not otherwise have interacted. This led to Christian conversion. Second, the civil war so devastated Dinka agropastoralism that it

---

[14] Terence Ranger, "New Approaches to the History of Mission Christianity," in *African Historiography: Essays in Honour of Jacob Ade Ajayi*, ed. Toyin Falola (Harlow, UK: Longman, 1993); Emma Wild-Wood, *Migration and Christian Identity in Congo (DRC)* (Leiden: Brill, 2008).

[15] South Sudan became an independent country on 9 July 2011. From 1973 to 1983 and from 2005 to 2011, it was an autonomous, self-governing region known as Southern Sudan. Since the activity in this book takes place prior to independence, I refer to the region as southern Sudan.

[16] Cherry Leonardi, *Dealing with Government in South Sudan: Histories of Chiefship, Community and State* (Woodbridge, UK: James Currey, 2013); Brendan R. Tuttle, "Life Is Prickly: Narrating History, Belonging, and Common Place in Bor, South Sudan" (Ph.D. dissertation, Temple University, 2013); Zoe Cormack, "The Making and Remaking of Gogrial: Landscape, History and Memory in South Sudan" (Ph.D. dissertation, Durham University, 2014).

caused many Dinka to look for new resources in a social environment in which it became clear that existing ways of life were no longer sufficient. One result was the widespread repudiation of existing religious beliefs in favor of Christian narratives. Older pieties were no longer seen as providing a secure basis for the new world in which Dinka found themselves. Third, the popular Dinka Christianity that emerged maintained deep resonance in its religious institutions and practices with the preceding non-Christian religion. The Dinka institution of prophecy, for instance, shaped how new Christians understood the Bible and Christian history, while Christianity shaped the work of a new generation of prophets. In a sense, then, religious change among the Dinka also involved a changing of religions, in that aspects of both Christianity and the non-Christian religion came together into a new creation. Fourth and finally, the new Dinka Christianity was rooted in the creation of a new narrative of sacred story and sacred place. New holy sites and new readings of Christian history and the Dinka past allowed Dinka to embrace Christianity.

The Dinka are one of several Nilotic people groups in southern Sudan. Many experienced some form of religious change during Sudan's second civil war. The focus of this book, however, is not only on the Dinka but more specifically on the large swath of Dinka territory that was allotted during the colonial period to the Anglican Church Missionary Society (CMS). This region straddles the White Nile River and includes the Bor, Twic, Ghol, Nyarweng, Agar, Cic, and Aliab subgroups. This book refers to Bor, Twic, Ghol, and Nyarweng as east-bank Dinka, and Agar, Cic, and Aliab as west-bank Dinka in reference to their location on the White Nile.[17] By focusing on the CMS mission sphere, the book also focus on Dinka Anglicanism. Although a large Catholic mission was active during the colonial period among Dinka further west, as were some some small evangelical Protestant missions, the energy of Dinka Christianity today is found in the Episcopal Church of South Sudan. Anglican churches are found in some of the country's most remote places. Dinka Catholicism is confined primarily to towns and larger conurbations and awaits further study.

---

[17] Political divisions in southern Sudan have frequently changed and, following the creation of new states in 2015, have changed yet again. The west-bank territory has often been part of a larger region known as Bahr el Ghazal, though more recently has been part of the smaller Lakes State. The east-bank territory has been part of a region known at times both as Upper Nile and Jonglei.

Dinka remember the civil war as a *riäk*, a supple word that can refer to drought, flood, epidemic or armed conflict and refers generally to spoliation, destruction, or catastrophe. Dinka said about the war what earlier generations said about the arrival of other outsiders: *"piny eci riäk"*—catastrophe has come to the land.[18] This *riäk* is the crucial variable in this analysis. It was the catastrophe of civil war that changed patterns of movement among the Dinka, forced them to look for new sources of power, cut them off from the larger world, and allowed for the emergence of a mixed Christianity that brought together different elements of religious expression into one church. When widespread religious change began among the Dinka, it followed patterns seen elsewhere on the continent. But it took the *riäk* to set the process in motion.

---

[18] Cormack, "Making and Remaking of Gogrial," 26–27.

1

Religious Encounter in the Anglo-Egyptian Condominium

In 1963, a prayer circular from the Church Missionary Society (CMS) comprehensively described the fruit of nearly a half-century of mission activity in southern Sudan. Among the Zande, Moru, and some other people groups who lived in the southernmost part of the country, the church was flourishing. Among the Dinka, the story was different: "The comparatively few Dinka Christians are to be found living near the old mission stations or in the district centres. The Gospel has made little impression on the Dinka people living in the villages and cattle camps."[1] It was an important observation about the associations of Christianity with a particular social landscape: the church was found in the locations that had emerged during colonial rule—district centers and mission stations—and not in the places that were at the center of Dinka social existence—villages and cattle camps. In the early 1960s, and in light of the growth of the church elsewhere in southern Sudan and sub-Saharan Africa, CMS saw the small Dinka church as a failure of missionary effort.

That prayer circular was one moment in the lengthy history of engagement between Dinka, European missionaries, colonial officials, and other outside forces that preceded the religious change that took place among Dinka during the 1980s and 1990s. In the century and a half between the arrival of the first outsiders in the region in 1828 and the beginning of the second civil war in 1983, two major themes

---

[1] David Brown, "From Whom Should We PRAY," inserted in *Sudan Diocesan Review* 16, no. 47 (Autumn 1963): 6.

emerged. First, Dinka religion was bifurcated between a network of towns and urban areas associated with Christianity (and to a lesser extent Islam) and a social landscape of villages and cattle camps that was at the center of Dinka religious practice. Religious change was therefore connected either to the expansion of government or the migration of Dinka out of villages and cattle camps. But the penetration of colonial rule in southern Sudan was always weak. Many Dinka shared the conviction that their way of life was superior and that there was little need to adopt new ways. As a result, in contrast to the movements of mass conversion across sub-Saharan Africa during the colonial period, religious change among the Dinka was modest, halting, and weak. Second, despite the fragility of religious change, there was nonetheless by 1983 a small Dinka Anglican church in southern Sudan. It was a church and a faith that was closely associated with education and the educated, was strongly gendered in that women struggled to find a place, and above all remained tied to a social landscape of towns and other government centers that continued to be foreign to many Dinka.

This chapter and the next one jointly consider the evolution of Dinka religious practice over this long period before the outbreak of the second civil war. It is a period that is divided into two stages: first, in this chapter, the early decades of the twentieth century before World War II when governance in southern Sudan remained weak and missionary activity sputtered; second, in the next chapter, the years after World War II when more resources were devoted to the region and a church began to take shape. The early 1960s witnessed the opening years of Sudan's first civil war and saw the beginning of new processes of migration that took large numbers of Dinka, particularly young people, out of their historic social landscape. The rocky expansion of governance in the 1970s between Sudan's civil wars further changed patterns of migration and laid the groundwork for the expansion of Christianity that took place during the second war. But long before Christian missionaries arrived, Dinka in southern Sudan had evolved their own religious beliefs and practices that were well suited to the environment in which they lived. It is there that the story of Dinka religion must begin.

THE DINKA

The Dinka are a Nilotic people group who live in a region that stretches from the east bank of the White Nile River around Bor to the northwest as far as Abyei and Aweil. A separate pocket of Dinka also exists farther north along the Nile near Melut and Renk. They know themselves as *Muɔnyjieng* or simply *Jieng*, which means "the people."[2] These regions of the Upper Nile have historically been impassable. The Sudd, a mass of vegetation that blocks, diverts, and narrows the river, long stymied explorers from the north. Until well into the nineteenth century, many Dinka were largely isolated from the wider world. Nonetheless, it is possible to reconstruct some aspects of Dinka society and religion in this period.

In broad terms, African political and social systems have been divided into those that possess centralized authority, administrative machinery, and judicial institutions and those that do not. The Dinka, along with the neighboring Nuer, have long been considered to be in this latter grouping of "stateless societies."[3] Dinka society was regulated by a segmentary lineage system in which kinship ties and territorial grouping took a central role in political organization.[4] The basic unit of societal organization was the *wut* (pl. *wuöt*) or cattle camp.[5] It is a term that refers both to territory—the specific location where cattle are gathered during particular times of the year—and also to kinship—the social grouping that comprises immediate agnatic relations. Various *wuöt* could and did come together to form sub-tribes and larger groupings, but the core unit remained local. The result was a Dinka society that was acephalous and noncentralized. Across the wide geographic

---

[2] Throughout this book, I use "Dinka" rather than "Jieng," in line with other scholarship. In doing so, I acknowledge the contested and potentially pejorative origins of "Dinka."

[3] M. Fortes and E. E. Evans-Pritchard, "Introduction," in *African Political Systems*, ed. Fortes and Pritchard (London: International African Institute by Oxford University Press, 1940), 5.

[4] Evans-Pritchard's study of the segmentary lineage system among the Nuer laid the groundwork for much subsequent work on other Nilotic peoples, esp. Evans-Pritchard, *The Nuer: A Description of the Modes of Livelihood and Political Institutions of a Nilotic People* (Oxford: Clarendon, 1940). Among the Dinka, the earliest studies of this system are by Godfrey Lienhardt, "The Western Dinka," in *Tribes without Rulers: Studies in African Segmentary Systems*, ed. John Middleton and David Tait (London: Routledge & Regan Paul, 1958), 97–135.

[5] Other authors translate *wut* as "cattle village," arguing that "cattle camp" suggests impermanence. I follow common usage here and agree that cattle-keeping is a year-round activity. See Brendan Tuttle, *Life Is Prickly: Narrating History, Belonging, and Common Place in Bor, South Sudan* (Ph.D. dissertation, Temple University, 2013), 13.

FIGURE 1.1
Dinka cattle camp, c. 1960. Used by permission of Cambridge University Library, Royal Commonwealth Society Collection.

range of Dinka territory, there were and continue to be approximately 25 different sub-groups of Dinka and at least four main and mutually intelligible dialects.[6]

Across Dinka territory, some commonalities existed. The importance of the *wut* indicates the centrality of cattle to Dinka life, which outside observers have long noted:

> The [Dinka] build better houses for their cattle than they do for themselves, and take more trouble over the smoke-fires to keep the mosquitos away from the cattle than from themselves. They will sing to a favourite bull if he is restless at night, will groom him and play with him and pretend to be driven off by his horns when he leads out the herd in the morning, sacrifice small bulls to his honour and health, carve an elaborate tethering peg for him, deck him with long tassels fixed to the ends of his horns and with a collar of bells round his neck.[7]

Cattle were the currency that were exchanged in marriage and cemented family alliances. They were sacrificed in religious ritual and used to pay

[6] Lienhardt, "Western Dinka," 102.
[7] G. W. Titherington, "The Raik Dinka of Bahr El Ghazal Province," *Sudan Notes and Records* 10 (1927): 175.

debts and atone for misdeeds. Men became closely associated with a particular cow, caring for it, shaping and decorating its horns, and ultimately taking their name and identity from it.

Dinka have also long been united by a similar lifestyle, that of the transhumant agropastoralist. The Nile River and its tributaries guided Dinka life. Seasonal flooding shaped the movement of people. As rivers rose, Dinka and their cattle moved away from the rivers and into the *toc* (seasonal grazing land). As the waters receded during the dry season, the search for water drove people back closer to the rivers. The extent of this seasonal movement varied across Dinka territory. On the east bank, where elevation gain is minimal, flooding has been a significant factor. On the west bank, there is greater elevation gain and more permanency to settlements, though there is also seasonal flooding in tributaries of the Nile. Across Dinka territory, seasonal movement was complemented by agriculture in villages, some of which had a great deal of permanency.

This network of cattle camps and villages formed a social landscape that was central to what Dinka valued and considered important in their lives. To be engaged in this means of production was how Dinka knew how to survive in a difficult and unyielding environment. It was what they taught their children as well. Cattle camps in particular took on special significance as the social heart of Dinka life:

> Whatever its difficulties, being in a cattle-camp is a source of dignity and pride. When visiting a cattle-camp, usually in the evening, a Dinka feels its superior atmosphere from a distance as he sees a beacon of cow-dung fires reaching into the sky and marking the location of the camp. As one draws nearer, the singing of the men, the dancing of the children, the bellows of the herds, the jingling of the bells, the jokes and laughter all indicate the profound difference between the jubilant air of the cattle-camp and the subdued atmosphere of the home.[8]

Cattle camps were where significant cultural activities took place: Dinka men composed songs, groomed cattle, prepared religious objects, and sacrificed animals, all practices at the center of Dinka society.

Dinka religious beliefs and practices were a response to this landscape and environment. In an unforgiving terrain and with no state to guarantee one's existence, Dinka religion centered on the search for security and a measure of control. The anthropologist Godfrey Lienhardt's

---

[8] Francis Mading Deng, *The Dinka of the Sudan* (Long Grove, Ill.: Waveland, 1984/1972), 85.

classic work on Dinka religion from the mid-twentieth century is titled *Divinity and Experience*, a title that makes clear the extent to which Dinka religious beliefs are rooted, first and foremost, in the concerns of this world and the experience that shapes their lives. Dinka religion is "phenomenological rather than theological, an interpretation of signs of ultra-human activity rather than a doctrine of the intrinsic nature of the Powers behind those signs."[9] Although there could be considerable diversity in practice on such matters as male circumcision, political leadership, marriage practices, and conflict resolution, many Dinka can point to common cultural attributes, particularly in regard to religion. The Dinka scholar and diplomat Francis Mading Deng argues that the best way to see the Dinka is as politically diverse but united by "their physical characteristics, their ethnocentric pride, and their striking cultural uniformity."[10]

Lienhardt used the word "divinity" to refer to various spirits and powers in Dinka religious belief. In Lienhardt's terminology, the various divinities "image" or embody particular social experiences. Overarching all is the divinity *Nhialic*, commonly referred to as creator and father, who embodies the experience of a single community of humans: "In Divinity [i.e., *Nhialic*] the Dinka image their experience of the ways in which human beings everywhere resemble each other, and in a sense form a single community with one original ancestor created by one Creator."[11] A rightly ordered social world is a reflection of the values embodied by *Nhialic* and it is this order that Dinka religious practice seeks. The essential unity of *Nhialic* means that Dinka understand the single high gods of other religions, including Christianity, as *Nhialic* but under another name.[12]

Although *Nhialic* has an overarching importance, the primary focus of Dinka religious practice has historically been on a series of lesser divinities. One set of lesser divinities has wide geographic range. Lienhardt refers to these as free-divinities. They image experiences common across Dinka territory; the free-divinity Deng, for instance, is associated with rain. Other lesser divinities are more local in scope. *Yïeth* (sing. *yath*) are often associated with ancestors and are specific to a clan or

---

[9] Godfrey Lienhardt, *Divinity and Experience: The Religion of the Dinka* (Oxford: Clarendon, 1961), 32.
[10] Deng, *Dinka of the Sudan*, 2.
[11] Lienhardt, *Divinity and Experience*, 156–57.
[12] Lienhardt, *Divinity and Experience*, 56.

wut. A local divinity in this way images the experience of agnatic kinship.[13] Another range of lesser divinities are known as *jak* (sing. *jɔk*) and are regarded as independent local divinities.[14] Among Dinka Bor, for instance, the *jɔk Lierpiɔu* provided an enduring symbol for people of that sub-tribe. The range of divinities, therefore, allowed Dinka to image the experience of both good fortune and bad fortune. Moreover, it provided the space for flexibility and variation in Dinka religious practice. Indeed, many of these lesser divinities were believed to have initially been foreign to the Dinka, and adopted and grafted into religious practice over a period of time.[15] While there was some difference in religious practice between east-bank and west-bank Dinka, the key point is the centrality of these lesser divinities to Dinka religious practice. On the east bank in particular, *jak* were especially important to religious practice, so this book generally refers to non-Christian Dinka religion as the religion of the *jak*. Although an imperfect and incomplete description, the phrase indicates the way in which these lesser divinities were the focus of much religious energy.

The primary religious practice for Dinka was animal sacrifice, ideally of a cow though occasionally of other domesticated animals as well. In the communal act of sacrifice, Dinka could rectify a life situation that had gone wrong by embodying the proper experience of community that is represented by the divinity.[16] Sacrifice was often linked to particular locations, notably a *wut* or a village home. Lienhardt tells the story of a Dinka man who became sick while traveling. He felt a pressing urgency about returning home because it was only there that he thought he could sacrifice properly.[17] Both villages and cattle camps have shrines or other objects of religious devotion, such as a particular tree, a collection of sticks, or a peg used to tie down cattle at night. These objects became part of the devotion of Dinka religion. In addition, there were other activities associated with sacrifice, notably singing, a popular and competitive activity among a people with a weak material culture. These practices reinforced the importance of the Dinka landscape. The social landscape of cattle camps and villages at the center of Dinka society was also a sacred landscape.

---

[13] Lienhardt, *Divinity and Experience*, 167.
[14] Deng, *Dinka of the Sudan*, 122.
[15] Lienhardt, *Divinity and Experience*, 164.
[16] Lienhardt, *Divinity and Experience*, 291.
[17] Lienhardt, *Divinity and Experience*, 105.

Sacrifice and other religious ritual required a diverse class of holy people and religious specialists who historically fell along a rough continuum. On the lower end were local *tit* (sing. *tiët*) whose success depended on their reputation for efficacy in healing and sacrifice. Further along were *bëny bith* (master of the fishing spear), more common among west-bank Dinka, whose role was tied to the spear used in sacrifice to kill the animal. At the higher end of the continuum were *ran ë Nhialic* (person of Divinity) or those whom Lienhardt and other scholars have called prophets. Such prophets are believed to be possessed by a free-divinity or even *Nhialic* and, as a result, had regional appeal. Both *bëny bith* and prophets had not just religious roles but political ones as well. The dispersed and unstructured nature of political authority among the Dinka meant that the Dinka lacked a single locus of sovereignty and instead wound up with multiple centers of authority in the form of ritual experts. In concert with other older men, ritual experts exercised leadership and made decisions about, for instance, cattle movement, sharing grazing lands with others, or when to fight against opposing lineage groups and other enemies.[18] While there were regional variations in these leadership practices, there was overall little sense of positional authority. Political authority and leadership was rooted in personal charisma as well as a sense of spiritual authority.[19] Some *bëny bith* were persons of great prominence. Others were minor figures, predominantly local. Prophets, by contrast, were intensely political. As *Nhialic* represents the ideal community, so the prophet works toward a regional peace among Dinka and in doing so embodies the experience of *Nhialic* and confirms his true inspiration.[20] In the conflictual setting of southern Sudan in the nineteenth and twentieth centuries, to make such a claim was to be a political actor. For the Dinka, religious and political authority could easily overlap.

The only immortality that Dinka religion knew was that which came from the survival of one's name through one's children. Sons, therefore,

---

[18] Jok Madut Jok, *Militarization, Gender and Reproductive Health in South Sudan* (Lampeter, UK: Edwin Mellen, 1998), 109.

[19] Francis Mading Deng, "The World of the Dinka: A Portrait of a Threatened Culture," in *Traditions, Values, and Humanitarian Action*, ed. Kevin Cahill (New York: Fordham University Press, 2003), 68.

[20] Douglas Johnson, *Nuer Prophets: A History of Prophecy from the Upper Nile in the Nineteenth and Twentieth Centuries* (Oxford: Clarendon, 1994), 27–28, 33.

were greatly prized because they could bear their father's name into a subsequent generation. Eldest sons were particularly prized and given preferential treatment. Daughters could be married and, in so doing, generate cattle, which could be used for sons to contract legitimate marriages. But collective rights to a cattle herd could easily lead to generational tensions. A father might want to use cattle for multiple marriages for himself while sons, particularly those born after the eldest, were unable to marry because of insufficient cattle.

Dinka agropastoralism and religion allowed the Dinka to survive in an unyielding environment. But beginning with the annexation of Sudan in 1828 by the Ottoman Empire, ivory merchants and slave traders from Europe and the Middle East began to move past the obstacles in the river and make contact with southerners. The interaction intensified in the 1850s with the creation of permanent slave-trading centers on the west bank of the Nile. While it was the many smaller people groups in the region that bore the brunt of the trade, many western Dinka were also affected by this intrusion of new forms of governance. The opening up of southern Sudan introduced a novel religion as well. Catholic missionaries began sporadic efforts in southern Sudan, including a station among the Dinka at Holy Cross on the Nile River, founded in 1858. High mortality rates among these missionaries ensured that their impact was negligible and that their stations were soon abandoned. In the 1880s, the messianic Islamic figure Muhammad Ahmad bin Abd Allah proclaimed himself the Mahdi, conquered much of Sudan, and expelled the slave traders and remnants of the missionaries. This ensured that many Dinka were forcibly made aware that there were larger forces at work beyond the Nile floodplain.

The nineteenth century saw tremendous internal change in southern Sudan as well. In the "Nuer Conquest," the Nuer people expanded eastward across the Nile, absorbing many other peoples—notably including some Dinka—in a "python-like" fashion that confounded later attempts by the British to delineate firmly between people groups.[21] The subsequent overlap of these identities, and evidence for intermingling between

---

[21] Sharon Hutchinson, *Nuer Dilemmas: Coping with Money, War, and the State* (Berkeley: University of California Press, 1996), 37; see also Johnson, *Nuer Prophets*, 20, and Raymond C. Kelly, *The Nuer Conquest: The Structure and Development of an Expansionist System* (Ann Arbor: University of Michigan Press, 1985).

the two has long preoccupied anthropologists.[22] More significantly for this book, it raises an important question as to whether it is possible to study the Dinka in isolation from the Nuer. As will become apparent, policies pursued during the British colonial period drew sharp distinctions between Dinka and Nuer, making permanent what had been a fluidity in location, practice, and identity.[23]

For Dinka, the series of intrusions in the second half of the nineteenth century became remembered as a *riäk*, the time when "the land was spoiled and did not hold."[24] This period also saw the first reports of Dinka from foreigners. What was frequently noted in these reports was the "pride" of the Dinka. In a pejorative used against pastoralist and other African peoples who chose not to disrupt their own modes of production simply because outsiders had arrived, these reports also noted their "laziness." A Catholic missionary wrote—perhaps not entirely verbatim—of his encounter with a west-bank Dinka elder who disdainfully said he would not do agricultural work: "Am I slave? Being the owner of so many cows, it would be shameful for me to work. I am powerful! Therefore, that gives me the right to do nothing."[25] In spite of the incursions of outsiders, it was still possible to survive and thrive by the standards—marriage, sons, cattle—of Dinka culture. The rhythm of village and cattle-camp life could remain the same. For those who were not already powerful in society, some Dinka and other southerners were able to establish useful relationships with these outsiders, particularly in the communities that grew up around the slaving centers.[26] Overall, however, and particularly on the east bank of the Nile, the incursions of the outsiders remained, in the grand scheme of

---

[22] E.g., Peter J. Newcomer, "The Nuer Are Dinka: An Essay on Origins and Environmental Determinism," *Man* 7, no. 1 (1972).

[23] Douglas Johnson, "Enforcing Separate Identities in Southern Sudan: The Case of the Nilotes of the Upper Nile," in *Les ethnies ont une histoire*, ed. Jean-Pierre Chrétien and Gérard Prunier (Paris: Karthala, 1989); Robert O. Collins, *The Southern Sudan in Historical Perspective* (London: Transaction, 2006), 29–30.

[24] Quoted in Deng, *Dinka of the Sudan*, 111.

[25] Anton Kaufmann, *Das Gebiet des weissen Flusses und dessen Bewohner*, translated and compiled in *The Opening of the Nile Basin: Writings by Members of the Catholic Mission to Central Africa on the Geography and Ethnography of the Sudan, 1842–1881*, ed. Elias Toniolo and Richard Hill (London: Hurst, 1974), 155.

[26] Cherry Leonardi, *Dealing with Government in South Sudan: Histories of Chiefship, Community and State* (Woodbridge, UK: James Currey, 2013), 31–39.

things, modest. It was still possible for many Dinka to resist significant change. Dinka life remained calibrated for survival in a difficult part of the world. Incursions by foreigners came along the region's rivers. Dinka could easily retreat to the *toc* where outsiders struggled to survive.

European Mission in Southern Sudan

The British general Lord Kitchener defeated the Mahdiyya in 1898 at Omdurman. The victory led to the establishment of the Anglo-Egyptian Condominium, an ostensibly joint arrangement between England and Egypt for rule of Sudan, but one in which, in practice, the British predominated. The British were interested in Sudan because of the Nile River and its downriver importance to Egypt. Southern Sudan was important only insofar as the British had to see off rival claims from first the French and then King Leopold of Belgium to ensure the Nile waters were not disturbed.[27] Unlike other parts of sub-Saharan Africa, "neither Christianity nor commerce nor civilization played any part in the decision by British officials to seize the Upper Nile."[28] Once Britain's claims were secure from rival powers around 1907, southern Sudan received little nonmilitary attention. This was in contrast to the north, into which the Condominium invested resources to turn it into a productive colony that could pay for its own administration. As late as 1934, a senior Condominium official described the Bor region as "almost literally . . . a backwater. So far as is known it contains nothing in any exportable quantity which the outside world requires."[29]

The attention the Condominium did give the south was largely military and used to subdue rebellious populations. In Nilotic territories, these pacification campaigns were particularly brutal. In January 1902, the Agar Dinka of the west bank under the leadership of a ritual expert rebelled against Condominium rule. The British responded with a scorched-earth campaign, destroying villages, confiscating cattle, and killing leaders. The rebellion was put down, but in the aftermath many Agar died of hunger. It was the "peace of the dead."[30] In 1919, the Aliab

---

[27] Robert O. Collins, *Land beyond the Rivers: The Southern Sudan, 1898–1918* (New Haven: Yale University Press, 1971), 1–45.
[28] Collins, *Land beyond the Rivers*, 324.
[29] R. T. Johnston, "Bor District Handing Over Report," 14 April 1934 (Sudan Archive Durham [hereafter SAD] 639/12/32).
[30] Collins, *Land beyond the Rivers*, 88–91.

Dinka began a similar rebellion, which was put down with similar force. In addition to these open rebellions, some Dinka also expressed opposition to the Condominium in other ways. In 1921, many Dinka gathered around a lake near Akot, fired by fervent religious hope in the imminent return of a messianic figure.[31] Around the same time, farther west, the prophet Ariandhit emerged as a focus for opposition to Condominium rule. Although his was not a military movement, the British still feared rebellion and suppressed him in 1922. Two threads united these bursts of activity. The first was the connection between religious leadership and opposition to British rule. In a stateless society, some religious leaders were political ones as well. The second thread was the weakness of the Condominium. Its weak presence in southern Sudan meant that it generally lacked the resources to adequately provide security and other services in return for the taxes it exacted. It was the lack of such provision that contributed to the outbreaks of rebellion. In general, the major experience that many Dinka had of outsiders was in these punitive and destructive "patrols" carried out by the Condominium.

Christian missionaries were among the first Europeans to return to Khartoum following Kitchener's victory. The Verona Fathers' Mission (VFM) was a Catholic order that traced its roots to the earlier generation of missionaries in southern Sudan. But the VFM was not alone. Many English Christians had interpreted the 1885 death of Charles Gordon in Khartoum at the hands of the Mahdi as a martyrdom. The Church Missionary Society, an evangelical Anglican organization, had been raising funds for the Gordon Memorial Sudan Mission (GMSM) since Gordon's death. Their deliberate goal was to convert Muslims. Now, they believed, they had an opportunity.

But Condominium officials worried that Christian proselytism in northern Sudan might spark a return of religious-inspired resistance to foreign rule. Lord Cromer, consul-general of Egypt, directed the missionaries south. He wrote to CMS headquarters in London in 1904, "The time is still distant when Mission work can, with safety and advantage, be permitted among the Muslim population. . . . The case of the southern provinces of the Sudan is widely different. In these regions, not only is there no reason for imposing any restrictions on missionary enterprise, but the Sudan Government would welcome the co-operation of missionaries in

---

[31] V. H. Fergusson, "The Holy Lake of the Dinka," *Sudan Notes and Records* 5, no. 2 (1922): 163–66.

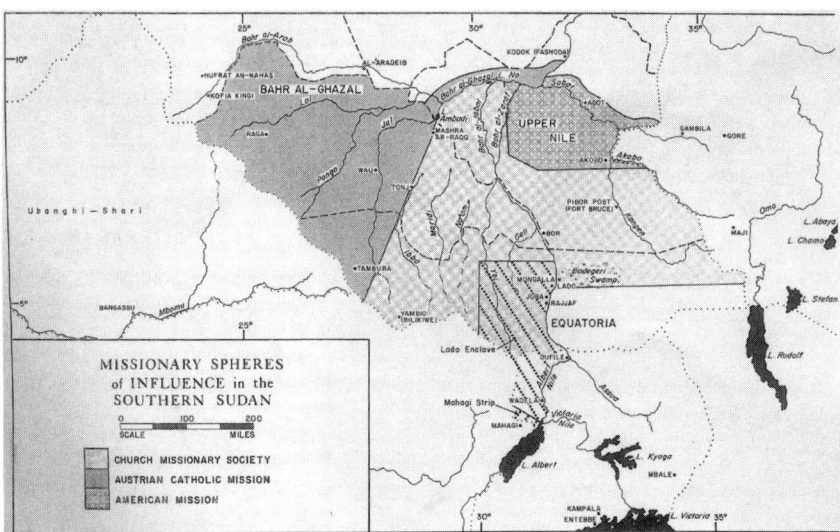

MAP 1.1
Mission spheres during the Condominium era. Robert O. Collins, *Land beyond the Rivers* (New Haven: Yale University Press, 1971), 294. Used by permission.

the work of civilisation now being undertaken."[32] Missionaries, Cromer saw, could usefully compensate for the Condominium's nonexistent social policy in southern Sudan. Cromer divided the south into spheres to prevent overlapping effort and competition between mission organizations. Missionaries protested, both at their exclusion from active work in Khartoum and at the limits of spheres, but they quickly made plans to move south. Dinka territory was split between Anglican and Catholic missionaries, with CMS' sphere encompassing the east-bank territory and the west bank as far as Tonj, west of Rumbek. The Catholic territory was farther west, centered on Wau and Aweil.

The first Anglican mission station in southern Sudan was founded in early 1906 at Malek, a few miles south of Bor on the east bank of the White Nile. The site had been selected because of reports that it was in the middle of the territory of the Dinka Bor. Unbeknownst to the team of six young missionaries, however, Malek was a significant spiritual location for many Dinka in the region. A ritual expert named Bior was based in the area and was linked to the powerful divinity *Lierpiɔu*. As one senior

[32] Quoted in Brian de Saram, *Nile Harvest: The Anglican Church in Egypt and the Sudan* (Bournemouth, UK: Bourne, 1992), 105.

Dinka figure from the region later recalled, "To tell Bior that his own divinity was not good, to disregard it, was foolishness."[33] The group of missionaries did themselves no favors either. So inexperienced were they at international travel, they almost missed their train from London and would have missed their ship from Marseilles after getting lost in the city but that it sailed late.[34] One was a skilled carpenter but in the flood plain of the Nile, there was no suitable wood to work with.[35] The early years of the mission were dominated by the group's lack of resources, poor health, and above all the crippling mismatch between the missionaries' enthusiasm and their inexperience of the world outside England. Within 18 months, five of the initial six had been sent home, felled by poor health and the difficulty of the work. The one who remained was a young priest named Archibald Shaw. By default, he became secretary of the mission, a position he held for the next three decades.

During that time, Shaw implemented a strategy similar to that of other Protestant missionaries in sub-Saharan Africa: erect mission stations, provide education and health care, and use the resulting encounters as an opportunity for evangelization. Medical work among the Dinka was always sporadic, languishing as a result of the combination of unqualified missionaries and the difficulty of acquiring the necessary supplies. CMS established an important hospital at Lui among the Moru in the 1920s, but health-care provision among the Dinka remained weak.

Education, by contrast, was at the heart of mission policy for the entirety of CMS' time in southern Sudan. Beginning at Malek but then spreading across its sphere, CMS concentrated on establishing schools at its mission stations and, in time, networks of "bush schools" in the villages around each station. Education and evangelism were interwoven. Children—particularly boys, the focus of the effort—could not become Christian, it was believed, until they could read the Bible themselves. Thus, they would be taught to read and so come to be Christian. Moreover, by creating a group of young, educated Christians, the students would become missionaries themselves, both at home and in their new stations in life. Archibald Shaw, in words that would be remembered by future generations of Dinka, wrote to his superiors in London that

---

[33] Abel Alier, in-person interview by Marc Nikkel. Location uncertain, 1989 (transcript in NSCCA).

[34] Archibald Shaw diary, 17 October 1905 (CMSA ACC111 F2/1, 2–3).

[35] Lilian Passmore Sanderson and Neville Sanderson, *Education, Religion and Politics in Southern Sudan 1899–1964* (London: Ithaca, 1981), 52.

"Christianizing among the Dinka must be done by Dinka missionaries."[36] But there were few Dinka families interested in sending students to mission schools, either at Malek or, in time, at other Dinka stations. Ritual experts like Bior rightly saw the mission schools as competitors. One Dinka church leader later recalled the stories that were told of this first inter-religious encounter, how Bior was believed to "do something of magic so that the child . . . will not go ahead [to school] and will return to the camp. He tried to discourage education because he said that this man is going to take our children away."[37]

More significantly, nothing about the presence of missionaries or Condominium officials made Dinka question the centrality of cattle to their livelihood. One missionary realized that "the European, being unlearned in the traditional lore of cattle as treasured by the Dinka, is considered to have little to teach or worthy of imitation."[38] The Dinka had no reason to adjust their sense of what was needed for success in life. A Condominium official in Bor advised CMS in 1907 that "the Dinkas have in their own eyes everything that they can possibly want bar perhaps clothes & of course their neighbours' cattle & other possessions."[39] Content with their way of life and having outlasted all previous outsiders, few Dinka saw any need to change simply because British missionaries had arrived. Some of the children who did come to school were orphans or from poor families and were consequently less invested in the existing system. Other families sent children, but often the ones they regarded as least valuable and intelligent and so unlikely to succeed in Dinka society. Abel Alier, who would later become an important political leader in independent Sudan, was sent to the school at Malek but he was the only one of his mother's 10 children and one of two of his father's 17 who was sent to school. He was the ninth child, neither the eldest nor the youngest and so relatively inconsequential to his family according to Dinka social roles.[40] His father had little to lose by sending him to the missionaries.

---

[36] Archibald Shaw to CMS General-Secretary Baylis, 31 August 1911 (CMSA G3, S/01, 1911); quoted in Collins, *Land beyond the Rivers*, 305.

[37] Nathaniel Garang Anyieth, in-person interview by Marc Nikkel. London, England, 12 March 1990 (transcript in NSCCA).

[38] A. L. Kitching, *From Darkness to Light: A Study of the Pioneer Missionary Work in the Diocese of the Upper Nile* (London: SPCK, 1935), 13.

[39] Inspector Jennings-Bramely to CMS, 5 April 1907 (CMSA G3 S0).

[40] Abel Alier, *Southern Sudan: Too Many Agreements Dishonoured*, 2nd ed. (Reading, UK: Ithaca, 1992/1990), 1; Lienhardt, *Divinity and Experience*, 82.

In 1930, with its punitive expeditions mostly complete, the British enacted what became known as the Southern Policy. Access to the south was to be restricted, and the region governed through local intermediaries who represented self-contained tribal units. To work, however, this plan required educated southerners through whom the British could rule. As the only schools in the region belonged to the mission organizations, the Condominium began to offer educational subsidies. CMS, which constantly struggled to finance its operations, welcomed the new support and began to open further mission stations. For the Dinka, the most significant station was at Akot on the west bank. Opened in 1929, it was the first lasting CMS station among Dinka on the west bank.

But colonial modernity had still not penetrated deeply into Dinka territory. One Condominium official noted in 1934 that salt was still not "an article of common consumption with any Dinka."[41] He noted that the greatest help the Condominium could give to the missionaries would be to "become more direct in touching the people's lives . . . thereby the road to the people's heads and hearts [would be] broken in by Govt. . . . [T]he Mission would not ungladly see a more intense administrative effort to shake the Dinka out of his age long static calm."[42] In a situation like this, it is not surprising that the new energy behind education was not matched by any appreciable increase in interest for it among the Dinka. At Malek, the education inspector newly appointed by the Condominium learned that "attendance at both school and outschools are affected by the periods of the cattle camps. Outschools cannot be reopened till boys return from the cattle camps. . . . The development of outschools is a very slow and often disappointing business."[43] Of those who attended, some were there unwillingly. On his visit to Malek, the inspector found 10 new students. Two were relatives of government officials in Juba, several came through the "influence" of the local district commissioner, and only one came of his own initiative. Without the intervention of the local district commissioner, the inspector noted, "It would not be unfair to say that . . . the school would be reduced to very small numbers. Of the new boys only two are Bor Dinkas. This section of the tribe indeed have no enthusiasm for education."[44]

[41] R. T. Johnston, "Handing Over Notes on Bor and Duk District," 13 April 1934 (SAD 639/12/59).

[42] Johnston, "Handing Over Notes," 13 April 1934 (SAD 639/12/76).

[43] A. G. Hickson, "Report on Malek Elementary School," 19 March 1937 (SAD 664/13/47).

[44] Hickson, "Report on Malek" (SAD 664/13/47).

FIGURE 1.2
Roll call at Malek school, c. 1940s. Used by permission of Cambridge University Library, Royal Commonwealth Society Collection.

Beyond their work in education, CMS missionaries also sought to build church communities. But their approach created challenges. As evangelical Anglicans, CMS missionaries preached a form of Christianity that emphasized the conviction of sin, belief in the saving power of Jesus Christ, and hope of eternal life in heaven. Conversion required a complete repudiation of existing religious beliefs. In order for a Dinka to become Christian, he—and virtually all of the new converts were male—could no longer sacrifice to *jak* and, indeed, had to destroy his shrines. Such a policy lengthened the social distance that new converts had to travel to become Christian. For instance, the ways in which sacrificial meat was distributed in Dinka society embodied social relations. To refuse to participate, as converts were required, was to cut oneself off from wider society. The difficulty of crossing this social distance and converting to Christianity is evidenced in the missionaries' frequent complaints about "backsliding" among their new converts. Missionaries wrote home despairing of how converts took multiple wives, drank alcohol, and continued to participate in family sacrifices.

Conversion was marked by baptism, concerning which CMS established stringent policies.[45] At a bush school, a student could make *gäm ë tök*, the "first promise," and assert that they wished to learn more about Christianity. After a period of study, they would make *gäm ë rou*, the "second promise," and be admitted to a baptism class. Finally, after further preparation, they would be baptized.[46] The process could take well over a year, and even then some converts struggled to read the Bible. The first Dinka to successfully make his way through this process was Jon Aruor, who was baptized at Malek in 1916, a decade after CMS arrived. In Aruor's case and in others, missionaries suspected converts had simply memorized the necessary passages and answers to demonstrate their faith and prove they were ready for baptism.[47] The link between literacy and baptism was particularly strong. If a convert could not read the Bible on his own, how was he to deepen his faith after baptism along the evangelical lines which CMS desired? Given the paucity of resources invested in education for women, this link between literacy and baptism ensured that early converts to the Dinka Anglican church were almost exclusively male.

Even as CMS struggled with the Dinka, it found success elsewhere. By 1917, missionaries could report that at Yambio among the Zande people, there were "thirty Catechumens and nineteen Enquirers. . . . Among those who live on the Mission Stations readiness to learn is as marked in the case of the Azande as it is absent in that of the Jieng."[48] In 1920, CMS tried to hand over its work in Malek to Australian missionaries of the Sudan United Mission (SUM), the organization founded in the early twentieth century to support the work of the evangelist Karl Kumm. SUM had begun work among the Dinka Padang in Melut in the far north of Dinka territory in 1918. Though CMS tried to put the best spin on its work at Malek, the reputation of the Dinka preceded them and SUM declined the offer.[49] A 1925 fundraising publication exhaustively detailing CMS' work in southern Sudan does not once use the word *Dinka*, or

---

[45] Richard Gray, *Black Christians and White Missionaries* (New Haven: Yale University Press, 1990), 64.

[46] Kitching, *From Darkness to Light*, 32.

[47] Archibald Shaw, letter home, 4 November 1917 (CMSA ACC111 F1/6).

[48] C. A. Lea-Wilson and A. G. King, report of GMSM, 1917 (CMSA G3/S/O/1916–1919).

[49] "Memorandum on C.M.S. Work Amongst the Dinkas," no date, c. 1920 (CMSA S1/L1/291–292).

mention Malek, the first station.[50] The work elsewhere in southern Sudan was more promising. It was only the intervention of the Condominium and its subsidies that ensured CMS' Dinka work continued.

Revival, Renewal, and Retreat

The first three decades of Anglican mission activity in east- and west-bank Dinka communities, spanning the period from its inception to the outbreak of World War II, had only limited impact on the Dinka and particularly limited impact on Dinka religious life. In 1934, the outgoing Condominium governor at Bor concluded that the Dinka had shown an "almost complete indifference . . . to the 30 years old presence of the Mission in their midst at Malek—an indifference which in all the circumstances may be said to amount to ill will." As for the school, "so far as can be seen from the conduct of daily affairs Mission teaching and influence have had no effect on Dinka custom or life."[51] For the Dinka, it was largely a calculation of utility: few Dinka saw anything worthwhile in what the missionaries had to offer. This judgment, in turn, was related to the relatively weak penetration of Condominium regulation in their lives. What Dinka Christians there were largely came from poor, unconnected backgrounds or peripheral places in their families. The symbolic Dinka Christian in this period was Daniel Deng Atong, who had been born a Mandari, orphaned, and raised as a Dinka at the mission station at Malek by Shaw. Shaw kept a careful eye on Deng Atong, ensured he was educated at mission schools, and then sent him for teacher training. In 1940, he was one of the first two southern Sudanese to be ordained a deacon. Yet his life to that point represented the marginal social position many Dinka Christians occupied within their own communities.

East Africa was the site of many movements of Christian conversion in the nineteenth and twentieth centuries, but the Dinka stood isolated from these trends. In other African contexts, young people were able to use Christianity as a means of challenging gerontocratic hierarchies in societies. But such challenges were most effective when they resonated with other tensions created by the economic, social, and political changes set in motion by colonialism. In southern Sudan, few such changes were taking place. Like other pastoralist peoples across the region, the weak

---

[50] Diocese of Egypt and Sudan, *Our Church's Work for the People of the Sudan* (Khartoum: n.p., 1925).

[51] Johnston, "Handing Over Notes," 13 April 1934 (SAD 639/12/33, 75).

penetration of Condominium rule meant that for Dinka the calculus of success and survival had not changed sufficiently to require an alternative system of religious belief and practice. Missionaries continued to report on the persistence of Dinka shrines and religious objects long after they arrived. The *jak* remained at the center of Dinka religious life.

Yet one moment did indicate that religious change was not impossible—and it came as a discomfiting shock to CMS missionaries. In 1938, spurred in part by the teaching of the missionary Richard Jones, new Christian fervor spread among many Moru and Zande peoples from a center at a mission school at Loka in Equatoria.[52] Those already in the church as well as new converts were encouraged to publicly confess sins, repent, and turn to God. Some new converts turned on the missionaries, criticizing their leadership and resenting the control they sought to exercise. From Yambio, one missionary wrote that the new energy was "mixed with the queerest doctrines and the most fanatical separatism amounting almost to hatred of those who disagreed with them. . . . Many of the time-honored methods and institutions of the Society had also been ruthlessly swept away. . . . There was crisis after crisis and at times it looked as though there was going to be a break away and a separate cult formed."[53] CMS invited Joe Church, the missionary in Gahini, Rwanda, where the so-called East African Revival originated, to visit. Church had welcomed the Gahini revival and wrote home that he found the missionaries in Sudan to have an "over cautious attitude . . . [that] had left them somewhat perplexed and disheartened."[54]

Daniel Deng Atong was teaching at the school in Loka and was caught up in the new religious energy. He brought this energy with him when he was sent to the mission station at Akot to work with a new missionary, John Collison. On Collison's arrival at Akot, the church consisted of a small congregation of students who were compelled to attend. Otherwise, "interest in the gospel was practically non-existent. Education to a large degree was unwanted and yet this was the means by which the CMS hoped to reach the people."[55] The revivalist preach-

---

[52] Andrew Wheeler, "Richard Jones and the Sudan Revival of 1938," *Anglican and Episcopal History* 71, no. 2 (2002).

[53] Arthur Riley, letter to friends, 31 October 1939, in papers of A. Morris Gelsthorpe (CMSA ACC/300/O1).

[54] Joe Church, circular letter, 28 March 1939 (CCCWA JEC 1/4/5).

[55] John Collison, "The Christian Church on the West Bank of the Nile, 1938–1940," 1, personal recollections written in April 1981 (NSCCA).

ing of Deng Atong and other students who came with him led quickly to new interest in Christianity. In early 1939, an outbreak of cerebrospinal meningitis meant that the government closed all schools. This freed teachers to be full-time evangelists, and, energized by the new revival, they engaged in a wide-ranging evangelistic campaign in the villages around Akot.[56] For a time, the congregation grew to over a thousand. Rather than consisting solely of students, the church now held "old men and old women. . . . [and] young men, unclothed, armed with their spears, boys with spears, all typical hunters of these tribes."[57] The church began to spread outside the mission station as well, with new congregations gathering at bush schools. One missionary reported that "the Gospel message has got outside the cloister wall. We have baptised a number of adults still living in their own environment, whereas in the past the Christians have been almost exclusively schoolboys or employees of the mission station."[58]

Several aspects of revival activity presaged later developments in the life of the church. First, in contrast to CMS' usual practice, the revival featured the "temporary abandonment of liturgical services and set prayers."[59] Second, it was almost entirely led by people who were not ordained. Deng Atong's ordination was imminent and some of the CMS missionaries were ordained, but most of the activity was carried forward by lay evangelists who visited villages and led prayer services. Third, the revival led to new musical compositions. Two composers in particular stand out, Ater Bai and Daniel Ayup. Neither were students; instead Bai worked on the mission station and Ayup was "a real cattle camp Dinka."[60] But both began composing Christian hymns in a form that was not that different from songs that would have been composed in a cattle camp except that they incorporated Christian themes. So innovative were these hymns that they provoked controversy among missionaries as to whether to allow them to be sung in church. Such debates were somewhat beside the point. The energy of the revival spread the hymns among new converts regardless of what missionaries said. As missionary Leonard Sharland later recalled, "The

---

[56] Collison, "Christian Church on the West Bank," 2 (NSCCA).
[57] Morris Gelsthorpe, circular letter, 1939 (CMSA AF/35/59/G3/S1/sub-file 9).
[58] Edward Arnold, "Akot Station Report 1942" (CMSA AF35/49 G3/S/g1).
[59] Collison, "Christian Church on the West Bank," 6 (NSCCA).
[60] Leonard Sharland, letter to David Brown, 31 March 1970 (SAD 865/3/17).

theology of spontaneous choruses would horrify a theologian but warm the evangelist!"[61]

The impact of the revival was felt in Dinka areas beyond Akot. In the early 1940s, after his ordination, Daniel Deng Atong was sent back to the east bank, first to Malek and then to a new quasi-mission station at Kongor among the Twic Dinka, north of Malek. The energy of the revival went with him. In 1947 he wrote that "the work at Kongor is flourishing well, and the number of adherents continues to rise. There are about a dozen people ready for baptism, and two of these have already been baptized out there."[62] When the missionary bishop visited that same year, he found 500 students at Kongor, "most of whom come in from surrounding cattle camps and homesteads for instruction every week."[63] New songs were also composed at Kongor, though as there were no European missionaries around, few of them made it into a compilation of songs that was published in the 1950s.

Almost as quickly, however, the energy of the revival faded. The strict policies on baptism and the prerequisite of literacy remained largely in place. Combined with the small number of people who could prepare converts for baptism, this meant that few of those newly interested in Christianity were drawn into the life of the church. Within a short period of time, Akot returned to its previous state, a disappointing station with a student-dominated congregation. A visitor in 1946 reported that "education is not appreciated, neither is there enthusiasm for the Christian message. . . . [Teachers] are regarded as strangers."[64] At Kongor, the enthusiasm ebbed as well.

The revival coincided with the retirement of Archibald Shaw in 1939. His decades-long labors had resulted in several publications in the Dinka Bor dialect, including an abbreviated version of the Book of Common Prayer in 1930, a compendium of stories from the Old Testament in 1935, and a complete New Testament in 1940, just after his retirement. But there were few Dinka Christians to use these resources. The contrasting fortunes of the CMS mission in southern Sudan is revealed in statistics from 1946: at Yambio among the Zande, there

[61] Sharland, letter to David Brown (SAD 865/3/18).

[62] Daniel Deng Atong, "Malek Report," *Southern Sudan Mail Bag* 1, no. 4 (1947): 12.

[63] Letter from Oliver Allison, 30 May 1947, *Southern Sudan Mail Bag* 1, no. 5 (1947): 28.

[64] Unsigned, "Akot Report," c. 1946 (CMSA AF35/49 G3/S/g1).

were 48 outschools with 1300 students; Juba, the growing commercial center of the south, had 60 outschools with 1527 students. In Malek, by contrast, there were 8 outschools with 98 students; at Akot, 9 stations with 113 students.[65] In comparison with the rest of the region, the early decades of CMS involvement with the Dinka had produced little appreciable religious change. But the end of World War II brought with it a new approach to colonial governance and Western missionary strategy. These shifts led some Dinka to look again at what Christianity offered.

---

[65] "Annual Report on Southern Education for the Year 1946 by Mr. D. H. Hibbert—Asst. Director of Education (South)" (SAD 664/13/10).

2

A Scattered Church

Independence, Civil War, and Migration

Prior to the outbreak of the second civil war in 1983, religious change among the Dinka was associated with the movement of Dinka out of the social and religious landscape of villages and cattle camps at the heart of their society. Young men became Christian by leaving a village and moving to a mission station or urban center. In the period before World War II, there was little incentive for this movement to happen. After World War II, however, the British approach to southern Sudan began to change. The early years of Sudan's independence brought with it new pressures that increased the incentive for migration. These factors meant that an indigenous Anglican church began to take root among the Dinka in the 1960s and 1970s. It was this fragile church that would begin to grow dramatically during the years of civil war in the 1980s and 1990s.

The End of the Missionary Period

Across Africa, the end of World War II brought with it a new approach to colonial and missionary activity. There was a new emphasis and new focus on training indigenous political and ecclesiastical leadership to take over from foreigners. These changes affected how the British approached southern Sudan. The Southern Policy restricting outside involvement in the region was officially abandoned in 1946. The 1947 Juba Conference controversially secured the southern region's place in the entire country, but northern Sudan began at a great advantage, given the years of educational and economic investment that the south had not seen. Colonial officials realized they could no longer neglect the south and began to take steps to expand governance and economic structures across the south. In Dinka territory, this intrusion of modernity took several forms. Markets began a slow and fitful expansion beyond district centers, opening up the possibility of trade in cattle and the sale of agricultural surplus. The Yirol Co-operative Marketing Society among the Aliab Dinka, for instance, created new economic opportunities for some people in the region.[1] On the east bank, a new district commissioner arrived in Bor in 1946 and in the next decade built a hospital and Bor's first quay, and opened two new primary schools for boys.[2] Between 1949 and 1953, scientists and researchers of the Jonglei Investigation Team ranged across the region to investigate the possibility of bypassing the Sudd by building a canal across east-bank Dinka territory and ensuring more water reached downriver users.[3] While work did not begin on the project at this point, it was one of many unmistakeable indications that Dinka could no longer live without interruption from outsiders.

The colonial government also began to substantially increase its investment in education. In 1926, the first year the Condominium offered subsidies to mission agencies, it spent £3,000. By 1947, the amount was £65,000, a figure that rose to £250,000 in 1951 and £750,000 by 1954, with additional funds spent on capital projects.[4] One of the most significant projects was Rumbek Senior Secondary School, opened in 1949, the first nonreligious secondary school in the south. It was situated in Rumbek primarily because it was a central location for the entire region. But putting it directly in Dinka territory meant that Dinka could no longer avoid the fact that education was now a part of life in southern Sudan. Nor could they miss seeing the benefits and new resources that accrued to those who were educated.

The greater intrusion of colonial rule shaped the opportunities open to Dinka, particularly Dinka young people. More began to seek education. Reuben Maciir Makoi, who would become an important church

---

[1] Southern Development Investigation Team, *Natural Resources and Development Potential in the Southern Provinces of the Sudan: A Preliminary Report by the Southern Development Investigation Team 1954* (London: Sudan Government, 1955), 29–30.

[2] Pengko Pilot Project, Technical Note no. 9, *The Social and Economic Setting of Rural Bor Dinka* (Arnhem, the Netherlands: ILACO, December 1979), 23.

[3] Robert O. Collins, *Shadows in the Grass: Britain in the Southern Sudan, 1918–1956* (New Haven: Yale University Press, 1983), 347–64.

[4] Southern Development Investigation Team, *Natural Resources and Development Potential*, 150.

leader on the west bank, first went to primary school in the 1940s when his family moved to Rumbek for medical care for a relative. When his family moved back to their village, Maciir remained behind, eventually working his way through secondary school and teacher training college in Akot. Along the way, like many students before him, he was baptized and became a Christian. His parents were displeased with his decision to stay in school, and Maciir at various points had to sneak away from home to return to school at the end of holiday periods.[5] Maciir, however, like other converts of his generation, was not the oldest son and so was relatively "expendable" in the eyes of his family. Increasingly, however, some families began ensuring that their more promising children were sent to schools. Whole communities began to be interested in education as well, with some chiefs and other leaders actively seeking out educational opportunities for their people. Leonard Sharland, who became the senior CMS missionary among the Dinka in the 1940s and 1950s after Shaw's retirement, noted a transition in the late 1940s: "There is no rush yet but the chiefs realize that education has come among them and is a factor of first rate importance."[6] Western education might not produce skilled pastoralists but it was increasingly recognized as a means of achieving prestige.[7] Such views on education were not universal. On the east bank, a Condominium official had a mixed report: in the area around Duk Faiwil, for instance, the chief was "very anxious" to have a school and was eager to discuss how to improve the village school. Just a little south in Baidit, however, the school was abandoned and being used as a refuse dump.[8]

For CMS, the period after World War II was a time of change as well. In September 1946, members of what was still known as the Gordon Memorial Sudan Mission adopted a "realignment plan" that included a commitment to make a renewed effort at "pioneer evangelism among the Nilotics."[9] This was a frank acknowledgement that the mission effort

---

[5] Reuben Maciir Makoi, in-person interview by Jesse Zink. Juba, South Sudan, 22 September 2013.

[6] Leonard Sharland, annual letter from Akot, 11 September 1947 (Sudan Archive Durham [hereafter SAD] 865/2/18).

[7] Lilian Passmore Sanderson and Neville Sanderson, *Education, Religion and Politics in Southern Sudan 1899–1964* (London: Ithaca, 1981), 264.

[8] J. W. Meadows, "Report of Inspector of Education, Upper Nile Province," 1 April 1949 (SSNA BD13/17.D.1–17.G.1).

[9] Gordon Memorial Sudan Mission Standing Committee Minutes, 16–18 September 1946 (Church Missionary Society Archive [hereafter CMSA] AF/35/59/G3/S2/1946–1949).

to date among the Dinka, the primary Nilotic people who fell in CMS' sphere, had failed. Missionaries were reassigned from stations in Equatoria to new stations among the Dinka. A new station near Yirol was opened in 1947 to be a more centrally located site for teacher-training work. In 1945, CMS founded its first school to train clergy that, in 1947, became known as Bishop Gwynne College. There was some indication that CMS was now finding more success. At Kongor, the influence of the revival from the early 1940s was still being felt, and there was a small but substantial Christian congregation. In 1954, a visiting missionary recalled a Sunday morning service in which "300 young men came in from surrounding cattle camps, and having sung their own Christian songs to their own music, and having listened to four sermons, returned to continue their life among their cattle, passing on their way the spirit hut of their forefathers, now deserted."[10] Such stories of modest church growth were largely exceptions. Elsewhere on the east bank at Malek, the origin of CMS work, the church continued to be dominated by students. In 1951, Daniel Deng Atong went through the baptism register and counted 450 baptisms in the history of the station, of which 300 had been students.[11] Sharland reported that at Malek, "there is no local church there apart from the few employees of the Mission and school. The outschools have been disappointing. It appears that services are not even attempted in some of them. . . . In short, I think we should face the fact that the East Bank Dinka area is still a Missionary area."[12]

Putting greater resources into education furthered the divide between the landscape of towns and mission stations on the one hand, and villages and cattle camps on the other. To be a student meant, as it had for Reuben Maciir, leaving one's own village for anything beyond the most basic education. In 1946, Sharland, who lived in a house in the center of Rumbek, noticed the cattle camps were competing with the schools for attention: "Neither the Christian message nor the opportunity of schooling has attracted more than a few Dinkas, and these for the most part are the less fortunate members of the tribe, such as orphans and otherwise

---

[10] Brian de Saram, "Bewildering Change," *Southern Sudan Mail Bag* 2, no. 5 (Spring 1954): 3.
[11] Daniel Deng Atong, "The Church of Christ in the Sudan," *Sudan Diocesan Review* 3, no. 11 (October 1951): 23.
[12] Leonard Sharland to GMSM Secretary in Juba, 20 June 1955 (CMSA AF/35/59/G3/S1/sub-file 3/1955–1959).

FIGURE 2.1
Church service at cattle camp on east bank of Nile River, c. 1950.
Cambridge University Library, Royal Commonwealth Society Collection,
CMS/9/1/17. Used by permission.

poor folk. . . . The cattle camp attracts the young men."[13] A decade later, he reported that in Dinka territory there were "vast areas as yet unevangelised." Of particular concern was the church's lack of impact on cattle camps where, he noted, "the real Dinka are to be found."[14] All this was particularly frustrating to CMS missionaries who were aware of the contemporaneous East African Revival. One missionary asked his supporters to pray it would spread to the Dinka: "It's no good trying to pretend that the Dinka Church is healthy and flourishing—it isn't."[15]

CMS had succeeded in creating a small group of Dinka church leaders, lay and ordained, chief among them Daniel Deng Atong. But they were used primarily to continue mission policies, staffing schools and mission stations. Having themselves rejected Dinka religious practices, these Dinka Christians continued to insist on the complete repudiation of existing practices prior to baptism. At Kongor, Deng Atong reported

[13] Leonard Sharland, annual letter, 1946 (SAD 865/2/15).
[14] Leonard Sharland, "Southern Sudan Christian Council, C.M.S. Report," c. 1956 (SAD 865/3/7).
[15] Brian de Saram, letter to supporters, *Southern Sudan Mail Bag* 1, no. 10 (February 1949): 12.

that when the school was started, "the first thing these learners did was to clear away from their huts and courtyards anything that had any connection with the worship of their gods, i.e. things like pegs driven into the ground on which oil or bones of victims sacrificed to the god or gods are poured, or placed under them. At Duk those who believed and became learners gave permission to the Christians to burn down the 'spirit hut.'"[16] Whether it was conveyed by British or Dinka evangelists, the message was that Christianity involved moving away from one's traditions and the location where those traditions were centered, the village and cattle camp. As students made progress and attended schools farther from home, it became less likely that students would be willing to return to their home village as Christian evangelists. A colonial official noticed the trend: "not very many boys who had once tasted the sweets of learning would return to hoeing fields or herding cattle."[17]

The frustration that missionaries experienced makes clear the persistence of the religion of the *jak*. Education and colonial governance had an expanded reach, which made more Dinka aware of Christianity. But it was regarded as a religion of young people. Indeed, among some Dinka the Christian God became known as *Nhialiny de mithke tukul*, "God of the students." If a Dinka boy enrolled in school, it was accepted that he might become a Christian. But there was no thought that the conversion would have any serious implications for anyone else in the student's family who was not also in school. Amos Awan de Gak left his home near Kongor to go to school in Malek in the early 1950s. When he returned home as part of an evangelism campaign, he remembers that the people in the villages he visited scoffed at them: "Oh, these naughty students. We send you to school and you come back and say there is somebody who has been killed and he is called Jesus and he is our redeemer. If he is the son of God, why would God allow his son to be killed?"[18] Even if Dinka elders were inclined to listen to Dinka youth talk about religion, so many mission students were from "the lower strata of society" and were not the kind of people "the average Dinka would regard as leaders."[19] Around Bor, *Lierpiɔu*, the divinity

---

[16] Daniel Deng Atong, "Report on Kongor and Duk Area 1943" (CMSA AF/35/59/G3/S1/sub-file 9).

[17] T. R. H. Owen, "Sudan Days," c. 1960 (SAD 769/11/52).

[18] Amos Awan de Gak, in-person interview by Jesse Zink. Juba, South Sudan, 4 April 2013.

[19] Leonard Sharland, annual letter, 1946 (SAD 865/2/15).

associated with Malek when CMS arrived in 1906, continued to exercise strong influence. Fighting between different Dinka sub-groups in 1945 and afterwards led the British to arrest a number of Dinka around Bor and to seize the spear sacred to *Lierpiɔu*, which was believed responsible for the violence. The spear was put in a jail in Khartoum.[20]

Sudan gained its independence on 1 January 1956. Even before then, however, there were signs of brewing trouble. A mutiny in Torit in August 1955 and other outbreaks of violence across the south indicated the dissatisfaction that many southerners felt with the emerging power dispensation. In the decade leading up to independence, the lack of investment in the south was demonstrated by the small number of southerners who were able to take administrative and governance positions. When a new Legislative Assembly was opened in Khartoum in 1948, it was determined that there were only 15 to 20 Nilotic people who were educated enough to participate.[21] Such exclusion fed southern discontent, and by 1963 rebels primarily from the Equatoria region were in revolt against the government, a war that would last until 1972.

These early years of independence were also a time of decreasing Western missionary influence. In a moment of great hope, Daniel Deng Atong had been made bishop in 1955, as the first Sudanese Anglican bishop. Leonard Sharland returned to England in 1959 and was not replaced by a European, marking the moment at which Anglican missionary work among the Dinka passed entirely into the hands of Dinka clergy. Deng Atong was suspended and removed from office in 1960 due to a mental breakdown and alcohol abuse. The Sudanese government began restricting missionary activity before ultimately expelling all foreign missionaries in 1964. CMS lamented this loss, but by that point it had only a half-dozen missionaries in the south. In Deng Atong's absence, the Dinka church was led by a small number of Dinka clergy who were primarily in urban areas, both because that was where Dinka Christians were and because the war had forced them there. In 1964, amid war, the school and mission station at Malek were destroyed. In 1965, the mission station at Akot was attacked and destroyed.

Six decades after European missionary activity began, a Dinka church did exist, comprised mostly of students, former students, and those who had come to live in towns or near mission stations. But it was small in comparison to the church among other people groups. When the

---

[20] Pengko Pilot Project, *Social and Economic Setting of Rural Bor Dinka*, 51–52.
[21] Collins, *Shadows in the Grass*, 428–29, 436.

expatriate bishop Oliver Allison made a confirmation tour of the south in 1960, he conducted 4,028 confirmations, but only 329 of those were Dinka, nearly the same as the number of Moru confirmations, though the Moru are a much smaller ethnicity.[22] It was statistics like these that prompted Leonard Sharland, as he prepared to leave Dinka territory, to write that there was plenty of "virgin soil" in Dinka cattle camps.[23] Despite efforts to replace it, the religion of the *jak* endured.

"Scattering" North

In the early 1960s, seasonal flooding of unusual intensity overwhelmed east-bank communities, particularly those of the Twic, Ghol, and Nyarweng Dinka around Kongor, Duk Faiwil, and Duk Fadiet. In the decade following 1961, and particularly between 1961 and 1964, vast areas of cultivable land were lost and cattle herds were decimated from loss of pasture and greater susceptibility to disease. These stresses, in turn, pushed the Dinka social system to the breaking point and led to widespread migration by many young men.[24] It is a time now remembered as a *pawɛɛr* ("scattering"). Many began to move toward the cities of the north, particularly Khartoum, in search of work, either in large agricultural schemes or in construction. By 1971, 60 percent of Khartoum's population over the age of 15 consisted of migrants from other parts of the country.[25] It was not an easy existence: "To a great extent these folks have a difficult time here. Jobs are not plentiful and these people are not trained to do much and so have to become laborers. Living conditions are hard and many of them have to live with little if any shelter."[26] The migration of the 1960s was a novel development for the Dinka. For the first time, large numbers of young Dinka men from the east bank were leaving cattle camps and villages and engaging with life in cities and towns.

---

[22] Oliver Allison, "The Bishop's Letter," *Sudan Diocesan Review* 13, no. 36 (1960): 5.

[23] Leonard Sharland, "Rumbek: Centre of Dinka Rural Deanery," *Sudan Diocesan Review* 11, no. 31 (Summer 1958): 11.

[24] Paul Howell, Andrew Mawson, and Sjöerd Zanen, "Recent Change among Nuer and Dinka Peoples of the Jonglei Area," in *The Jonglei Canal: Impact and Opportunity*, ed. Paul Howell, Michael Lock, and Stephen Cobb (Cambridge: Cambridge University Press, 1988), 255–58.

[25] Nour El-Din Ahmed Maglad, "An Empirical Analysis of Rural-Urban Migration in the Sudan," *Sudan Notes & Records* 64 (1983): 53.

[26] "Extracts from Circular Letters from the Rev. and Mrs. Leander Finley of the American Mission, Omdurman," *Sudan Diocesan Review* 14, no. 40 (1961): 18.

Many of the young Dinka men had not been students prior to their arrival in these cities. But in Khartoum and elsewhere there was a new enthusiasm for education. The skills of agropastoralist survival that had been useful in cattle camps were no longer helpful in a place like Khartoum. The need to be able to read and communicate was now readily apparent. This new situation posed a challenge for the church. Anglican churches in Khartoum and other northern cities in the 1960s were primarily chaplaincies to British expatriates. As the population of southerners increased, it became clear that the church needed some form of response. The close connection between Christianity and education meant that it was not surprising that a primary means by which the church responded to this new influx of migrants was through education. In 1961, missionaries in Omdurman reported, "Nearly every Church is doing something in the way of giving lessons in evening classes . . . but the number is so great that it is necessary to plan and set up some definite scheme whereby they will be reached."[27] Much of the impetus for these educational efforts, particularly among Anglicans, came not from missionaries but from Dinka themselves. In the evenings, migrants assembled themselves for education in Dinka, English, and the Bible, led by those who had been educated in CMS schools in the south and had also migrated to Khartoum. One of those first leaders was a young man named Daniel Deng Bul from the Kongor area who had had a few years of schooling before moving north. When he arrived in Khartoum, he found Dinka classes going on: "I was a teacher with them teaching [Dinka] dialect only. I was well trained in our own dialect and I know it properly. Through teaching . . . I was really very happy to teach the gospel."[28] Education and Christianity remained closely linked, with enthusiasm for the former leading to new openness to the latter. But it was not only education that young migrants found in these church-based clubs. They also found a way to develop a communal identity. In the midst of the Muslim-dominated north, they found in the clubs a place "where they could speak their vernacular language, sing in their own idioms and so affirm, or assert, their identity in an alien environment."[29]

---

[27] "Extracts from Circular Letters from the Rev. and Mrs. Leander Finley," 18.
[28] Daniel Deng Bul, in-person interview by Robin Fisher. Port Sudan, Sudan, 1985 (transcript in NSCCA).
[29] Marc Nikkel, "Aspects of Contemporary Religious Change among the Dinka," *Journal of Religion in Africa* 22, no. 1 (February 1992): 80.

The Anglican congregation in Khartoum North became a central gathering point for young Dinka migrants. At first there were few clergy to provide leadership. The first civil war, however, changed that situation. Reuben Maciir Makoi, who had once defied his parents to seek education, had been ordained in 1960 and placed in charge of the Akot mission station. When it was destroyed in 1965, he was forced to flee to Khartoum. On arrival, he was put in charge of ministry to Dinka.[30] Maciir had been deeply influenced by CMS and he modeled his ministry on that of the Anglican mission. The Dinka congregation in Khartoum North became a sort of mission station, sending out people to found prayer centers and outstations in other parts of the growing urban area, not unlike the bush schools that surrounded mission stations in the south. The Dinka congregation grew, from 10 people at its first service in 1966 to more than 500 at its main service in 1983, with thousands more connected through prayer centers and outstations around the city.[31] Maciir returned to the south in 1975 and was replaced by John Malou Ater, who also came from the west-bank communities around Rumbek and had been educated in CMS mission schools. Maciir, Malou, and other CMS-educated lay leaders of the Khartoum congregation provided a direct link between the mission period and the church in an independent Sudan.

But leaders from the CMS era were too few to accommodate the growth of the church. The Khartoum North congregation emphasized training new leadership from among the large group of new church members with no direct connection to CMS. In the mid-1970s, with the war over, some of these new church members were sent south for training at Bishop Gwynne College in Mundri and returned as ordained clergy. It was the first generation of Dinka clergy who had not been guided to ordination by European missionaries. Among the first was Daniel Deng Bul, the young man who had been teaching the Dinka language in the north. When he arrived at Bishop Gwynne College, one of his teachers remembers that he would spend his spare time in the army barracks in Mundri where there were Dinka soldiers, "doing what the Dinka Christians were always doing in those early days and that was starting night classes, in which you learned the Dinka language so you could read the Bible in Dinka and get properly rooted."[32] When he

---

[30] Allison, "Bishop's Letter," 9.

[31] "Dinka Congregation-Khartoum: Annual Report for 1983" (SAD 812/9/15).

[32] Andrew Wheeler, in-person interview by Jesse Zink. Guildford, England, 13 December 2010.

graduated, Deng Bul returned to the north where he was sent to Port Sudan to extend what had been an expatriate congregation to include migrant populations from elsewhere in Sudan. His strategy emphasized education through a network of small church centers: "we could see a lot of Christians were not being educated and we founded it to teach young people so they could read the Bible and write. . . . The school also teaches them Christian culture."[33] The pattern of outstations and education was mirrored in other northern cities. Numerical growth became a primary focus of the church. The Khartoum congregation, for instance, organized periodic door-to-door evangelism campaigns and other forms of direct evangelism. What was being created across the north among this Dinka diaspora was the beginnings of a religious movement. Rather than an institutional church that was closely connected to CMS missionaries, there was new energy around Christianity, some of which was contained in growing church structures but much of which simply swirled through Dinka communities in Khartoum.

In the south, the brunt of the devastation of the first civil war was borne by the peoples of Equatoria, in the far south of the country. But Dinka areas were also affected and some Dinka joined Equatorians in seeking refuge across international borders, particularly in camps in northern Uganda. Displaced Anglican clergy began to recreate church life with the help of the Anglican Church of Uganda, and the church began to grow. A Sudanese cleric wrote to Bishop Allison from a refugee camp that "God is doing wonderful things among the people here. Many who were not previously worshippers have become true worshippers. The refugee years have proved a blessing to many who are coming to the Lord's side."[34] Dinka were a minority in these camps but some were still affected by this new religious enthusiasm. One young convert was named Nathaniel Garang Anyieth. Garang had been born and raised in a cattle camp near Bor in the late 1930s. As a third son, he was sent to attend school at Malek and then Rumbek Secondary School. He was baptized, but there is little indication that he was anything other than one of the growing number of disinterested young Christians in this period. After fighting with the southern rebel movement in the early years of the war, he sought refuge in Uganda. In his own telling of the story, it was in Uganda that he truly became a Christian, helped along

---

[33] Daniel Deng Bul, in-person interview by Robin Fisher. Port Sudan, Sudan, 1985.

[34] Quoted in Allison, "Bishop's Letter," 6.

by the active life of the church as well as a born-again moment that clarified his own sense of religious identity. While in Uganda, he developed a relationship with a group of expatriate Christians who funded his theological education at Nairobi Pentecostal Bible College in Kenya. When the war ended, he returned to the church of his early education, presented himself to Anglican leaders, and became the priest in charge of the Anglican congregation in Bor in May 1974.[35] One of his first tasks was to preside at the funeral of Daniel Deng Atong, the first Sudanese Anglican bishop, who had lived out his days since his deposition in near poverty in Malek. It was a symbolic passing of the torch from the priest and bishop who represented the high points of the CMS period to the priest and soon-to-be bishop whose formative religious experiences were independent of CMS. When Garang arrived in Bor, "there was no church, [only a] few children pray[ing] in the court[yard]."[36]

The years of Sudan's first civil war, therefore, are also the years of the first significant religious change among the Dinka. A combination of ecological, economic, and political factors created new streams of migration and displacement. Some young men headed for the cities of the north in search of alternative livelihoods. Others were forced by the war to seek refuge abroad. In both cases, this movement led to a greater openness to Christianity. Exposure to a wider world beyond cattle camps, combined with the recognition of the need for new resources that came from education, led many people to consider Christianity afresh. Moreover, in the contested environment of northern Sudan, Christianity provided the basis for a new communal identity.

Although Christian adherence was growing, it was only due to the movement away from Dinka villages and cattle camps. The landscape of Christian belief remained largely the same as it had been for the previous half century. The growth of Christianity in the 1960s happened where such growth always had happened: in the towns, cities, and now refugee camps that were the result of the growth of governance structures. To be a Christian still meant that Dinka had to leave the landscape in which they had been raised. That more Dinka were making this decision to leave meant there were more Dinka Christians, but it did not change

---

[35] This summary of Garang's life is based on John Chol Daau's unpublished research.

[36] Nathaniel Garang Anyieth, letter to Commissioner of Jonglei Province, 9 May 1978 (SSNA BD 31/46/B/1).

the historic pattern in which Christianity was separate from the Dinka social landscape. Indeed, Dinka leaders on the east bank prevailed on Sudan's new president Gaafar Nimeiri to return the spear of *Lierpiou* to its home in 1970. Its return home was greeted with widespread sacrifice. The end of the civil war in 1972 was attributed to the return of the sacred spear.[37]

The Addis Ababa Agreement

The 1972 Addis Ababa Agreement ended the first civil war by establishing a southern region with a large measure of self-government and control of its internal affairs. But it was a weak regional government, one beset by factionalism and rivalry, and which struggled to deliver services to its population.[38] Still, the relative stability of the 1970s allowed for the expansion of services across the region. While progress was always uneven and fragile, the combined efforts of the new regional government and international organizations led to schools, roads, and an enlarged governmental presence in previously isolated communities.[39] Moreover, there were new opportunities for migration out of Dinka territory. Such changes led to continued religious change.

The expansion of education was a major goal of the Addis Ababa period. By 1982, there were 24 primary schools in the Bor District and 31 in the Kongor District, a significant increase in the number of schools in these communities during the colonial period.[40] The impetus for building many of these schools came not from the government but from members of individual communities. Visitors to east-bank communities

---

[37] Pengko Pilot Project, *The Social and Economic Setting of Rural Bor Dinka*, 52; Douglas H. Johnson, "Indigenous Religions in the Sudanese Civil Wars," paper presented at "Workshop on Religious Conflict and Development in Africa and Asia" at School of Oriental and African Studies, 31 October 1997 (SAD 306/8/151).

[38] Terje Tvedt, "The Collapse of the State in Southern Sudan after the Addis Ababa Agreement: A Study of Internal Causes and the Role of the NGOs," in *Short-Cut to Decay: The Case of the Sudan*, ed. Sharif Harir and Terje Tvedt (Uppsala, Sweden: Nordiska Afrikainstitutet 1994), 69–104.

[39] John W. Burton, "When the North Winds Blow: A Note on Small Towns and Social Transformation in the Nilotic Sudan," *African Studies Review* 31, no. 3 (1988).

[40] "Report on the Progress of Education in Jonglei Province for Academic Year 1982/1983," 17 July 1982 (SSNA SR/ME/No 81). Equivalent figures for west-bank schools are unavailable due to the wartime destruction of records from Bahr el Ghazal province.

in the 1970s frequently mentioned the enthusiasm for "self-help" projects, that is, projects undertaken at the initiative of the community and using local methods of construction. In Duk Fadiet, a visitor found that "Good self-help is going on at this centre. A girl[s'] school is being built and the people are ready to build more if they can be assured of teachers; especially they pleaded for a boy[s'] school which the Minister of Education has agreed to assist if they can build the facilities."[41] The weakness of the government, the difficulty of transporting building materials, and a host of other problems meant that construction often lagged well behind enthusiasm. But the trend line toward greater educational opportunities was clear.

Given the continued close association of education and the church, the expansion of the former led to growth in the latter. In contrast to the mission outschools of a previous generation, which had emphasized preparation for baptism, the priority of these new schools was secular education. In many such schools, however, there were teachers or other lay people serving as chaplains. When new church congregations were gathered, they often first met close to the schools. For instance, when a new school was founded in Pacong on the west bank shortly after the Addis Ababa Agreement, one informant remembers how the church there first met under a tree next to the school. One of the teachers served as an evangelist to the students and introduced many to the church.[42] The model of mission established by CMS endured in this new period.

The church also followed the expansion of government in other areas of society. In 1981, Anglicans began a new congregation in Awerial, at a site not far from where missionary bishop Guy Bullen had been killed in a plane crash in 1937. The decision to expand to Awerial, it was reported, was made possible only by the government's decision to build a road to the community and to begin to offer primary education. The government had also dug several wells, which meant people were beginning to gather around the school.[43] Nor was Awerial the only community where such church growth was taking place. In 1983, the bishop of Rumbek reported a gradual expansion of church centers like the one

---

[41] "Report on Visit to Bor District by Sayeds Michael Tawil, Dr. Justin Yac Arop and Mading de Garang," 10–13 February 1975, 4 (SSNA SR/ME/no. 9).

[42] Petro Marial Thon, in-person interview by Jesse Zink. Pacong, South Sudan, 18 September 2013.

[43] Benjamina Yugusuk, "Aliab Visit" (NSCCA).

at Pacong. He listed seven such centers, all in places that had recently founded schools and were connected to the expanding road system.⁴⁴ It was a similar situation on the east bank. Residents at Anyidi built a school as a self-help project in 1973. A few years later, they built a church with the support of the local chief. The chief had no religious interest in Christianity but saw that building a church attracted positive attention from authorities in Bor and "would make the station famous."⁴⁵

As the reports on "self-help" indicate, the expanded provision of education and other government services coincided with a shift in attitudes among Dinka. There was a growing awareness of the importance of education. If some Dinka had once thought they could outlast the changes imposed by outsiders, that belief was no longer tenable. In a new dispensation, education was seen as a useful resource for a family to have access to. Sending at least a single male child—though rarely still the first-born—to school had now become valued. Such education could lead to positions in the government and so help Dinka gain access to the levers of state power. The proliferation of schools and the decline of familial resistance made it easier for a new generation of Dinka young men to attend school than it had been in previous generations.

But education was not universally embraced. The benefits of Christianity were still not immediately obvious to all in what remained an agropastoralist community. One informant who grew up on the east bank in the early 1980s remembered that while there were more schools provided by the government, "many people at that time, they don't recruit children to the school. If you recruit your child to the school, who will take care of the cattle? And who will help you in cultivation? These are the sources of life at that time."⁴⁶ The rhythm of Dinka life demanded a set of skills that formal education could not provide. In the villages and cattle camps of the Dinka social landscape, attitudes toward education and thus Christianity were changing, but the change was by no means overwhelming.

The impact of modernity was felt in other ways beyond simply education. In 1976, Bor became the capital of the new province of Jonglei, and the presence of institutions of government increased.

---

⁴⁴ Report from Benjamina Yugusuk in *Sudan Church Review* 7, no. 29 (Spring 1983): 4.

⁴⁵ Pengko Pilot Project, *Social and Economic Setting of Rural Bor Dinka*, 135.

⁴⁶ James Nhial Maler, in-person interview by Jesse Zink. Bor, South Sudan, 6 April 2013.

Markets continued to expand their reach, and basic commodities like salt, cooking oil, and grain began to be available for purchase. Whereas once a colonial official had noted the absence of salt in Bor, the Addis Ababa period was one in which outside capital and commerce penetrated the Dinka traditional economy.[47] There were also more foreign nongovernmental organizations assisting in the rebuilding effort. The distance between rural Dinka life and the new dispensation became clearer: "The coming of donor agencies, nuclei of prosperity and high technology, and their projects to Bor Dinka daily make the Bor Dinka realize the tremendous gap there is between their own situation and that of the outside world."[48] A new class of leaders began to emerge, and their value was rooted in their ability to mediate between modern institutions of governance and local life in villages and cattle camps.[49]

The intrusion of modernity also created possibilities for migration out of Dinka territory, particularly for young men. Younger sons who found their ambitions for marriage and economic independence frustrated by the claims that older male relations made on cattle could now look for work in a town and so begin to build up their own cattle wealth independent of gerontocratic hierarchies.[50] A report on Bor Dinka in 1979 found that a large number of young men were leaving rural areas for towns. When asked, they gave two reasons for the move: "problems at home" and "opportunities to improve the family's living conditions."[51] The social and economic impacts of this change were complex and varied. Fewer laboring men in villages had a negative impact on agricultural production. It was unclear whether cattle purchased with wages earned in urban labor were subject to the same patterns of communal ownership

---

[47] George Tombe Lako, "Social Differentiation and the Market: The Case of Kongor in the Jonglei Canal Area," Development Studies, Occasional Paper no. 12, University of East Anglia, May 1981, 34.

[48] Pengko Pilot Project, Technical Note no. 20, *Bor Dinka: Prospects for Development* (Arnhem, the Netherlands: ILACO, November 1981), 44.

[49] Pengko Pilot Project, *Social and Economic Setting of Rural Bor Dinka*, 46; Cherry Leonardi, *Dealing with Government in South Sudan: Histories of Chiefship, Community and State* (Woodbridge, UK: James Currey, 2013), 148–53.

[50] Sharon E. Hutchinson, *Nuer Dilemmas: Coping with Money, War, and the State* (Berkeley: University of California Press, 1996), 63–83; Lako, "Social Differentiation and the Market," 28–29.

[51] Pengko Pilot Project, *Bor Dinka: Prospects for Development*, 47.

that had historically applied to herd management. This resulted in weakened kinship ties across the region.[52]

What was clear, however, was that the patterns of development during the Addis Ababa period were reinforcing those that had begun during the floods of the early 1960s. For the first time, there was a growing group of Dinka who lived in urban areas outside of the east- and west-bank communities in which they had been raised. As had been true in Khartoum in the 1960s, the migration to the larger conurbations led to an increased demand for education. Indeed, the demand for education by these migrants became so great that schools began to complain their students were too old. Primary schools for students aged 6 to 12 found they had students over the age of 20. Secondary school students were older than 30.[53] Young men who had missed out on education in their home communities now sought it out where it was available. It was in these towns that the church was strongest, and so urban migration often led to religious change. One informant grew up in an east-bank cattle camp in the late 1960s and early 1970s. When it became clear that his family did not have the cattle necessary for anyone beyond his older brother to be married, he left his village and went to Juba for work. In the process, the informant became involved in an evening education class and eventually was baptized.[54] This informant and others like him were part of a growing group of young, relatively educated Dinka Christians. In Juba and elsewhere, they became part of a larger Christian youth movement that had been shaped by the first civil war and was heavily influenced by Ugandan evangelicalism.[55] But the Dinka were always a small minority in this movement, and their conversion did nothing to dissolve the long-standing associations of Dinka Christianity with urban areas. Christians remained a minority among the Dinka and within the church, and were still, by and large, separated from the sacred landscape in which they had been raised.

---

[52] Howell, Mawson, and Zanen, "Recent Change among Nuer and Dinka Peoples of the Jonglei Area," 267–69.

[53] Regional Ministry of Education, Southern Region, "Memo: Age Control in Schools," 13 September 1974, 1 (SSNA SR/ME/No. 13/117.D.6/A).

[54] Reuben Akurdit Ngong, in-person interview by Jesse Zink. Bor, South Sudan, 12 April 2013.

[55] Roland Werner, William Anderson, and Andrew Wheeler, *Day of Devastation, Day of Contentment: The History of the Sudanese Church across 2000 Years* (Nairobi: Paulines Publications Africa, 2000), 479–82.

FIGURE 2.2
Bishop Daniel Deng Atong with the Rev. Kedhekiah Barac Mabior at the latter's ordination as deacon in Rumbek, Palm Sunday 1957. Cambridge University Library, Royal Commonwealth Society Collection, CMS/9/1/45. Used by permission.

In the north, Dinka young men often joined the congregation in Khartoum North or one of its satellites. In the south, urban Dinka Anglican life was under the control of Khedekia Barac Mabior, who functioned as an archdeacon in the Diocese of Rumbek though he was based in Juba and had oversight of the Dinka congregation there. Like his near contemporary Reuben Maciir Makoi, Barac had followed the traditional CMS path to ordination: educated at a mission school, and trained as a teacher before studying for ordination at Bishop Gwynne College in the 1950s. Barac was ordained by Daniel Deng Atong in 1957 and, like Maciir, held firmly to CMS practices like lengthy baptismal preparation, an insistence on literacy for new converts, and worship according to the translated Book of Common Prayer. In the Addis

Ababa period and amid new religious influences in Juba, Barac found that he needed to guard this tradition closely. Barac ordained Nathaniel Garang and sent him to Bor in 1974. In 1977, Garang was joined by Paul Nhomlau, who was also from the east bank, and who had studied with Garang at Nairobi Pentecostal Bible College in Kenya. While there, Nhomlau had become involved in an East African Pentecostal association affiliated with the Assemblies of God in England. Contention soon ensued. In his preaching Nhomlau condemned the sinfulness and lack of commitment of his congregation, and there was soon concern that the congregation was departing from Anglican traditions. In 1981 Barac expelled Nhomlau from the church and insisted that Garang step away from his ministry in Bor for a year and attend Bishop Gwynne College to learn Anglican traditions. Garang complied, but Nhomlau founded his own congregation, which was one of the first congregations of what is now known as the Sudan Pentecostal Churches.[56]

This work in Bor and other regional centers received support from urban Dinka congregations, which were beginning to consider deliberate evangelism campaigns to their former homelands. This was prompted in part by the return home of young men who had first traveled to Khartoum and other northern cities in the 1960s. As they returned to their villages, they brought with them the new faith they had been taught in the north and began to share it with their family members.[57] More significantly, newly converted Christians in Juba and elsewhere began making targeted evangelism campaigns in rural areas. Two young men, Samuel Majok Deng and Joseph Akol Gak, were so committed to the work that they left Juba permanently and returned to the east bank to live as evangelists, Majok among the Dinka Ghol and Akol among the Nyarweng. Both Majok and Akol were Dinka Bor. They made particularly effective evangelists and teachers because the New Testament and prayer book translations left behind by CMS had been translated into their dialect. Informants who were living in these communities at this time remember being aware of new Christian activity. Its impact was mixed. On the east bank, one informant remembered seeing an itinerant Christian evangelist. He asked his friends, "'What is

[56] Werner, Anderson, and Wheeler, *Day of Devastation, Day of Contentment*, 485.

[57] Marc Nikkel, "Christian Conversion among the Jieng Bor," in *Religion and Conflict in Sudan*, ed. Yusuf Fadl Hasan and Richard Gray (Nairobi: Paulines Publications Africa, 2002), 164.

that man doing?' Some people who know him say, 'Oh, he is Christian. He is preaching the good news.' I did not know what was the good news at that time. So it was not a big issue for me."[58] Other Christian evangelists were greeted with confusion and incomprehension. Still, with the arrival of Nathaniel Garang in Bor in 1974 and Reuben Maciir in Rumbek in 1975, there was ordained leadership on both the east and west banks. There were also new resources for the work: in addition to sending people, the Dinka congregations in Juba and Khartoum also financially supported the ministry in Bor.[59]

The enduring connection of education and Christianity meant that Dinka Christianity continued to be a strongly male religion. In statistics from the mid-1970s, the number of girls enrolled in school lagged far behind boys. Fewer than a third of students were female.[60] The basic obstacle was that education for girls was less valued than it was for boys. Educated boys could generate more cattle wealth for a family; girls reached their earnings potential simply by being marriageable. Mary Alueel Garang, who would emerge as a key leader of the east-bank Christian conversion movement in the 1980s, spent a short period in Malakal as a child in the 1970s, and briefly attended school. "But I was taken, snatched from the town, to be taken home. At that time, the Dinka say, 'Our girls cannot be in towns. We need our girls to be in the cattle camps.' So I was taken from Malakal to the cattle camp."[61] One route to Christian conversion that did exist for women was if they married an educated "town man," and so moved from a village or cattle camp and crossed the urban-rural divide. But this path was not necessarily smooth. Many churches preserved the requirement for a lengthy period of pre-baptismal catechesis. One female informant who married a town man recalled that while it generally took educated men two years of preparation prior to baptism, twelve years elapsed between her first

---

[58] Gabriel Chol Kuany, in-person interview by Jesse Zink. Phoenix, Arizona, 27 June 2012.

[59] Nathaniel Garang Anyieth, in-person interview by Andrew Wheeler and Roger Schrock. Location uncertain, 14 September 1991 (transcript in NSCCA); Isaiah Majok Dau, *Suffering and God: A Theological Reflection* (Nairobi: Paulines Publications Africa, 2002), 58.

[60] "Summary Statistics for Junior Secondary Schools, 1974/75" (SSNA SR/ME/No. 9/17.B.1).

[61] Mary Alueel Garang Nongdit, in-person interview by Jesse Zink. Bor, South Sudan, 14 April 2013.

church attendance and her baptism, seven of which were devoted to baptismal preparation as she struggled to learn to read the Bible and catechism.[62] Despite the obstacles, some women were nonetheless becoming Christian. In a sign of things to come, of the seven new church centers on the west bank in 1983, two were being led by women evangelists.[63] On the east bank, Khedekia Barac licensed two women as lay readers.

The 1970s had seen change in the governance of the Anglican church as well. In 1976, the Episcopal Church of the Sudan (ECS) was established as a separate province of the Anglican Communion. Both the east- and west-bank Dinka communities were contained in the Diocese of Rumbek, one of the new province's four dioceses, which also included the proportionately larger Moru church around Mundri. A 1980 listing of clergy in the diocese named 41 pastors, 14 of whom were Dinka: 7 in east-bank churches, 4 in west-bank churches, and the balance in various urban congregations associated with the diocese.[64] Dinka were a minority in ECS, and Christianity was a minority faith among Dinka.

But there was an undoubted increase in Christian commitment among many Dinka. The expansion of governance and new opportunities for migration meant that Dinka Christianity continued to grow along the lines of earlier generations, as a male-dominated church, closely linked to education, and concentrated in urban areas. In 1983, on the eve of the second war, the ECS Archbishop Elinana Ngalamu visited Bor and other east-bank towns. He reported being welcomed by large crowds and sensing "a great desire for spiritual assistance and guidance." The bishop of Rumbek confirmed 523 people on the trip, a large number but far fewer than the 1,375 he confirmed that year in the smaller Moru archdeaconry.[65] The basic dynamics of Christianity were beginning, slowly, to change as a result of new development and new movement, both from north to south and within the south. But the enthusiasm the archbishop encountered was not yet widespread. Instead, a consistent picture of Anglican life among Dinka of the east and west bank before the second civil war emerges: congregations composed primarily of those who had been to school were found along the main roads

---

[62] Martha Kuei Marier, in-person interview by Jesse Zink. Rumbek, South Sudan, 19 September 2013.

[63] Report by Benjamina Yugusuk in *Sudan Church Review* 7, no. 29 (Spring 1983): 4.

[64] Benjamina Yugusuk, letter to Oliver Allison, 31 May 1980 (NSCCA).

[65] Report by Elinana Ngalamu in *Sudan Church Review* 8, no. 29 (1983): 7.

and in the growing towns. In the villages and cattle camps, by contrast, "there was no church, whether a preaching centre or sub-parish."[66]

Agropastoralist Christianity

In his history of the African church, Adrian Hastings writes that the people groups with the most "negative" response to Christianity were the agropastoralists of East Africa, such as the Nuer, Turkana, or Maasai. The social structure "provided an almost total bar to the kind of religion the Western missionary had on offer."[67] The Dinka had a similar response to Christian missionary activity. The Anglican church that was created among the Dinka during the mission period and in the years following was closely tied to education, associated with towns and other urban areas, and strongly gendered toward men. As a result, it was a small church, since for much of this period many Dinka placed little value on education and centered their social existence in villages and cattle camps.

Studies of Christianity among other East African pastoralist peoples show clear parallels with the Dinka experience.[68] For the Dinka and for others, it was the marginal in society who were most likely to convert, but in converting many separated themselves from their communities and cultures. This is in contrast to the experience of nonpastoralist peoples in East Africa, many of whom actively sought out religious change and were able to use Christianity as a new form of societal power.[69] As Hastings argues, the social structure of pastoralist societies—stateless, amorphous, and lacking in easily identifiable political or commercial centers—confronted missionaries with a conundrum they could not easily resolve. European missionary strategy centered on creating stations and bringing people to those stations. Among a sedentary, agrarian

---

[66] Abraham Mayom Athiaan Deng, in-person interview by Andrew Wheeler and Roger Schrock. Location uncertain, 14 September 1991 (NSCCA).

[67] Adrian Hastings, *The Church in Africa, 1450–1950* (Oxford: Clarendon, 1994), 325.

[68] Dorothy L. Hodgson, *The Church of Women: Gendered Encounters between Maasai and Missionaries* (Bloomington: Indiana University Press, 2005); Richard Waller, "They Do the Dictating and We Must Submit: The Africa Inland Mission in Maasailand," in *East African Expressions of Christianity*, ed. Thomas Spear and Isaria N. Kimambo (Oxford: James Currey, 1999), 83–126; and Peter Rigby, *Persistent Pastoralists: Nomadic Societies in Transition* (London: Zed, 1985).

[69] Derek Peterson, *Ethnic Patriotism and the East African Revival: A History of Dissent, c. 1935–1972* (Cambridge: Cambridge University Press, 2012).

people, such strategy met with success. Among a people like the Dinka, such strategy met with failure. In the terms of Robin Horton, pastoralists are particularly well suited to resist the pressures of the macrocosm. Dinka could always move deeper into the *toc*, as they always had in response to the presence of unwelcome outsiders. In southern Sudan, the weakness of colonialism meant that the pressure to reckon with social change was lessened in comparison to other parts of the continent.

In 1906, when Malek mission station opened, Dinka religious life centered on cattle, cattle camps, and a series of primarily local divinities. By 1983, when the second civil war began, it was possible to distinguish a trend of modest growth in Christian adherence among the Dinka. There were Christian churches in east- and west-bank communities under the leadership of Dinka clergy. Nonetheless, much of the old religion remained. The spear sacred to *Lierpiɔu* remained in the Bor region under the care of ritual experts. Church services continued to be dominated by younger people, and younger men in particular. Had the second civil war not happened, the continued rural-to-urban migration and increased penetration of modernity would likely have resulted in a gradual expansion of Christianity to the point of its becoming a substantial—but not majority—religious presence and retaining its close connections with education and governance centers.

But the civil war did happen. This *riäk* suddenly intensified and altered Dinka religious life.

3

Like a Rain Which Comes Suddenly

Grassroots Religious Change in Sudan's "Liberated Areas"

In 1991, eight years into Sudan's second civil war, Anglican priest Abraham Mayom Athiaan was asked to describe what Dinka Christianity had been like before the war began. He recalled that "the churches . . . were only along the road and they were not inside, in the villages. And they did not take in the chiefs and elders."[1] The strength of the church was concentrated among Dinka who had left the rural areas, as Nathaniel Garang Anyieth remembered: "The church grew steadily in the town[s] [but not] in the village. Christianity was still for the elite."[2] By the late 1980s, however, the situation had changed dramatically. Mayom used a natural image to describe the transition: "[Christianity] has come like a rain which comes suddenly."[3]

In the 1980s and early 1990s, the religious allegiance of many Dinka in the former Anglican mission sphere rapidly changed. In less than a decade, Christianity entered the sacred landscape of the Dinka in a way that it had never before. Whereas prior to the war Anglican Christianity was the faith associated with education and urban areas, during the war Christianity became a religious movement in the rural heartland of Dinka territory on the east and west banks of the Nile River. There are numerous ways to measure this transition—number of congregations,

---

[1] Abraham Mayom Athiaan, in-person interview by Andrew Wheeler and Roger Schrock. Location uncertain, 14 September 1991 (transcript in New Sudan Council of Churches Archive [hereafter NSCCA]).
[2] Nathaniel Garang, letter to CMS General Secretary, c. 1992 (NSCCA).
[3] Abraham Mayom Athiaan, interview by Andrew Wheeler and Roger Schrock. Location uncertain, 14 September 1991.

baptisms, hymns composed—but the simplest way to describe the change is this: coincident with the early years of Sudan's second civil war, a majority of Dinka in the former Anglican mission sphere came to understand their religious identity not in terms of the religion of the *jak* but in terms of the religion of the students, Christianity.

This transition cannot be comprehended apart from understanding the societal stresses induced by the onset of the second civil war. The civil war created new patterns of movement that facilitated religious change and lowered barriers that had previously existed between Christianity and Dinka culture. The combined impact was to make religious change easier. At the same time, the war challenged the religion of the *jak* and clarified the value of what Christianity had to offer. The stress the war placed on the religion of the *jak* caused Dinka to reevaluate its claims and led to a shift in religious identity. The movement that resulted from this shift in religious identity had much in common with earlier mass conversion movements, particularly those of Christian independency elsewhere in the continent. Yet Dinka Christianity remained part of a mission denomination, the Episcopal Church of the Sudan. At a grassroots level, these mass conversion movements share similar basic features. The war remained the defining variable. In the areas of Dinka territory where the war was more severe, religious change proceeded furthest and fastest.

The Return to War

The Addis Ababa Agreement that ended the first civil war began to deteriorate in the early 1980s. President Gaafar Nimeiri mandated that Islamic law apply to the entire country, sought to divide the autonomous southern region into three separate states, and redrew internal boundaries to put newly discovered oil resources under his control. Even without such action, the southern regional government had become enmeshed in a debilitating conflict with ethnic dimensions. Many Equatorians began to resent the outsize role taken by Dinka in the politics of the region. This was particularly notable in Juba. As the capital of the south it had an increasing number of Dinka in what had historically been a Bari community. Many Equatorians supported Nimeiri's redivision policy as a way to reclaim Juba for themselves. The redivision, therefore, led many Dinka to leave Juba. Some moved to Malakal, capital of the new Upper Nile region, Bor, Rumbek, and other regional centers. The movement toward Juba that had begun in the 1970s began to be reversed.

Low-level violence during the late 1970s and early 1980s among unreconciled rebels from the first civil war was the first sign of the breakdown of the Addis Ababa Agreement. But it is an army mutiny in Bor in May 1983 that is commonly regarded as the outbreak of the second civil war. The mutineers fled to Ethiopia and organized the Sudan People's Liberation Army (SPLA). Unlike the rebel movement of the first civil war, which was largely led by Equatorians, the SPLA was regarded from the start as a Dinka-dominated movement. Its leader, John Garang, was a Dinka from Twic county, north of Bor. His senior lieutenants were other Nilotic people, Nuer and Dinka from both banks of the Nile.

The outbreak of violence led to movement and displacement among southern Sudan's peoples. Some people moved toward urban centers, including Juba, Wau, Malakal, and especially cities in the north like Khartoum. But for Dinka the most significant impact of the war was to intensify movement away from Juba and away from towns altogether. In the early years of the war on both the east and west banks, the Sudan Armed Forces (SAF) sought to hold towns and concede rural areas to the SPLA. By 1986, Bor, Malakal, Juba, and Rumbek were SAF garrison towns. The heavily Dinka cast of the SPLA meant that the SAF looked with suspicion on any Dinka male; those who remained in towns were at risk of their lives. In Bor, for instance, the SAF attacked the church compound in December 1985. Jacob Akei, a church evangelist, was killed, and "all the population in the town left to the countryside because of the killings. No one was left in the town, only the government soldiers."[4] Attacks like this one provoked an exodus of Dinka men and their families from southern towns. Those who fled tended to be educated. Some had worked in government, agriculture, health care, or other extension work.[5] They fled from the road system where the damage of the war was concentrated and returned to the rural villages and cattle camps that they had left for school or work. In the language of the SPLA, these became known as the "liberated areas" that were the vanguard of a "New Sudan." The displacement undid the growth of church institutions that had begun in the 1970s. The bishop of Rumbek wrote in July 1985, "all villages along the roads were destroyed. Yirol town [is] now

---

[4] Nathaniel Garang, letter to CMS General Secretary, c. 1992 (NSCCA).
[5] Kosti Manibe, "The Agony of the Family," in *War Wounds: Development Costs of Conflict in Southern Sudan*, ed. Nigel Twose and Benjamin Pogrund (London: Panos Institute, 1988), 122.

completely destroyed; only army are living there. Two of our pastors . . . are in cattle camps with their families without homes. . . . [A]ll the local church buildings in these places were burnt and people are now living far away from the roads."[6] For Dinka, the war effectively "put an end to urban activity."[7]

The urban-to-rural displacement brought educated, Christian Dinka into close, sustained contact with uneducated, rural Dinka. The new arrivals found few others like them. One lay Christian informant had been in Juba for more than 15 years when the war forced him to return to his village. He remembered that the only Christians he found in his home village "were the people who deserted the towns. Those who were at home were not believers."[8] The newly displaced had been shaped by the experience of urban living and brought this knowledge with them as they returned to life in their home villages. This encounter led to the growth of Christianity. For instance, one informant was baptized in 1984 after learning about Christianity from young people who moved to her village from Bor, sang Christian songs, and worshipped together.[9] It was a pattern that was repeated elsewhere on both banks of the Nile. As Abraham Mayom Athiaan recalled, "people who were inside the towns went out to live in the countryside and they teach people about the word of God. [People listened] because they are their own people. Before they said that he was . . . the God of the students. But nobody [had] taught them starting from their own cultures."[10] Before the war cut off communication between Juba and the SPLA–controlled areas, reports began to come in that new village prayer centers were being established where there had been none before.[11] The displacement of the war began Christianity's shift from being an urban, educated faith to being a rural, popular one.

[6] Letter of Benjamina Yugusuk, 8 July 1985, printed in *Sudan Church Review*, 12, no. 29 (1985): 3, 4.
[7] African Rights, *Great Expectations: The Civil Roles of the Churches in Southern Sudan* (London: African Rights, 1995), 9.
[8] Gordon Aboi Ajith, in-person interview by Jesse Zink. Bor, South Sudan, 13 April 2013.
[9] Mary Alueel Garang Nongdit, in-person interview by Jesse Zink. Bor, South Sudan, 14 April 2013.
[10] Abraham Mayom Athiaan, interview by Wheeler and Roger. Location uncertain, 14 September 1991.
[11] Report of Benjamina Yugusuk, printed in *Sudan Church Review* 15, no. 29 (1987): 8.

The war also had a significant impact on the leadership of the church. Since the foundation of the Episcopal Church of the Sudan (ECS) in 1976, both the east- and west-bank Dinka communities had been included in the vast Diocese of Rumbek, which incorporated a variety of ethnic groups and stretched from Bor to Aweil and as far south as Mundri. The bishop, Benjamina Wani Yugusuk, was a non-Dinka from Equatoria, which meant that the Dinka congregations were effectively under the control of Archdeacon Khedekia Barac Mabior. In 1984, Nathaniel Garang Anyieth, who had been sent to Bor by Mabior in 1974, was consecrated bishop of the new Diocese of Bor. In Garang, the east-bank church had a single, strong leader, who had been trained in a Pentecostal college in Nairobi but retained a loyalty to the Anglican church of his youth.

FIGURE 3.1
Bishop Nathaniel Garang Anyieth meeting a member of his diocese, c. 1992.
Collection of Nathaniel Garang Anyieth. Used by permission.

On the west bank, leadership was divided. Yugusuk left Rumbek in 1985 for a meeting in Juba and, because of the war, was never able to return. Instead, leadership came to be shared—often contentiously—between Reuben Maciir Makoi, Benjamin Mangar Mamur, and, later, Abraham Mayom Athiaan, all priests and not (initially) bishops. Each had a long history of involvement with CMS schools and training. There, however, the similarities ended. Maciir was a Jur-Beli, one of the small people groups on the edge of Dinka territory, and spoke fluent Dinka, had a Dinka wife, and was regarded as Dinka by many church members. He was a first-generation Christian who had been nurtured by CMS through education to ordination and church leadership roles in Khartoum and Rumbek. Benjamin Mangar, by contrast, was a second-generation Christian, raised in an Anglican family. When he studied in Khartoum and later Cairo in the 1960s and 1970s, he was introduced to and became an eager proponent of charismatic experience and worship. He returned to Rumbek in the late 1970s as a teacher at Rumbek Senior Secondary School, where many people thought it odd how often he read the Bible and how energetically he prayed.[12] Abraham Mayom had been educated but not ordained at Bishop Gwynne College in the early 1980s and spent the first years of the war in refugee camps in Ethiopia before returning to the west bank in the early 1990s. He had family connections to local SPLA leadership and at times used these connections to strengthen his own position in the church.

The early years of the war, therefore, separated the leadership of ECS. On the one hand, there were leaders like Yugusuk, Barac Mabior, and Archbishop Elinana Ngalamu, who were confined to Juba, Khartoum, and trips abroad. These urban church leaders would soon divide among themselves, leading to a church schism that was only fully healed after Ngalamu's death in 1992. They were in contact with international supporters but were largely disconnected from events in SPLA-controlled areas. On the other hand were the rural church leaders like Garang, Maciir, and Mangar, all of whom personally experienced the displacement of war. Mangar Mamur, for instance, was teaching in Rumbek in 1984 when it became clear that the town was going to fall to the SAF: "It was a choice: you either join the government soldiers and go to Khartoum or you go to the SPLA-controlled zones. I opted to go to the

---

[12] Hilary Garang Deng, "The Second Revival among the Dinka Anglicans in South Sudan, 1970–2010," unpublished manuscript (2016), 39.

FIGURE 3.2
Reuben Maciir Makoi, c. 1994. Collection of Marc
Nikkel. Used by permission of Durham University Library.

SPLA–controlled zones."[13] Garang stayed in Bor until 1985 when the church compound was attacked and then fled to the SPLA–controlled areas. These rural church leaders were isolated from the church hierarchy, which meant they were free to adapt church policies in response to what they encountered. The war, therefore, had two impacts: by displacing urban populations to rural areas, it brought new knowledge of Anglican Christianity into rural Dinka areas; by cutting off these rural areas it created a distance between the grassroots level and church hierarchies. The result was that Christianity could become a genuinely popular movement.

[13] Benjamin Mangar Mamur, in-person interview by Jesse Zink. Rumbek, South Sudan, 11 September 2013.

A Growing Church

In its early years, the burden of the civil war fell most heavily on areas of Bahr el Ghazal closest to the north-south border. The Khartoum government armed militias and sent them to attack Dinka territories around Aweil, Abyei, and elsewhere, creating streams of displacement toward Khartoum and Ethiopia. It was from these regions that news of the civil war first began to reach Western audiences with reports of massacres, enslavement, and the widespread destruction of villages. In east- and west-bank communities in the former CMS sphere, by contrast, many Dinka were still able to follow a pattern of life that was broadly similar to what had obtained prior to 1983. This was particularly true in the late 1980s when SPLA advances made victory seem possible and prevented the SAF from bringing the war to Dinka homelands in any meaningful way. As late as April 1991, a visitor reported "a high degree of peace and security . . . throughout most parts of the east bank of the Nile."[14] A group from the United States Agency for International Development reported that while there were pockets of malnourishment and drought, "the populace was quietly farming, fishing, and tending cattle."[15]

This comparative stability allowed Christian lay people and clergy to conduct a wide-ranging evangelism campaign, though one that was tempered by the need to work for survival. Reuben Maciir remembered, "I left Rumbek town when the town had fallen. . . . [Then] I was working among the Christians around Rumbek, preaching the Gospel in the cattle camps. . . . I was based in my home area because I had to make sure I had something for my family to eat. I had to cultivate first, then preach the Gospel, then come back and do some work. . . . I was traveling only on foot."[16] Although CMS missionaries had once made fitful efforts at "itineration" and town-based Christians in the 1970s had funded rural evangelism campaigns, the evangelism of the 1980s was the first sustained Christian effort to take place in the sacred landscape of the Dinka. Rather than having to move to a mission station or a town, rural Dinka could hear—again and again—the Christian message in their cattle camps and villages.

---

[14] Andrew Wheeler, "Report on a Visit to the Episcopal Church of the Sudan in the SPLA Administered Areas of Southern Sudan: 12th–18th April 1991," 2 (NSCCA).

[15] Quoted in J. Millard Burr and Robert O. Collins, *Requiem for the Sudan: War, Drought, and Disaster Relief on the Nile* (Oxford: Westview, 1995), 295.

[16] Reuben Maciir Makoi, in-person interview by Marc Nikkel. Thiika, Kenya, 10 February 1994 (transcript in personal files of Marc Nikkel).

The basic evangelical strategy centered on the formation of new "preaching centers." Although Maciir, Mangar, Mayom, and Garang were the senior leaders, much of the initial leadership came from lay people, who took responsibility for gathering people in a common spot, such as under a tree, for worship. One interview with a female evangelist took place in her church, which consisted of a cleared area under a large tree with some wooden benches. The informant remembered that it was in locations like these that worship first began: "We come and cut trees like this," indicating the church, "and put benches like this for sitting. After that, when people have come we were praying under the tree. Even there is no bench like this, they just come with a mat and put it down and sit and pray. They just sit under the tree. That is the way they worship."[17] Leaders at the preaching centers would actively seek out people to join them. Another female evangelist recalled that shortly after fleeing to the rural areas in 1984, she began to gather a new congregation. "I used to take the jar of the water and use it as a drum. . . . I used also to go under a tree and pray with the children. . . . Then the people came and I preached to them."[18]

The senior church leaders became involved when there was a demand for sacramental ministry, above all baptism. They found their services in great demand. One informant recalls starting a congregation in July 1986. By August, more than 300 people were ready for baptism.[19] When a preaching center had sufficient numbers to sustain itself, a leader from within the new converts would be appointed and the initial evangelist could depart to start more congregations. There were never enough educated, ordained clergy to lead the new congregations. Instead, the criteria for church leadership were more basic: "When we got a big tree in a certain place near a certain house, we selected a person who could sing the Christian songs in a Christian way. We put him there to train people how to sing those songs and to explain those songs into the Bible."[20] One result of this policy was that the new Christian leaders were relatively

---

[17] Mary Aruay Majak, in-person interview by Jesse Zink. Rumbek, South Sudan, 13 September 2013.

[18] Martha Yar Mawut, in-person interview by Jesse Zink. Akot, South Sudan, 15 September 2013.

[19] Martha Kuei Marier, in-person interview by Jesse Zink. Rumbek, South Sudan, 19 September 2013.

[20] Petro Marial Thon, in-person interview by Jesse Zink. Pacong, South Sudan, 18 September 2013.

uneducated and untrained. Whereas before the war, the Anglican church insisted on extensive education prior to ordination, now the lay evangelists and congregational worship leaders were often new Christians themselves. Indeed, many worship leaders were only just beginning to learn to read: "What we taught them was the Dinka alphabet. But afterward, each and every one of them has to go and develop their own reading. There was no chalk and blackboards. . . . You write it on the ground so that they can learn it."[21] The inexperience was not a great hindrance. The major communal act for Christians at these preaching centers was their worship and it was necessarily uncomplicated. Few copies of the Anglican prayer book circulated in the SPLA–controlled areas as only a few people who had fled urban centers brought copies with them. As a result, formal, liturgical worship was largely set aside. Instead, the central activities of worship were singing, praying, Bible-reading, preaching, and healing. In general, the Eucharist was de-emphasized, as much because of lack of resources as any other reason.

Part of the appeal of Christianity was that it seemed to address real problems faced by Dinka in a war zone. In the new Christian communities, the utility of Christianity was seen in part in matters of health and welfare. The war had significantly reduced the already limited provision of biomedical health care. Many Dinka already believed that religious practice could have salutary impacts on health. The growth of the church, therefore, offered sick people two options: approach a ritual expert in the religion of the *jak* or approach the church. The key difference between the two was that the former required sacrifice to be made, while the latter did not. As resources became scarcer during the war, it became harder to justify the expenditure of an animal for sacrifice; Christianity became more appealing. One informant recalled: "Those who worship *jɔk*, the leader of that *jɔk*, when another person get sick, he used to say, 'OK, if you don't bring a bull or a cow or whatever, this person will die.' . . . But with people in the church, a person get sick, the church leaders they just come, they pray, they touch him, and that is all."[22] Another informant remembered a song that was particularly helpful in evangelism. Its lyrics said that even if a person does not have an

---

[21] Petro Marial Thon, interview by Zink. Pacong, South Sudan, 18 September 2013.

[22] Mary Aruay Majak, interview by Zink. Rumbek, South Sudan, 13 September 2013.

animal their sick child does not have to die; the church could provide a solution.[23] Health and Christianity were already connected in the minds of many people because of how CMS had operated dispensaries as part of its mission stations, although not always successfully. During the war, the connection between healing and Christianity remained, but with one change: "The medicine [now] is prayer," as Abraham Mayom recalled.[24]

Christian healing was only an effective evangelism tool insofar as it was believed to be efficacious—and converts could tell dramatic tales of miraculous healings and other instances of apparent divine intervention. On the west bank, Reuben Maciir developed a particular "speciality" in praying for women who were unable to conceive and who later gave birth after his ministrations. Maciir cited over 30 instances in a 1994 interview. More generally, he said, "I am being treated as a doctor. By night people will be coming to me, saying 'Pastor, pastor, my child is dying.' Or, if it is a big person, they will ask me to go to the house. They will wake me and ask me to go to the house to pray, but in all this the Lord is doing wonders."[25] Healing prayers became a central function of Christian religious leaders and a necessary part of every worship service. New converts began to demand it of their leaders, as Abraham Mayom recalled: "So, after church services, after prayers, you have to go to the healing section. You have to put your hand on a person [or] he will be unhappy and he will not even go to his or her house, unless the pastor has put his hand on his head."[26] Christianity was undercutting the religion of the *jak* by offering an alternative to animal sacrifice. The change had a significant impact on church growth. One researcher who visited the west bank in the mid-1990s concluded that a major positive reason for the acceptance of Christianity was its "practical efficacy," known most of all in the field of health.[27]

Miraculous healings were one part of a larger belief that miracles were occurring that favored the new Christians. The belief became widespread, for instance, that Christians were protected from the violence

---

[23] Daniel Kon Malwal, in-person interview by Jesse Zink. Bor, South Sudan, 5 April 2013.
[24] Abraham Mayom Athiaan, interview by Wheeler and Schrock. Location uncertain, 14 September 1991.
[25] Reuben Maciir Makoi, interview by Nikkel. Thiika, Kenya, 10 February 1994.
[26] Abraham Mayom Athiaan, interview by Wheeler and Schrock. Location uncertain, 14 September 1991.
[27] Field notes of Michael Medley, taken near Akot, 28 December 1995.

of the war. At the end of December 1984, the market in Pacong was attacked while Christians were in church for Christmas celebrations. Seven people were killed in the market, but people in the church were not.[28] Numerous informants could recall examples like this in which it was believed that Christians were spared from death because of their new religion. On another occasion, a group of Christians was brought before a traditional court to answer charges that they were corrupting young women by encouraging them to convert. When the Christians arrived, they sat down and sang a song:

> A very strong wind came, very cold, very cold wind, and came and stirred the people. So the whole group of chiefs, they stood up automatically by themselves and those who were behind the chiefs, they ran away, and they said that God is [protecting the] people. . . . And that tree, where people were praying, they made a church centre just near that court, and that place was surrounded with grass. And fire came from very far to burn all the areas, all the trees, that church was safe, even a single piece of leaf was not burnt. . . . So people were converted from that.[29]

These stories are remembered by Christians, so there is an inescapable element of self-justification in them. But what is significant is not how or whether the events occurred as described, but that they were regarded as interventions by the same God who was acting in miraculous ways through the healing prayers of Christian leaders. They were interpreted as ratification of the novel program the Christians were advancing. Christianity was coming to be seen as beneficial. As this belief took hold, preaching centers spread across east- and west-bank communities.

Education

The preaching centers that spread from village to village were the core unit of church growth and the focal point of religious life. But the church took additional steps that had the effect of placing itself at the center of the communities in the SPLA–controlled areas. As Christianity spread, the church expanded its educational offerings, particularly on the west bank. Given the well-established connection between education and Christianity, it was not surprising that churches would seek to educate

---

[28] Petro Marial Thon, interview by Zink. Pacong, South Sudan, 18 September 2013.

[29] Abraham Mayom Athiaan, interview by Wheeler and Schrock. Location uncertain, 14 September 1991.

FIGURE 3.3
Church school in the west-bank community of Kharic, 1991. Collection of Marc Nikkel. Used by permission of Durham University Library.

their members. New Christians needed to learn to read the Bible for themselves so that they could deepen their faith. Indeed, one informant remembered that "it is difficult for those who don't read the Bible after [they convert]. They can be persuaded by others to come back to *jɔk*. . . . Some return if there is not a teacher."[30] But the war provided additional motivation for the church's engagement in education. Government services in the SPLA–controlled areas ceased to function during the war. The SPLA-affiliated Sudan Relief and Rehabilitation Association did seek to offer primary education, but its efforts often foundered. In a reversion to the pattern of the Condominium years, the church became the primary provider of education. A 1991 report listed 135 church schools on the west bank, though a 1997 report listed only 60.[31]

[30] Peter Bol Arok, in-person interview by Marc Nikkel. Kakuma Refugee Camp, Kenya, 27 February 1994 (transcript in personal files of Marc Nikkel).
[31] Abraham Mayom Athiaan Deng, interview by Wheeler and Schrock. Location uncertain, 14 September 1991; "Minutes of the Seventh General Assembly of the New Sudan Council of Churches," 17–18 April 1997, Lokichogio, Kenya (NSCCA).

Yet the church's access to resources was limited. Pictures of one school in 1991 show several barely clad children gathered around a single adult. There is no building, blackboard, writing implements, or books. The resource limitations meant that the education the church offered was basic, sporadic, and primarily focused on Dinka literacy. The teachers were often not trained as such but were educated people displaced from urban areas. Teaching happened in situations ranging from formal classes for children when circumstances permitted to *ad hoc* classes for adults whenever they happened to be gathered. The lack of resources did not detract from the urgency of the efforts: "If you have [a] chance of gathering some people in [one] place, you have to continue the teaching," said Abraham Mayom.[32] In part, the urgency came from the historic connection between education and Christianity. As it had during the CMS period, literacy education continued to facilitate Christian conversion, a fact that church leaders were well aware of. Reuben Maciir recalled: "To keep them like this [without being able to read] is like a commander who don't know how to open his gun, and don't know how to use it. Our gun is the Bible, and a pastor cannot just sit, sing songs and pray without reading the Bible."[33]

The urgency was also due to the growing recognition of education's importance among non-Christian Dinka, an importance that was underlined by the impacts of the war. Displacement is a function of one's inability to preserve one's position. In such situations, it is natural that people would look for new means to prevent further displacement. This explains why many Dinka men joined the SPLA and fought the Khartoum government. Guns are perceived as one source of power. Increasingly, however, Dinka perceived that education and literacy—a "gun" of a different sort in Maciir's view—were a major source of power in which they were deficient. One informant recalled, "now . . . someone can take [what is] yours by force, and if you are not educated it can be taken. Now the Government can make laws by force. But if you have a son who is educated, he can get clothes and bring [them] to you."[34] Another informant said, "Here everybody wishes to be a Christian to learn to read and write. . . . We can get something from those who are

---

[32] Abraham Mayom Athiaan Deng, interview by Wheeler and Schrock. Location uncertain, 14 September 1991.

[33] Reuben Maciir Makoi, interview by Nikkel. Thiika, Kenya, 10 February 1994.

[34] Informant unidentified, in-person interview by Michael Medley. Near Akot, Sudan, 30 December 1994 (transcript provided by Michael Medley).

educated, so tomorrow we can tackle our own problems by ourselves."[35] This view was consonant with views expressed during the later colonial period: the education of sons would redound to the family's benefit. But the war broadened the interest in education beyond male children. One visitor to the Rumbek area in 1997 encountered a local leader who told her, "I have arrived at a river bank . . . and to cross I need education and the church as ferry boats. The *jak* and hunger are the river over which people must cross."[36] The comment expresses both the close connection between education and the church and the new importance with which education was viewed. And as more people sought education, they more naturally saw themselves as Christian as well. The eagerness for education generated by the conditions of the war led to a new openness to Christianity as well. Moreover, the increased interest in education shows how the church was taking on a new centrality in Dinka society. It was the one institution that attempted to provide—in however haphazard and poorly resourced a way—what many Dinka now regarded as important. The link between education and Christianity meant that as desire for the former grew, so too did the latter.

YOUTH

From students in mission schools to young people who had moved to Khartoum in the 1960s, young people had historically been a major part of the Dinka Anglican church. Unlike other situations in sub-Saharan Africa in which Christianity could amplify and become part of other socioeconomic changes, however, in southern Sudan there was insufficient economic change for the young people to challenge existing generational patterns. By the beginning of the second civil war, however, generational relations began to change and so too did religion. Nathaniel Garang Anyieth, in reflecting on the early years of the Christian conversion movement on the east bank, remembered, "it start[ed] from the youth and not from big people."[37]

The turmoil of the war in southern Sudan called into question existing religious beliefs and practices. It also allowed young people

---

[35] Quoted in African Rights, *Great Expectations*, 10.
[36] Quoted in Lillian Craig Harris, *Keeping the Faith: Travels with Sudanese Women* (Nairobi: Paulines Publications Africa, 1999), 114.
[37] Nathaniel Garang Anyieth, in-person interview by Marc Nikkel. London, England, March 1990 (transcript in NSCCA).

to challenge a system that did not accord them status or position. Such a challenge was understood in terms of the recognition that Christianity was more powerful than the religion of the *jak*. One informant sought baptism in 1987 at age 16 after a confrontation with a *tiët* at a fishing camp. The informant was singing a Christian song he had learned when the *tiët* told him to stop because his throat was being strangled by the song. The informant realized, "What I am singing is making sense and I am not a Christian. God is more powerful than this *jɔk*." When he returned home from the fishing camp, he sought baptism.[38] Many other informants remember a confrontation with a figure of the religion of the *jak* as a key moment in the process of conversion.

The church also offered a new form of social connection. Informants remember the songs and games they learned when they first attended churches. As one recalled:

> The activities in the church were new. So we were excited to dance as a Sunday School and we were impressed also with the birth of Christ during Christmas. So this is the new [things] and we see Christians they are always happy. . . . That's why many kids went to the church and played. They didn't go for the prayers, but they just go for the entertainment during the dancing of Sunday School.[39]

The age-group structure of Dinka society facilitated this; Dinka young people would encourage others in their age group to attend church with them, pointing to the social aspects of it as a particular attraction.[40]

The war brought with it a change in the profile of converts. In the 1970s, it was middle sons who left home when it became clear that their families could not afford for them to be married and life in the towns provided an economic alternative. There, many converted to Christianity. During the years of the second civil war, however, the new converts came to include older sons who had positions of prominence in rural society. Petro Marial Thon, who would later become one of the first pastors ordained on the west bank during the war, was the oldest son in his family and had never received formal education. He was highly regarded

---

[38] Samuel Galuak Marial, in-person interview by Jesse Zink. Juba, South Sudan, 20 April 2013.

[39] James Nhial Maler, in-person interview by Jesse Zink. Bor, South Sudan, 6 April 2013.

[40] Gabriel Garang Machot, in-person interview by Jesse Zink. Bor, South Sudan, 7 April 2013.

among his peers as a songwriter and prominent figure in cattle camps. Yet he was drawn to Christianity in the early years of the war after an evangelist came to his cattle camp. Although his father rejected the new faith, saying that Christianity was "the religion of young people" and so not suited to the heir who was to carry on his father's name, Marial Thon nonetheless was baptized, drawn by the opportunities offered by the new faith.[41]

These young converts became important evangelists for the church. After his baptism, Marial Thon became an itinerant evangelist throughout the cattle camps. Nathaniel Garang remembered that when he was isolated on the east bank in the 1980s, young people played a key role:

> The youth guided me. I would be in one village and a group of young people would say, "Bishop, there are three thousand people a week's journey from here. They need you." I would go there . . . training some of the leaders, and ordain them to lead the church. Then another group of youth would find me and say, "Bishop, there are thousands waiting for you at such and such places." . . . I would then leave and go and teach and minister and ordain.[42]

The result of this evangelical activity was that Garang found something that had rarely been seen in Dinka territory in the past: "now you find [young] people praying in the [cattle] camp. They go to that [cattle] camp and then make their prayers."[43] Through some young people, Christianity was entering the sacred landscape of the Dinka.

REJECTING THE *JAK* AND SEEKING BAPTISM

The embrace of Christianity meant the rejection of the religion of the *jak*. As had been true since the time of CMS, new converts had to destroy the items in their homes that represented their *jak*. In what became a quasi-liturgical act, Christians would gather and sing while burning the shrines, cattle pegs, and other items of religious belief. One informant gave a detailed description of the process:

> We go to the compound and circle it three times. Then we meet in the middle of the compound with the leader at the centre and announce the reason

---

[41] Petro Marial Thon, interview by Zink. Pacong, South Sudan, 18 September 2013.

[42] John Chol Daau, unpublished research on Nathaniel Garang Anyieth, 92.

[43] Nathaniel Garang Anyieth, interview by Nikkel. London, England, March 1990.

for coming: "We have come to burn the *jɔk*, uproot the *jɔk*, because this member of the house has said they don't want *jɔk* anymore." Then the person who converted is given a chance to speak, saying why they want to get rid of the *jɔk*. We read passages from the Bible and sing songs. Then we pray: "Give us power to uproot the *jɔk*. Father, with your son Jesus Christ and the Holy Spirit we are now going to clear them away from here." Then we begin to uproot the [items sacred to the *jɔk*], split [them] into pieces, and whatever is left for the *jɔk* as an offering—groundnut paste, the fat of a cow. All is brought out and burnt. We are singing the entire time. After we burn it, those people in the compound are brought into the centre and people pray for them, touch them as they kneel down, and put their hands on them: "God we thank you for bringing this family in to your flock. We are now commending them into your care. Give them your strength and the feeling that you are with them. You are replacing *jɔk*. Give them this feeling. This compound is now your place since your crosses have been planted here." Then we put crosses in the holes where the things of the *jɔk* were and many small crosses are put on the huts around there. Then people pray and disperse.[44]

It is unclear how welcome this activity was. Informants remember that it was often led by young people, including young women, and not the head of household. This may simply be a reflection of the association of Christianity with younger people and the emergence of a younger generation as leaders in the church. Or it may confirm what the anthropologist Sharon Hutchinson noted, that "some Nuer and Dinka converts to Christianity have occasionally resorted to destroying the religious shrines of non-Christians in an effort to end 'the worship of false gods.'"[45] One informant remembered being confronted by a SPLA commander who said that Christians "come by force and pull them [*jak*] out and burn them without any permission."[46] Church leaders denied this and insisted

---

[44] Reuben Akurdit Ngong, in-person interview by Marc Nikkel. Location uncertain, 14 May 1995 (transcript in personal files of Marc Nikkel). Similar descriptions are given by other informants and in other sources; Sharon Hutchinson, *Nuer Dilemmas: Coping with Money, War, and the State* (Berkeley: University of California Press, 1996), 327–29; and Lilly Sanders Ubbens, "Chasing after the Cross: The Early Life of Rev. John Chol Daau" (M.A. thesis, Trinity School for Ministry, 2011), 22.

[45] Sharon Hutchinson, "Sacrificing Childhood: The Impact of Sudan's Unresolved Civil War on the Lives of Nuer and Dinka Women and Children," unpublished paper, August 1998, 23 (copy in NSCCA).

[46] Martha Yar Mawut, interview by Zink. Akot, South Sudan, 15 September 2013.

they would not destroy a *jɔk* without agreement of the household.⁴⁷ Still, some tension must have existed between the new religion and the old.

At first, the destruction of the *jak* appears to be a sharp confrontation with the religion they represented. In fact, however, it represents a reinterpretation of religious belief. Christians taught and believed that *jak* were now undermining Dinka welfare, a point considered at greater length in chapter 5. Dinka had to fight back by destroying the shrines of the *jak* and converting to Christianity. Crucially, however, the destruction of the shrines did not mean that the *jak* ceased to exist or had never existed in the first place. Rather, the destruction of a shrine was believed to anger the *jɔk* and invite its retribution. Abraham Mayom said that new converts "feared that *jɔk* will return again if I am not baptized. Baptism means he has changed from the old ways and turned to the new ways. Jesus will be his protector. The cross will be his protector and he will put it in his house. . . . If Christ is in his heart, then the *jɔk* will not come."⁴⁸ Such protection became part of the appeal of Christianity. In several instances, conversion gained momentum because neighbors of a Christian convert would seek baptism, fearing that if the convert was protected from the *jɔk*'s retribution, punishment might be visited on the neighbors instead. (In at least one instance a man sought baptism not only for himself but for all of his cattle as well.⁴⁹) Such beliefs began to change habits of association. Reuben Maciir recalled how Christians would gather in one cattle camp, while "[t]hose who are not believers are asked to have their own camp. If we stay together, [they] will let the devil come and tempt my children, because [they] will do those things unbelievers are doing and those things are not allowed with us here."⁵⁰ Maciir sees this in a largely positive, uncomplicated light. In her work on the Nuer, Sharon Hutchinson has argued that Christian evangelists drove wedges between converts and non-Christian Nuer, sharply dividing communities.⁵¹ Without contemporaneous anthropological work on

---

⁴⁷ Nathaniel Garang Anyieth, interview by Nikkel. London, England, March 1990.

⁴⁸ Abraham Mayom Athiaan Deng, interview by Wheeler and Schrock. Location uncertain, 14 September 1991.

⁴⁹ Marc Nikkel, "The Cross as a Symbol of Regeneration in Jieng Bor Society," *Land of Promise: Church Growth in a Sudan at War*, ed. Andrew Wheeler (Nairobi: Paulines Publications Africa, 1997), 92, 102.

⁵⁰ Reuben Maciir Makoi, interview by Nikkel. Thiika, Kenya, 10 February 1994.

⁵¹ Hutchinson, *Nuer Dilemmas*, 311.

the Dinka it is hard to say more. What is important here is the way in which Dinka Christians were repudiating their belief in the efficacy of the *jak* but not the belief that the *jak* actually existed. The practices of the new Christians, therefore, could be seen to establish a measure of congruence between Christianity and the established beliefs, lowering the barriers to Christian conversion.

The number of new converts seeking to repudiate their *jak* and turn to Christianity placed new demands on the church. New converts wanted to be baptized quickly, but CMS had established clear practices regarding baptismal preparation, the importance of literacy and knowledge of the catechism, and the inadmissibility of polygynists to the church. These had largely been carried over by Dinka church leaders like Maciir and Barac in urban churches in the 1970s. But the pressure was real: one informant, for instance, in a version of a story that is repeated by many informants, recalled that he felt impelled to join the church by dreaming of a figure in white that appeared to him over many nights and told him to seek baptism.[52] If such a person turned up in church, not only would it have been difficult to refuse baptism to someone with such a strong sense that it was God's will, but the dearth of educated church leaders also made it difficult to provide the education and training that the church had historically insisted upon. The response to this tension was different on different banks of the Nile. On the east bank, Nathaniel Garang was the sole leader, had trained at a Pentecostal institution, and—crucially—was cut off from communication with Khedekia Barac in Juba, who only a few years earlier had intervened in Bor, expelled Paul Nhomlau, and sent Garang for remedial training in Anglicanism. Under Garang's leadership, the church acceded to the pressure for baptism and largely dispensed with extensive preparation. Baptism spread widely.

The situation on the west bank, by contrast, reflected the multiple centers of leadership. Reuben Maciir prized his CMS background and upheld the view that baptism must be preceded by a lengthy catechetical period. It was a view rooted in his understanding of what it meant to be Christian: "If you don't read and you just listen to what somebody is telling you, you cannot keep it. That is why I opened places all over the forest among the communities so that they read for two years before they are baptized so that they can [learn to] read and know the

---

[52] James Nhial Maler, interview by Zink. Bor, South Sudan, 6 April 2013.

meaning."⁵³ It was the view that had been held by CMS missionaries: in order to be baptized, one first had to demonstrate one had the skills to grow in faith. Benjamin Mangar Mamur, on the other hand, had been influenced by Pentecostalism in Khartoum, Egypt, and elsewhere, and believed that his role as a pastor was to bring new people to the church. Dispensing with baptismal preparation was acceptable to him. Mangar was also open to the idea of baptizing people in polygynous relationships: "I never asked whose wife are you. A person was just come to Jesus, I accept her as she was."⁵⁴ This extended to baptizing multiple wives of the same man as well as the husband to more than one woman. In general, however, the deprivation of the war meant that polygyny was relatively rare among Dinka because the cost of marrying and maintaining multiple wives was usually prohibitive. As a result, polygyny did not pose the sort of church-defining test to Sudanese Anglicans that it has elsewhere in sub-Saharan Africa. The key issue instead was baptismal preparation. When Abraham Mayom returned to the west bank in the early 1990s after several years in refugee camps in Ethiopia, he supported Mangar's position, arguing that the only condition for baptism was a person's repudiation of the *jak* regardless of literacy or marriage practice. If a person burned his *jak*, he said, that "means he has changed from the old system to the new system. And then he will be baptised in front of the people."⁵⁵ Catechesis and literacy education would come after, not before, baptism. In Mayom's words, "We know the minds of our people. If he says he believes, you believe him. He will not go back. Then we will teach them [after]."⁵⁶

The Mangar-Mayom position prevailed, in a parallel to the policy Garang followed on the east bank. In a sense, the overwhelming interest in Christianity demanded such changes. Many people were looking to Christianity for the protection of baptism and the opportunities they found in the faith. But there were too few educated people to provide

---

⁵³ Reuben Maciir Makoi, interview by Zink. Juba, South Sudan, 22 September 2013.

⁵⁴ Benjamin Mangar Mamur, interview by Zink. Rumbek, South Sudan, 11 September 2013.

⁵⁵ Abraham Mayom Athiaan Deng, in-person interview by Michael Medley, Dhiaukuei, South Sudan, 26 December 1994 (transcript provided by Michael Medley).

⁵⁶ Abraham Mayom Athiaan Deng, interview by Wheeler and Schrock. Location uncertain, 14 September 1991.

pre-baptismal preparation as it had once existed. If the church was to become a popular movement, it needed to alter its membership policies and tolerate a degree of doctrinal confusion so as to make membership easier. The approach to polygyny was more pragmatic than anything else. Without foreign missionaries to inveigh against it and with no clear biblical condemnation, there seemed little reason to oppose a practice that was embedded in Dinka culture. These changes were not without contention: there was significant disagreement between Maciir, Mangar, and Mayom during the war, and some educated Christians continued to lament converts' lack of knowledge. One told a visitor to the west bank during the war: "The stages of deepening involvement in the Church—baptism, confirmation, deaconing, priesting, consecrating of bishops—are being passed through without any deep understanding of the history and traditions of the church."[57] The contrast with the Akot-area revival of the late 1930s is striking. Then, many new people streamed into congregations. Missionary leaders insisted on pre-baptismal catechesis and lacked the necessary personnel to oversee it. In the 1980's and 1990s, Dinka again joined congregations in large numbers. This time, church leaders were cut off from external oversight and left to make their own decisions. This they did and in a way that contradicted what their missionary forebears had done.

The changing approach to baptism demonstrates one of the ironies of the Dinka conversion movement. The isolation that many Dinka on the east and west banks felt during the war encouraged them to turn to Christianity. Its association with education in particular encouraged converts to think that it was a way to cope with the impact of the war. Yet at the same time the church was loosening its relationship with education by easing the educational requirements associated with joining the church. In an important change from the mission period, many new Christians remained functionally illiterate. Moreover, part of the appeal of Christianity during the war was that people from rural areas were able to join the church and rise to positions of leadership in communities. Christianity was no longer solely associated with an urban elite. It was precisely this distance and separation from the urban hierarchy that allowed rural church leaders to loosen baptismal requirements. Informants remember that as word of what was happening in rural areas reached him, the Dinka archdeacon Khedekia Barac was distressed at the news. But the war made

---

[57] Quoted in African Rights, *Great Expectations*, 13.

him powerless to intervene. The church of the 1970s that Barac knew had been centered in towns and consisted of educated Christians who had endured a lengthy baptismal preparation period. The church of the 1980s was rural, growing, and made up of people who were looking for stability and power in whatever forms it might come.

Opposition to the Church

Christian conversion placed demands on its converts that were incompatible with their obligations to their family and society. One manifestation of this tension was in the distribution of meat after an animal sacrifice to a *jɔk*. A series of well-established customs governed which parts of the family received which parts of the meat. The distribution practices served to knit together the extended relations that were embodied in the sacrifice.[58] Many Christian converts, however, refused to participate in such a distribution, an act that was interpreted as a repudiation of one's relations and a challenge to social hierarchies. One informant remembered that his elders saw Christians "as their enemies because we are not abiding [by] their culture. . . . When there is a ceremony or sacrifice at the family level, then you as a member of the family, there is a need for you to be partaking. When you refuse, then the members of the family look at you as not loyal to them anymore."[59] Informants, particularly young ones, frequently recalled how senior male figures in their family sought to prevent them from attending church and being baptized.

Many of these older men also held positions of religious authority in Dinka culture. Beyond the familial and relational implications of Christian conversion there were, of course, religious implications as well. The shift away from sacrifice to healing prayer, for instance, limited the societal role of older men who had fewer sacrifices over which to preside.[60] Beyond that, having rejected the *jak*, Christians also had to reject the authority of the leaders who sustained the religion of the *jak*. Direct confrontation between Christian leaders and *tit* was one result. Nathaniel Garang recalled one such incident when people in an east-bank village built a church for the first time:

---

[58] Godfrey Lienhardt, *Divinity and Experience: The Religion of the Dinka* (Oxford: Clarendon, 1961), 23–25.
[59] Daniel Kon Malwal, in-person interview by Zink. Bor, South Sudan, 5 April 2013.
[60] Sharon Hutchinson, *Nuer Dilemmas*, 311.

> When the church was opened, then they [opponents of the church] tried to call *bëny bith* in order to let the church be disappeared but the *bëny bith* could not be able to overcome the church. . . . He said, "Now, *jɔk*, if the church here is taking your people, why [do] you not chase away these people? Why not kill these people?" So the church could still grow, with many people coming in. . . . So this one, people saw that this *jɔk* has no power. This made people enter in the church.[61]

Informants related many other stories of similar confrontations, in which it was perceived that Christian leaders defeated leaders of the existing religion. Again, these are stories told by Christians with a hint of self-justification. But the tension they describe between leaders of competing religious practices is accurate.

Yet one must not overstate the scale of opposition that Christianity encountered. Christianity was one of several changes altering the context of Dinka life during the war. While it challenged some aspects of Dinka culture, it also brought aspects that were increasingly seen as beneficial in the form, for instance, of education. For some people, Christianity came to be associated with the hoped-for post-war dispensation. At the outbreak of the war, a leading prophet figure on the west bank, Manyang Jok, was reaching the end of his life. He is remembered (by church informants) as realizing that he could do no more: "What is coming is a dangerous thing," an informant remembers him saying, "but I don't have the power to prevent it. Only you go to the church people. . . . You go to God's people. If they pray, God will answer them."[62] This story must be treated with caution as it cannot be confirmed by a non-Christian source. However, it is not uncommon elsewhere in the history of African Christianity for ritual experts and religious leaders to be among those who recognize the utility of Christianity and its potential future role.[63]

The war was bringing rapid social—not simply religious—change to Dinka society. The *riäk* visited on many Dinka communities had no parallel in living memory, putting the beliefs and practices that had

---

[61] Nathaniel Garang Anyieth, interview by Nikkel. London, England, March 1990.

[62] Abraham Mayom Athiaan Deng, interview by Wheeler and Schrock. Location uncertain, 14 September 1991.

[63] Robin Horton, "A Hundred Years of Change in Kalabari Religion," in *Black Africa: Its Peoples and Their Cultures Today*, ed. John Middleton (London: Macmillan, 1970), 204.

FIGURE 3.4
Christian community worshipping in a west-bank cattle camp, c. 1994.
Collection of Marc Nikkel. Used by permission of Durham University Library.

sustained Dinka society under unprecedented pressure. Those who had the most invested in the existing system, particularly older men and ritual experts, found the change more confusing. One priest informant recalled a conversation with an older man in 1990. Seeing the informant's clerical collar, the older man unloaded his frustration on him: "The church has spoiled the people here in the area. . . . Dr. John [Garang] went to the bush trying to liberate people. Then Bishop [Nathaniel] Garang also came up with another liberation saying he want to destroy *jak* and we are totally confused."[64] The older man lamented how young people were joining the church and how Christianity was changing expectations about what was appropriate for women. But the basic complaint was confusion over the rapid pace of change. Other older men may have seen the beneficial effects of Christianity but were not yet convinced of the need to convert. In the early years of the war, the religion of the *jak* still answered the questions that many Dinka men were asking.

[64] Stephen Mathiang Kuc, in-person interview by Jesse Zink. Bor, South Sudan, 9 April 2013.

A Popular Christian Movement

The early years of the civil war transformed the position of the church in Dinka society. Rather than being a marginal actor in urban areas, church leaders took what they had learned in towns and put their institution at the center of rural communities. One result was new church adherents in places where there had previously been few. One informant grew up in a cattle camp but lived in Rumbek for many years and became Christian. By the mid-1990s, she recalled with surprise, "you can even find the church in the cattle camp."[65] In the isolation of the war, Dinka in the SPLA–controlled areas were finding that the church was a main provider of social services, even if that provision was scattered, imperfect, and hindered by the war. The displacement caused by the war had brought Christians into sustained contact with non-Christian Dinka. As time passed, these Christians sought to establish the institutions of the church as they knew it in their new environment. In the midst of societal breakdown, the church was emerging as a source of order in society.

The early years of the civil war, therefore, saw the development of an isolated but nonetheless strong Christian movement that, deprived of its historic resources, improvised in terms of liturgy, worship, and practice, growing rapidly and establishing itself as a central actor in Dinka society. Given the fluidity of war and the rapidity of the growth, it is difficult to quantify such growth, but available numbers help paint a picture. A 1992 report from the Diocese of Rumbek, the first effort to record the growth in the region, named 235 parishes, sub-parishes, and praying centers in an area reaching from Yirol to Tonj. The same report claimed that three quarters of a population of over a million had been converted, though provided no means of verifying this claim.[66] On the east bank, a 1991 report from the Diocese of Bor, a smaller region than Rumbek, listed 30 parishes with a combined 117 sub-parishes.[67] Another way of measuring the growth is in the need for clergy. The small group of ordained priests

---

[65] Informant's identity uncertain, in-person interview by Michael Medley. Near Akot, Sudan, 28 December 1994 (transcript provided by Michael Medley).

[66] "Statistics of Churches in the Diocese of Rumbek," 17 January 1992 (NSCCA).

[67] Nathaniel Garang, "Diocese of Bor 1991 Report" (NSCCA). At the first general assembly of the New Sudan Council of Churches in 1991, Nathaniel Garang reported there were 120 churches, but many other preaching centers under trees. (Wheeler, "Report on a Visit to the Episcopal Church of the Sudan in the SPLA Administered Areas of Southern Sudan," 4.) Such discrepancies are no doubt due to the challenge of keeping track of congregations when travel between areas was

at the outset of the war was insufficient to meet the new demand. On the east bank, the church had a bishop in Nathaniel Garang who was not hesitant about ordaining new clergy, even if they had little training. By 1991 on the east bank, there were about 75 pastors, a ten-fold increase from the 7 east-bank clergy in a 1981 report. Most of the new clergy "were ordained without full Bible school training."[68] When writing about the church, Dinka church leaders quoted Matthew 9:37–38—"there is a large harvest, but few workers to gather it in"—and said that "the population which looks up to them [clergy] for pastoral and spiritual assistance is too great to be served by the few pastors and priests who are now trying to shepherd this flock."[69] The west bank lacked a resident bishop until the mid-1990s, and its leadership came primarily from a small handful of clergy and many unordained people.

The growing Christian movement was a popular movement. Unlike Dinka Anglicanism of an earlier generation, this new Christianity drew its energy not from an educated elite but from the grassroots preaching centers. Indeed, the description of Dinka Anglicanism offered here—public reading and preaching about Scriptures, aggressive rejection of existing religious objects, and hymn singing (the subject of chapter 5)—is reminiscent of descriptions of Christian independency, the quintessential African popular Christian movement.[70] It is not uncommon now to attend Dinka church events and see long columns of women clad in white, marching, singing, and waving crosses. It is strongly evocative of independent churches elsewhere in sub-Saharan Africa—yet the women are all members of ECS. Two examples make these parallels particularly clear. Christian independency has been understood, in part, as a reaction to the pressure of African religion and culture on churches.[71] One area in which this pressure is seen is matters of health and healing, traditional areas of concern for African religion. Many descriptions

---

difficult as well as the different measures of counting: it is not always clear what counts as a sub-parish and what as a preaching center.

[68] Diocese of Bor, "Project Proposal: C.M.S. Bible Institute, Malek, 1992 Programme," December 1991 (NSCCA).

[69] Nathaniel Garang and Abraham Mayom, letter to Mark Harris, 4 September 1990 (NSCCA).

[70] David Maxwell, "Christianity," in *The Oxford Handbook of Modern African History*, ed. John Parker and Richard Reid (Oxford: Oxford University Press, 2013), 270.

[71] Adrian Hastings, *The Church in Africa 1450–1950* (Oxford: Clarendon, 1994), 529–30.

of independent churches focus on their healing rituals and practices.[72] The healing practices of the growing Dinka Anglican movement mirrored those of an independent denomination yet were contained within a mission church. Leaders such as Reuben Maciir and Benjamin Mangar became respected for their healing powers, as if they were independent leaders, yet remained within a mission denomination they both valued deeply, though differently.

Independency has also been seen as a reaction to the rapid growth of Christianity with which mission denominations were unable to cope. Independent prophets offered baptism, the missionary's primary rite, because they thought it so important and because it was so much in demand: "while almost all missionaries reasonably insisted upon a quite lengthy baptismal preparation, the desire for instant baptism had become so great in some quarters that it almost generated prophetic baptizers to respond to it."[73] This describes Dinka Anglicanism during the civil war. The desire for baptism was so great that church leaders had little choice but to respond, but they did so within a mission denomination. Yet for all that Christian practice was changing in these east- and west-bank communities, one undeniable result of all this religious change was the strengthening of ECS, a denomination with historic and continuing mission ties. But it was strengthened only insofar as it was responding to the needs and pressures generated by the war.

The parallels between the Dinka Christian movement and other movements of Christian independency are due to many factors. One of these, surely, is the Pentecostal background of some of the leaders of the Anglican movement. Both Nathaniel Garang and Benjamin Mangar Mamur had significant exposure to Pentecostalism, the twentieth-century Christian renewal movement that is a collection of "vital and powerful idioms about illness and healing, evil and purity which make striking resonances with peoples sharing common historical experiences of marginalization from established religion."[74] Such ideas were clearly part of the Dinka conversion movement. Yet these Pentecostal ideas were put to work in a part of Africa that had not experienced overlapping Protestant mission work. When Mangar and Garang returned

---

[72] E.g., Matthew Schoffeleers, "Ritual Healing and Political Acquiescence: The Case of the Zionist Churches in South Africa," *Africa* 60, no. 1 (1991).

[73] Hastings, *Church in Africa*, 531.

[74] David Maxwell, "Historicizing Christian Independency: The Southern African Pentecostal Movement c. 1908–60," *Journal of African History* 40 (1999): 244.

to their home areas fired with Pentecostal fervor, they found that their people only knew one form of Christianity, Anglicanism. If they wanted to work with their people, it was only by working as Anglicans that they would be understood. As Mangar Mamur recalled, "If I got another denomination, they will say, 'No, no, no, he is not our man.' And then they will not listen to the Gospel."[75] Garang, similarly, returned from his study at a Pentecostal college in Kenya in 1974 and sought ordination in the Anglican church, even consenting to an additional year of training at Bishop Gwynne College.

This background helps explain why the history of the church in southern Sudan is marked by the absence of independent Christian movements. Even today, the religious scene in South Sudan continues to be overwhelmingly dominated by mission denominations—Catholic, Anglican, and Presbyterian—with only a small presence from Pentecostal and other churches. On one level, this is to be expected. The conditions that often led to the emergence of independency were absent in southern Sudan. If independency is to be seen as a reaction against ecclesiastical paternalism, there was little for southern Sudanese to react against. By the 1950s, much of the frontline mission work was in the hands of southern Sudanese who were also, in fits and starts, gaining more authority within the church.[76]

But to say that independent churches are absent from southern Sudan is not also to say that the energy that gives rise to independency is absent. In the conversion movement among the Dinka in the 1980s and 1990s, there was new energy, new enthusiasm, and new leadership for the Christian message. The practices of the church evoke those of independent churches. There is an essential continuity between movements of mission Christianity and movements of Christian independency.[77] At a popular level, discerning difference between the two is difficult. In the case of the Dinka, the war was a key factor. It was the war that effectively isolated these east- and west-bank communities from church hierarchies that may have intervened more aggressively had they known how practices were changing. It was also the war that raised serious

---

[75] Benjamin Mangar Mamur, interview by Zink. Rumbek, South Sudan, 11 September 2013.

[76] Hastings, *Church in Africa*, 528–31; See also Terence Ranger, "Christian Independency in Tanzania," in *Africa Initiatives in Religion*, ed. David R. Barrett (Nairobi: East African Publishing House, 1971), 122–45.

[77] Hastings, *Church in Africa*, 530.

questions about the efficacy of the religion of the *jak* and caused people to look at other options more seriously. Christian leaders, freed by the war, were able to respond to the needs generated in their local communities. Dinka Anglicanism on the east and west banks had the vibrancy and energy of Christian independency within an historic mission church.

War and Religious Change

Christian conversion in the middle of a civil war is, in part, a decision of personal security. When one has to flee one's home or is otherwise displaced, it is understandable to ask how one has come to be in such a position and how to avoid such a position in the future. This displacement created new opportunities for Christians to offer an alternative religious explanation to account for the situation. Mary Aruay Majak, a church leader on the west bank, remembered that when she first began to evangelize and encountered a hostile response, Dinka "were living in a very stable way, there was no problem, they were living in a peaceful [way]. But when the war was in all areas of South Sudan, there was no way except God."[78] People turned to Christianity because they perceived that the *jak* had failed to protect them. As one informant said, "The peace of the *jak*, their peace is a limited one. But for us in Jesus Christ, our peace is so much wider and is for a long time."[79] By turning to Christianity, many Dinka found answers—in the form of protection, healing, and community—that they were unable to find elsewhere. Christianity was associated with a constellation of values and attributes that were now regarded as valuable in Dinka communities in the SPLA–controlled areas. But the new needs among displaced Dinka would have mattered little if there had been no one to spread the Christian message. Displacement, therefore, was a key feature of religious change not simply because it caused many Dinka to look for new resources but because it displaced potential Christian evangelists, namely the educated and Christian residents of towns. For the first time, sustained Christian evangelism was taking place in the cattle camps and villages at the center of Dinka life. One informant remembered the significance of this: "those in the towns [have come out]—the word is God is now out [and] spread by people

---

[78] Mary Aruay Majak, interview by Zink. Rumbek, South Sudan, 13 September 2013.
[79] Martha Kuei Marier, interview by Zink. Rumbek, South Sudan, 19 September 2013.

[who were] in towns."[80] Displacement created a situation in which not only were people looking for new answers, they were also encountering evangelists bearing those answers.

The need for new resources that was created by the war is crystallized in a particular aspect of the church: its connection to a broader world outside southern Sudan and its role as a potential conduit of international aid. Prior to the war, it was not always immediately obvious to many Dinka what the non-Dinka world had to offer that might be valuable to them. In the war's early years, this attitude persisted in part because the east- and west-bank communities were so isolated. Fitful efforts at international relief in the 1980s struggled to deliver relief supplies to SPLA–controlled areas. Even when they succeeded, the east- and west-bank communities were often bypassed in favor of areas that were then bearing the brunt of the war, particularly along the north-south border. But by the 1990s, it was clearer to many east- and west-bank Dinka that international aid and support were necessary—and that the church could fulfill this role. Church and aid became associated with each other for many people. As one report noted, "Foreign aid . . . is almost a sacred sign of the churches' links internationally and of their perceived power to change things. . . . [I]t gives the church an almost mystical power that traditional religions cannot match."[81] In an area experiencing such severe shortages of food, clothing, and shelter, distributing aid became a freighted and complex exercise that gave power to those with access to resources. The Sudan Relief and Rehabilitation Association, affiliated with the SPLA, was active particularly on the west bank and took a role in directing the distribution of aid. But the church also took a role, in large measure because some of the aid was coming from religious organizations. Some informants remember that people joined the church because they believed it would offer them preferential access to relief supplies: "Some people among all these Christians are caring for personal material benefit because of relief items."[82] The distribution of relief supplies came to be an issue of dispute particularly within the west-bank church, as various leaders used the distribution to strengthen their own position at the expense of others. For a time in the

---

[80] Paul Manyuon Gak, in-person interview by Michael Medley. Dhiaukuei, Sudan, 4 January 1995 (transcript provided by Michael Medley).

[81] Hugh McCullum, "Ministering during War," *One World* 14 (June 1995) (NSCCA).

[82] Paul Manyuon Gak, interview by Medley. Dhiaukuei, Sudan, 4 January 1995.

1990s Abraham Mayom was able to use his family connections to and apparent membership in the SPLA to sideline Reuben Maciir and take greater control of the west-bank church. Disputes over the "manipulative use of relief supplies" ensued, and one informant noted, "Mayom is a politician. Reuben Maciir is really a religious man."[83]

Beyond aid that the church could command, belonging to the church also connected its members to a larger advocacy organization: "The Church . . . represented us to [the] outside, calling people outside that there were people in other areas suffering like us."[84] In part, this aid was in response to the formation in the late 1980s of the New Sudan Council of Churches (NSCC), an ecumenical organization in which Nathaniel Garang and Abraham Mayom took leadership roles. NSCC advocacy visits to the Vatican, the World Council of Churches, and England succeeded in highlighting the needs of southern Sudanese. These visits were repaid by the Archbishop of Canterbury, George Carey, who visited the west-bank church in 1994. Carey's visit is widely remembered nearly a generation after it took place: "He did not come to bring aid, speak out on human rights, or make peace. His simple message of solidarity was received with straightforward enthusiasm and joy."[85] Among the Dinka, the church had always been associated with modernity. The war represented a great intrusion of Western modernity into the rural Dinka heartland. By associating themselves with the church's international connections, Dinka could come to grips with that destructive modernity and find new resources in the middle of war.

For all the multiple reasons people had for converting, two reasons remain relatively muted in interviews with informants. When asked about the appeal of Christianity, few cite the classic evangelical reason of eternal life. This is not to say that people were not motivated to convert by the promise of eternal life, but that in interviews and other source materials it does not emerge as a prominent reason. When prompted, informants would agree that eternal life was a reason but it was rarely

---

[83] Andrew C. Wheeler, "Church Growth in Southern Sudan, 1983–1996: A Survey of Present Understanding," in *Land of Promise: Church Growth in a Sudan at War*, ed. Wheeler (Nairobi: Paulines Publications Africa, 1997), 26; Abraham Mayek, in-person interview by Michael Medley. Dhiaukuei, Sudan, 4 January 1995 (transcript provided by Michael Medley).

[84] Identity of informant uncertain, in-person interview by Michael Medley. Akot, Sudan, 30 December 1994 (transcript provided by Michael Medley).

[85] African Rights, *Great Expectations*, 33.

volunteered independently. The absence of such a narrative within southern Sudan highlights the pragmatic and "this-worldly" calculations that governed conversion to Christianity. Education, international connections, and a new understanding of the *jak* were the resources that Dinka needed to survive the war.

The other area on which informants are relatively silent is the role of Islam. Unlike the situation in the Khartoum area in the 1960s and 1970s, fewer people seemed motivated to convert as a way to assert one's identity against an Islamic hegemony. In part, this has to do with how Islam was manifest in the SPLA–controlled areas. In the north, Islam was a religious and political force, with the former at least as significant as the latter. In the south, by contrast, Islam was perceived primarily as a political force and "a facet of Northern 'Arab' domination. . . . Islam as a *religion* hardly registers on the horizon of the Church."[86] Islam was part of the general oppression southerners experienced from the north. The religious conflict that mattered was between Christianity and the religion of the *jak*, not Christianity and Islam. Given that the Sudanese civil war is often described in shorthand as a war of Christians against Muslims, such a finding is significant for the way that it confounds this narrative. As a religious matter, Christianity and Islam were not in conflict.

If the religion of the *jak* was a religion that offered explanations and control over the experiences that Dinka encountered in their daily lives, then this chapter has shown how the appeal of a new religion, Christianity, was that it continued to offer explanations for changed social circumstances. In preaching centers and schools across the region, Dinka converts associated themselves with a new modernity and joined the church. For the Dinka of the 1980s and early 1990s, the civil war reshaped how Dinka perceived the world and what they regarded as valuable for success in life. It is not surprising, therefore, that in recalling their decisions to convert to Christianity, informants highlight this-worldly reasons that emerge from the changed context of the civil war. The *riäk* of civil war generated a set of conditions that put in motion an intense period of religious change.

Indeed, the connection between civil war and religious change can be seen more clearly by examining where the experiences of east- and west-bank communities diverge. In the opening years of the war, there were broad similarities between the two regions. In 1991, however, the

---

[86] African Rights, *Great Expectations*, 39.

course of the war significantly changed, and the development of the church on each bank diverged. In August of that year, the SPLA split along ethnic lines. The Nuer commander, Riek Machar, announced that he was deposing the Dinka head of the SPLA, John Garang. Garang, however, retained the support of much of the SPLA, leading to conflict between rival SPLA factions. In November 1991, Nuer forces attacked Bor and the surrounding area, killing thousands and displacing hundreds of thousands. It is an event of central ethno-historical importance for east-bank Dinka and is remembered now as the "Bor Massacre." It left the Bor region devastated and almost uninhabited. Many east-bank Dinka fled west or south to camps for internally displaced people or farther to camps in Kenya or Uganda.

The Bor Massacre also changed the east-bank church. In part because of the preaching of a prophet named Kon Ajith, the subject of chapter 7, some Dinka interpreted the Bor Massacre as God's punishment on the Dinka for their devotion to *jak*. The proper response was to finally reject the *jak* and turn to God as made known in Jesus Christ. Seen in the terms of this chapter, the Bor Massacre was conclusive proof for many that new resources were needed to survive the war. In a 1992 interview, one priest explained the scale of conversion by saying that people "are looking for safety. They worshipped these traditional gods and the war took place. . . . And so they are fed up. The Christians told them the god they are worshipping will not protect them. The right god to worship is the one of Christianity; so they say they will try this god now. . . . They are looking for safety."[87] The profile of converts began to change. Whereas before 1991, converts were primarily drawn from younger populations, informants recall that the period after the Bor Massacre was one in which older men who had previously resisted Christianity now sought baptism. Younger people were now able to welcome their fathers into the church. In early 1993, Anglican priest John Kelei presided over a bonfire outside Bor in which over 3,000 items related to the religion of the *jak* were burned, including the spear sacred to *Lierpiɔu*. The spear had once been a central religious symbol to the people of Bor and was believed by some to have ended the first civil war. Kelei recalled that "the Bor Massacre, it was actually a part of evangelization. . . . After the Bor Massacre, old people find themselves vulnerable. There's

---

[87] Mark Akuien Gak, in-person interview by Marc Nikkel. Location uncertain, 16 June 1992 (transcript in NSCCA).

no cows that you can use to perform worship so the only option that came to people's mind was to join Christianity to give them a heart to continue, give them hope for their future."[88] The burning was a moment that symbolized the transition that east-bank Dinka had undergone. The religion of the *jak* had been almost completely abandoned in favor of Christianity. After 20 years there are few signs of the religion of the *jak* on the east bank.

Although the SPLA split affected west-bank communities, there was no single event there comparable in scale or destructiveness to the Bor Massacre. The church continued to be a provider of education and aid, and people continued to join it. But conversion was always less complete than it was on the east bank. Two older male west-bank informants interviewed in 1994 represent this. Each says he is open to Christianity and appreciates its role in society, but neither is baptized and shows no inclination to pursue that course: "That is a new generation. They need to go to church always because of God. I am staying here in my house as an old man."[89] Christianity is seen as a coming force but one that is not appropriate for older men. The west bank never had a mass movement of older men into the church in the way the east bank did in the wake of the Bor Massacre. That difference persists two decades on. Items of the religion of the *jak* remain on display and in use in west-bank communities. Church leaders on the west bank are aware that their church draws on a smaller percentage of society than the east-bank church does. The clear indications are that Christianity, while a much larger presence among west-bank communities than it was prior to the war, is weaker than the near-complete integration of the east bank.

There are many differences between the east-bank and west-bank churches. The latter had multiple leaders during the war, while the former had a single dominant leader. West-bank leaders are eager to point out that since CMS began its work at Malek on the east bank, Christianity has had longer to take root there. (Such an argument elides the fact that by the end of the mission period, the concentration of CMS' work among the Dinka was in west-bank communities.) While Dinka in both places shared broadly similar religious beliefs and practices centered on

---

[88] John Kelei, in-person interview by Jesse Zink. Bor, South Sudan, 16 April 2013.
[89] Informants' identity uncertain, in-person interview by Michael Medley. Akot, Sudan, 29 December 1994 (transcript provided by Michael Medley).

jak, yiëth, Nhialic, and other divinities, the relative emphasis was different. On the east bank, there was a greater proliferation of *jak,* which were consequently more central to religious practice. On the west bank, by contrast, there was less sense of a mediating force between Dinka and *Nhialic.* Therefore, for east-bank communities, conversion to Christianity represented a radical dismantling of traditional life, which needed an equally radical moment—the Bor Massacre—to complete the process. For west-bank communities, however, conversion was a more gradual process of coming to understand the identity of *Nhialic* with the Christian God.[90] But there is no escaping the conclusion that the different course of war on each bank had a strongly determinative effect. That conclusion is in keeping with what has already been seen about the way in which the catastrophe of the war forced many Dinka to consider new religious options. Where the war was more destructive, the conversion was more complete.[91]

Conclusion

The early years of Sudan's second civil war led many Dinka in the former CMS sphere to re-evaluate the claims and utility of the religion of the *jak.* No longer was it answering the questions to which Dinka needed religious answers. At the same time, Christianity became a serious alternative. The displacement of war caused many people to return to cattle camps and villages from towns and urban areas. The conditions created by the war sent many Dinka looking for new resources and opportunities. Christianity proved the truth of its claims by demonstrating its utility in fields such as education and health. The distance from church hierarchies created by the war allowed local church leaders to adapt Christian practices to respond to the situations in which they now ministered. The result was a shift in religious identity among many Dinka. Where the war was strongest—that is, where the pressures on the claims of the religion of the *jak* were perceived to be most acute— the religious identity of Dinka shifted most dramatically. The wartime

---

[90] Roland Werner, William Anderson, and Andrew Wheeler, eds. *Day of Devastation, Day of Contentment: The History of the Sudanese Church across 2000 Years* (Nairobi: Paulines Publications Africa, 2000), 559–60.

[91] A similar correlation was noted in relation to conversion to Protestantism during Guatemala's civil war: where fighting was fiercest, churches grew fastest. Virginia Garrard-Burnett, *Protestantism in Guatemala: Living in the New Jerusalem* (Austin: University of Texas Press, 1998), 131–32.

religious change among the Dinka created a Christian movement in that Christian ideas and rhetoric were both popular and widespread at the grassroots level. The Christianity that was practiced had many of the hallmarks of an independent Christian movement and yet Dinka Christians in these regions of southern Sudan saw themselves as members of ECS, an historic mission denomination.

Not only did the *riäk* of civil war displace many Dinka within southern Sudan, it caused many to leave the country altogether. Religious change also took place among these displaced populations, but in a different manner and with different emphases than the communities within southern Sudan. It is these displaced populations that are the subject of the next chapter.

4

Lost Boys, Found Church
Displacement and Conversion in Ethiopia and Kenya

For much of the 1990s, Ezekiel Diing was the senior Anglican cleric in Wau, a major town in the Bahr el Ghazal region. Wau had been in the mission sphere allocated to the Roman Catholic church, a fact attested to by the large Catholic cathedral in the center of town. The Anglican presence originated in a chaplaincy to expatriates during the Condominium period. When Diing arrived, it was a small church. The Episcopal Church of the Sudan (ECS) had consecrated its first bishop for Wau, John Malou Ater, in 1984, but in a sign of the weakness of the Anglican presence Malou was an Agar Dinka from the Rumbek area and not native to Wau. In 1986, Malou was killed when the SPLA shot down the plane he was traveling in. The war forced his successor to remain in Khartoum. In the 1990s, Diing established himself in Wau, but he was from even farther away: a Twic Dinka from the Kongor area.

During his time in Wau, Diing became aware of a new trend in the rural areas of Bahr el Ghazal: new converts were joining ECS. The main instigator of this religious change was not Diing himself but a group of young men from the Rek Dinka sub-tribe who had been displaced from their homes in the 1980s and sought refuge in camps in Ethiopia and Kenya. When they began to return home, they did so as Christian evangelists. Diing recalled their strategy: "They went with the music. When they were singing the songs, the songs attracted the young people, those who were not the typical Catholic. Then they started their church. . . . What helped them also, some of the people say, 'OK, these are our children. When they went, they were not Christian. Then they came and they are now Christian and they are ordained pastors.'"[1]

From its beginning in 1983, a central feature of Sudan's second civil war was displacement. The young refugees Diing encountered were among hundreds of thousands of southern Sudanese forced to leave their homes and seek refuge elsewhere. Some sought safety in remote, rural communities distant from towns and the road system. Others found it in government-controlled cities such as Juba or Khartoum. But a major stream of displacement was across international borders. By 1987, there were hundreds of thousands of refugees, a majority of whom were Dinka, in camps in southwestern Ethiopia. When the Ethiopian government was overthrown in 1991, refugee life shifted to new camps in southern Sudan, Kenya, and Uganda.

This refugee population was noteworthy in at least one regard: a large proportion was young males who were apparently unconnected to any family or adult support. Known first by international aid workers as "unaccompanied minors," in time this group of approximately 30,000 young people—a vast majority of whom were Dinka—became known as "The Lost Boys of Sudan." When they left their homes at various points in the 1980s, they represented the then-current situation: they were most familiar with the religion of the *jak* and had received little to no education. In the course of more than 15 years in refugee camps, they came to understand their religious identity primarily within Christian terms. And, as Diing recognized, they became agents of further religious change. As the course of the war began to shift in the 1990s, some of these young people returned to their homes as evangelists and began to expand the presence of Anglican churches in new areas.

This chapter parallels the previous one. Having traced the currents of religious change among Dinka who remained within southern Sudan, this chapter now follows the path of religious change among Dinka who were forced to flee across international borders. The unsettled, unsafe, and unstable life they encountered in refugee camps in Ethiopia set the context for religious change and provided an environment in which the church was able to emerge as a central social institution that counteracted other destructive tendencies also present in the refugee camps. When the course of the war shifted in 1991 and the refugees were forced to move to new

---

[1] Ezekiel Diing, in-person interview by Jesse Zink. 5 April 2013, Bor, South Sudan.

camps in Kenya and Uganda, the comparative stability of these new camps created an environment in which the church could consolidate its growth and begin to build the institutions made necessary by the rapid growth. It was from this base that some refugees began to return home and expand the reach of the church.

As the unaccompanied minors became known as "The Lost Boys of Sudan," they generated considerable sympathetic media attention. But it is while they were "lost" that they found—and built—the church.

Refugees, Recruits, and Converts in Ethiopia

From the beginning of the second civil war, the government of Mengistu Haile Mariam in Ethiopia was a principal supporter of the Sudan People's Liberation Army (SPLA). Leaders of the Bor Mutiny fled to Ethiopia in 1983 and it was there that they organized the SPLA. Ethiopia's influence was crucial in the emergence of John Garang de Mabior as head of the rebel movement. Southwestern Ethiopia became the headquarters of the SPLA and the base from which it launched its operations in Sudan.[2] But it was not only the SPLA that was present in southwestern Ethiopia. Southern Sudanese, primarily Dinka and other Nilotic peoples from SPLA-controlled areas, began arriving in Ethiopia as early as 1983 and finding refuge in camps established by the United Nations. In its early years, the burden of the war fell most heavily on western Bahr el Ghazal as the Khartoum government armed militias and sent them into the region. An escalation of violence in the area in 1987 and 1988 produced famine conditions and led to a sharp increase in the number of refugees. By 1988, there was a series of refugee camps in the region at Itang, Dimma, and Pinyudu (also spelled Panyido and Fugnido). By 1990, it was estimated that there were between 350,000 and 400,000 people in the camps, the majority of whom were in Itang, by far the largest camp.[3] A notable feature of this population was the large number of minors, particularly in Pinyudu, which had been established in part to care for this population of young people. A May 1988 census showed that 45 percent of Pinyudu's

---

[2] Douglas H. Johnson and Gerard Prunier, "The Foundation and Expansion of the Sudan People's Liberation Army," in *Civil War in the Sudan*, ed. M. W. Daly and Ahmad Alawad Sikainga (London: British Academic Press, 1993), 117–41. Peter Adwok Nyaba, *Politics of Liberation in South Sudan: An Insider's View* (Kampala, Uganda: Fountain, 1997), 50.

[3] Sharon E. Hutchinson, *Nuer Dilemmas: Coping with Money, War, and the State* (Berkeley: University of California Press, 1996), 6.

population of over 30,000 were male children between the ages of 6 and 15.[4] Virtually all of these children lacked adult caregivers. As a result, they became known as "unaccompanied minors" for they had walked without—apparently—adult supervision across southern Sudan to Ethiopia. In 1991, when the camps were abruptly closed, there were nearly 15,000 children in Pinyudu, 90 percent of whom were Dinka.[5] Thousands of other such children were in other camps.

Many refugees, but particularly the minors, arrived at these camps in very poor health. A fact-finding group of British Members of Parliament visited the camps in 1988 and found new arrivals "suffering from disease and malnutrition of a similar severity to that experienced in the 1984–85 famine [in Ethiopia]."[6] One international NGO worker remembered seeing on a visit to Pinyudu "only naked bodies, very thin, of boys, as far as the eye could see. They did not even have *tukls* [huts] to live in."[7] These were the young people who had survived the journey. Studies indicated that as many as one in five of the minors who set out from home died before reaching Ethiopia.[8] It was a sudden and abrupt transition from a life centered in a village or cattle camp to one dominated by international actors. In the terms of Robin Horton, the microcosm had been decisively shattered.

Studies of refugees often draw a simple causal line between war, violence, and displacement. A contemporaneous BBC report quoted a young Dinka man who fled when militias allied with the Khartoum government attacked his home: "Our houses and villages were set on fire by the government army. We were just looking for survival. No-one encouraged us to come. Either you escape or you die."[9] Several of the young

---

[4] UNHCR Technical Support Service, "Ethiopia: Unaccompanied Children in Fugnido: A Preliminary Study, 30 May–28 June 1988," TSS Mission Report 29/88, 1 (UNHCRA).

[5] Rädda Barnen, "The Unaccompanied Minors of Southern Sudan," November 1994 (NSCCA).

[6] House of Commons Foreign Affairs Committee, "Famine in the Horn of Africa," 12 May 1988, Session 1987–88, HC 297, xxvii.

[7] Human Rights Watch / Africa, *Civilian Devastation: Abuses by All Parties in the War in Southern Sudan* (New York: Human Rights Watch, 1994), 204.

[8] Sheila Rule, "Refugees from Sudan Strain Ethiopia Camps," *New York Times*, 1 May 1988.

[9] Mike Wooldridge, "Why They Fled," in *War Wounds: Development Costs of Conflict in Southern Sudan*, ed. Nigel Twose and Benjamin Pogrund (London: Panos Institute, 1988), 142. See also Rule, "Refugees from Sudan Strain Ethiopia Camps."

FIGURE 4.1
Dinka children in Pinyudu, c. 1988. Collection of Erik Gunnar Eriksson.
Used by permission of Star of Hope® and the estate of Erik Gunnar Eriksson.

people later wrote memoirs in which they attributed the displacement to the violence of war and the need for a safe place to seek education.[10] But even in the midst of war, displaced people retain agency, making displacement a more complex phenomenon than it initially seems.[11] In this case, displacement was both a response to the war and a strategy actively shaped by the SPLA. The rebel army recruited young men to Ethiopia to prepare them for future military service in training camps it maintained in close proximity to the refugee camps.[12] One informant recalled this in a matter-of-fact manner: "The SPLA commander on the east bank, Kuol Manyang, analyzed the situation and [saw] that the war

---

[10] See, for instance, Abraham Nhial and DiAnn Mills, *Lost Boy No More: A True Story of Survival and Salvation* (Nashville: B&H, 2004) or John Bul Dau with Michael S. Sweeney, *God Grew Tired of Us: A Memoir* (Washington, D.C.: National Geographic, 2007).

[11] Stephen C. Lubkemann, *Culture in Chaos: An Anthropology of the Social Condition in War* (Chicago: University of Chicago Press, 2008), 15–21.

[12] Carol Berger, "Southern Sudan's Red Army: The Role of Social Process and Routinised Violence in the Deployment of Underaged Soldiers" (D.Phil. dissertation, Oxford University, 2010).

will take time and the children will grow up without education. So Kuol talked to John Garang so that he can organize the children to be taken to Ethiopia for education. And Garang agreed with him. So he came up with a program that every male child will be taken to Ethiopia.... We have to be trained as SPLA fighters."[13] One young refugee remembers being recruited to Ethiopia by SPLA soldiers who told him "we could get guns and training and then return to help force the Arabs out of southern Sudan."[14] To the SPLA, the minors became known as *jiech amer* (Arabic: "Red Army") and were to be the force that aided them in the war. The SPLA sought to hide these purposes by stressing the importance of raising a generation of educated young people. A human rights NGO concluded, however, that "the SPLA recruited the boys for both education and military purposes, but attempted to conceal the military purpose."[15] It is claims such as these that make the "unaccompanied minor" label inappropriate; at least some of the children were accompanied and directed by the SPLA.

The majority of displaced male minors received military training at some point, some voluntarily, others not, in camps that the SPLA maintained close to the refugee camps. The training was harsh and difficult and featured extreme physical punishment, starvation, and forced labor.[16] Separated from their families and upbringing, the young people were trained in a way that was designed to destroy any mediating structures of community, loyalty and kinship that would obstruct the recruits' relationship with their military superiors.[17] The aim was to develop a "nihilistic attitude towards civilians and existing social structures."[18] As the *jiech amer*, these minors would be the vanguard of the new Sudan the SPLA was creating.

---

[13] Daniel Kon Malwal, in-person interview by Jesse Zink. 5 April 2013, Bor, South Sudan. Such views were also reported in news reports at the times, e.g., Jane Perlez, "Children Recruited as Manpower Pool," *New York Times*, 14 August 1991.

[14] Dau with Sweeney, *God Grew Tired of Us*, 43.

[15] Human Rights Watch, *Civilian Devastation*, 205.

[16] Berger, "Southern Sudan's Red Army," 110–11.

[17] Sharon E. Hutchinson, "A Curse from God? Religious and Political Dimensions of the Post-1991 Rise of Ethnic Violence in South Sudan," *The Journal of Modern African Studies* 39, no. 2 (2001): 315.

[18] Rolanda Oostland and Ronald Berkvens, *Sudanese Life Stories: Voices from Kakuma Refugee Camp* (Utrecht: Churches in Action & Pax Christi, April 1998), 34; Nyaba, *Politics of Liberation in South Sudan*, 55; African Rights, *Food and Power in Sudan: A Critique of Humanitarianism* (London: African Rights, 1997), 82.

Nor were the camps administered by the United Nations a safe refuge. Citing security, the SPLA and their allies in the Ethiopian government forbade international workers from staying in Pinyudu, Itang, and other camps overnight. This allowed the SPLA to seize food aid and redirect it to its soldiers, who were stationed in camps not far from the refugees.[19] In the camps themselves, the SPLA exercised considerable control over the life of the refugees. One refugee remembers that even as he was learning English, he was explicitly instructed not to use his new knowledge to speak to any non-Sudanese. If approached, he was to act shy and pretend not to be able to understand.[20] The SPLA leadership from time to time convened public gatherings in the refugee camps at which it executed alleged traitors as a demonstration of what would happen if its dictates were not obeyed. The result was an atmosphere that was "characterised by general fear, apathy, indifference and self-insurance. To stay alive became a cherished idea and this encouraged the culture of silence and insensitivity to all that was happening."[21] Calling the residents of these camps "refugees" was useful to the SPLA in that it encouraged the international community to respond with aid, which was then redirected towards the training and operational bases the SPLA maintained in safety from the Sudan government.[22]

THE CHURCH IN ETHIOPIA

The SPLA was not the only Sudanese organization active in the Ethiopian refugee camps. Among the refugees and recruits arriving in Ethiopia was a small number of Christians, including a handful of clergy from different denominations. Particularly after refugees began arriving in greater numbers in 1987, the presence of the church became widely apparent. By July 1989, a report from the camps identified five ordained Anglican priests (four of whom were Dinka), three ordained Catholic priests (two of whom were Dinka), and several senior commissioned evangelists, both male and female.[23] In total, there were nearly 40 lay and ordained church leaders from a variety of

---

[19] Human Rights Watch, *Civilian Devastation*, 207.
[20] Dave Eggers with Valentino Achak Deng, *What Is the What: The Autobiography of Valentino Achak Deng: A Novel* (London: Vintage, 2006), 326.
[21] Nyaba, *Politics of Liberation in South Sudan*, 67.
[22] African Rights, *Food and Power in Sudan*, 73.
[23] Open letter "To All Churches of Christ" from Dominic Matong Majok, Matthew Aguto Kuoi, and Abraham Mayom Athiaan, 9 July 1989 (NSCCA).

denominations and regions in southern Sudan. They were needed to serve a growing church. One of these was Abraham Mayom Athiaan, who had been educated but not ordained at Bishop Gwynne College in the early 1980s, displaced to the camps, and would later return to the west bank in the early 1990s. He wrote to a friend, "Our Lord Jesus is recreating his work in the refugee camps. . . . [T]here are many big churches in which one can accommodate over three thousand people."[24] At the center of these churches were the "unaccompanied" minors who turned to Christianity in part because of what it offered them in their new environment.

Most of the young people who arrived in Ethiopian refugee camps, whether from Bahr el Ghazal or the east-bank communities, were like the majority of Dinka: they were not Christian and knew little of Christianity before their arrival. But the religious change that had begun within southern Sudan meant there were a small number of lay evangelists among the unaccompanied minors who had converted before their departure from home. It was these lay evangelists who became an important factor in facilitating Christian conversion. Like church life in SPLA–controlled areas in southern Sudan, they began holding services under trees in the camps. This worship is described similarly to that of the preaching centers spreading in east- and west-bank communities. One informant recalled how "[t]hey organize[d] rallies in the evening. They [taught] songs. They [taught] the Bible. And most of the people [got] acquainted with [Christianity]."[25] One of the keys to the success of this evangelism was that it was local. The sheer size of the camps prevented the emergence of a single gathering place for preaching and evangelism. Instead, clergy leaders would train senior children to lead worship and Bible teaching in prayer centers in different parts of the camp. The lay evangelists began a regular schedule of daily preaching and teaching close to where the young people and others were living.

The energy in the new churches transcended denominational backgrounds, particularly in the early years. The Catholic catechist Joseph Pal Mut, a Nuer, arrived in Itang in 1987. Finding no established Catholic presence, he worked as an evangelist with a Presbyterian congregation, which had a strong presence among the Nuer. At that time, Anglican

---

[24] Abraham Mayom Athiaan, letter to Marc Nikkel, 13 June 1989 (NSCCA).
[25] Daniel Kon Malwal, interview by Zink. Bor, South Sudan, 5 April 2013.

Dinka were also meeting with the Presbyterian Nuer.[26] When the Dinka Roman Catholic priest Dominic Matong arrived in Itang, he noticed the new cooperation among churches: "The Roman Catholics have come to like being together [with other denominations]. The Roman Catholics are borrowing from the Anglican Christians. In an ecumenical service the Dinka sing the songs of the Nuer. They can sing back and forth. The Dinka sing in Nuer language, the Nuer in Dinka language. Roman Catholics, Presbyterian and ECS are all singing across language and denominational lines in their worship." Church services began to structure social life: "The social cohesion from the past is being replaced by the Church. There is no alcohol. The youth would be with us all evening. The Bor youth were singing Christmas songs. . . . They sing and dance."[27] In time, this trans-denominational enthusiasm would lead to the formation of the New Sudan Council of Churches, an ecumenical organization that in the 1990s began to advocate for peace in southern Sudan and reconciliation among warring factions.

The energy behind Christian worship and evangelism was paralleled by and related to the emphasis on education in the refugee camps. All young people, whatever the reason for their arrival in Ethiopia, shared a deep hunger for any form of schooling. The war had laid bare the disadvantage Dinka faced in their relations with the Khartoum government. Education was seen as *the* way to remedy this deficit. The enthusiasm for education was immense. Indeed, when a UN team began assessing education needs in Pinyudu in August 1988, it noted with surprise that refugees had started their own school system with 15,000 students and no external assistance.[28] The schools were basic and lacked resources. One report described the "crude long structures made of wood and/or mud for the children to sit on. Some do not even have that, and very few have blackboards."[29] One teacher remembered his students:

---

[26] Andrew C. Wheeler, "'Can You Announce the Darkness after You Have Seen the Light?' Catholic Catechists' Achievements in Upper Nile 1970–1996," in *Announcing the Light: Sudanese Witnesses to the Gospel*, ed. Andrew C. Wheeler (Nairobi: Paulines Publications Africa, 1998), 172.

[27] Dominic Matong, in-person interview by Nikkel. Rome, Italy, 11 October 1989 (transcript in NSCCA).

[28] UNHCR Technical Support Service, "Ethiopia: Assessment of the Psycho-social Needs of Children in the Fugnido Camp, 8–22 August 1988," TSS Mission Report 39/88, 3 (UNHCRA).

[29] UNHCR Technical Support Service, "Ethiopia: Unaccompanied Children in Fugnido," 4.

FIGURE 4.2
Classroom in Itang Refugee Camp, December 1990. Collection of Timothy Biles. Used by permission.

> We started with those who were from the village—they have not gone to school. So we have to start from there with Class 1. There was no blackboard, there was no chalk—nothing! So we were using ground for writing and sometimes there was no blackboard so we were using cartons that were used for bringing oil. We used charcoal to write on those. And most of the children they write on the ground. At that time when you go around you see many writings on the ground.[30]

No matter the lack of resources, the schools became the center of the minors' life and the place where they concentrated their energy. One refugee recalled the exhortation his teacher gave the class: "You must do better! You have nothing now, nothing but education. Don't you see this? Our country is in shambles, and the only way we can reclaim it is to learn! . . . While your older brothers fight this war with guns, when the bullets stop, you will fight the next war with your pens."[31] By 1988, there were 5,500 students in classes in Pinyudu, a small number relative

---

[30] Thomas Agau Kur, in-person interview by Jesse Zink. Bor, South Sudan, 8 April 2013.
[31] Eggers with Deng, *What Is the What*, 297.

to the total population of the camp, but large in comparison to the lack of educational opportunities in southern Sudan.[32]

As was the case within southern Sudan, the teachers in the camps were often not trained teachers, but southern Sudanese who had at some point received some measure of education. The close relationship between education and Christianity that was established during the colonial period meant that many of these teachers were also Christian. One informant remembered that he became Christian when he moved to Juba in the 1970s and began his education. The outbreak of war forced him to flee first to SPLA–controlled areas and then to Ethiopia. There, because of his background, he became a teacher.[33] Some of the educated Christians who fled towns in the early years of the war ended up in these Ethiopian camps, bringing educated, Christian Dinka into contact with rural, non-Christian Dinka. The teachers did not even have to see themselves as Christian evangelists. The dynamic in the camps was the same as that established by European missionaries a generation or more earlier: education led to conversion. The difference was that Dinka youth were now eager for education. Education became "virtually inseparable" from membership in the church.[34]

It was not only the schools that lacked resources, but the evangelists did as well. In 1989, one visitor reported that there were "virtually no Bibles . . . available."[35] In a similar fashion to the church within southern Sudan, there was no Eucharist, both because the new converts had not yet been confirmed but primarily because "there are no chalices, no vestments."[36] As a result, music was an important tool for Christian evangelism. Numerous informants remember the importance of songs in their process of conversion. One recalled, "They [evangelists] were teaching us about like the Ten Commandments, respect one another, love your God, love others as you love yourself. . . . But most of the time, they teach us hymns. But those hymns, when you go home, you wrote them down and sing them again. This is how we start knowing more about

---

[32] Rädda Barnen, "Unaccompanied Minors of Southern Sudan," 34; African Rights, *Food and Power in Sudan*, 80.

[33] Thomas Agau Kur, interview by Zink. Bor, South Sudan, 8 April 2013.

[34] African Rights, *Food and Power in Sudan*, 80.

[35] John Boyer, "Assistance to Sudanese Refugees in South West Ethiopia," November 1989, 8 (NSCCA).

[36] Abraham Mayom Athiaan, letter to Robert Runcie, 27 December 1989 (NSCCA).

God. And that is when I go to church and say, 'I want to be baptized.'"[37] Andrew Mayol Ajak, who became the senior Anglican cleric in Pinyudu in 1988, was explicit about the importance of hymns: "Spiritual songs which quote the Bible cement in what the evangelist says. The sermon happens but then the song makes it stay."[38] Hymn composition became a major activity in the refugee camps, and sharing songs became a major activity of the church. A song written in one part of the camp would be memorized or written down, taken to church leaders, and then, if approved, shared with other prayer meetings elsewhere in the camp. The hymns were important not just for the content they communicated but the form they represented. No matter how intensive or extensive the educational efforts, functional illiteracy remained the lot of a majority of Dinka. The skills of learning and transmitting songs, by contrast, were at the center of Dinka culture. In Ethiopia, songs became a primary form of Christian catechesis. Music allowed many Dinka to become Christian regardless of their ability to understand a written text.

The combination of lay evangelism, the emphasis on education, and the role of hymns led to new energy around Christianity among the communities of unaccompanied minors. What is striking about the life the Dinka young people created in Ethiopia is its parallels to the life they might have had had they stayed in Sudan and been sent to cattle camps. Cattle camp life revolved around groups of young people living together, caring for cattle, and composing songs about their cattle, their girlfriend, or their victory in a wrestling match. A UN report noted the parallels: "[T]he particular cultural patterns of the Nilotic ethnic groups in the camp seems to have made the adjustment to the camp easier. Most of the boys had previously experienced extended stays away from their families. . . . Support and guidance for boys in a cattle camp is provided by age-mates [and] older youths."[39] In some instances, the SPLA took advantage of the age-set division of Dinka youth to organize the movement of young people to Ethiopia.[40] While extended stays in cattle camps were unusual, in Pinyudu and elsewhere they became standard.

[37] Gabriel Chol Kuany, in-person interview by Jesse Zink. Phoenix, Arizona, 26 June 2012.

[38] Andrew Mayol Ajak, in-person interview by Jesse Zink. Juba, South Sudan, 4 April 2013.

[39] UNHCR Technical Support Service, "Ethiopia: Assessment of the Psycho-social Needs of Children in the Fugnido Camp," 5.

[40] Daniel Kon Malwal, interview by Zink. Bor, South Sudan, 5 April 2013.

Religious change in these refugee camps was aided by the unusual generational patterns of their populations. The religion of the *jak* was the domain of older men, who guarded their roles as religious and political leaders and sought to prevent religious innovation. But there were fewer older men in the Ethiopian camps. Many had either been unable to make the journey or were fighting for the SPLA. In the absence of older men, young boys were unconstrained by religious tradition and were unlikely to recreate the rituals and practices of Sudan in Ethiopia. Instead, there was space for religious experimentation. One informant said, "Spiritual ceremony is part of human life. So if you are separated from the other part, then you consider the alternatives that you can do. And if they see that there is another kind of ceremonial than the one they know, they join."[41] The protective function provided by the *jak* still needed to be filled, even if these divinities were absent in Ethiopia. In a context of war and displacement, Christian conversion was perceived to offer that protection.

Although the Anglican church was growing in the Ethiopian camps, it was aware of its distance from the church hierarchy. Abraham Mayom wrote letters to correspondents far and wide, including Archbishop of Canterbury Robert Runcie, asking for help and referring to the church as "a drowning person [who] always throws his arms about in desperate search for safety."[42] Even Bishop Nathaniel Garang, himself cut off from the church hierarchy in SPLA–controlled areas, was unable to visit Ethiopia. For the refugee populations and for the few church leaders, this meant that it was difficult to baptize new converts and impossible to confirm them. In 1988, however, Garang did send a freshly ordained Anglican priest, Andrew Mayol Ajak, to take leadership of the church in Pinyudu. When Mayol Ajak arrived, he found thousands of boys who had been prepared for baptism by lay evangelists and were waiting for a priest to administer the rite. On arrival, Mayol did 1,601 baptisms in two days.[43] Other Anglicans improvised. In the Itang camp, the Anglican lay leader Peter Bol Arok cast aside thought of apostolic succession and was ordained an Anglican priest by a group of Presbyterian elders.

---

[41] Daniel Kon Malwal, interview by Zink. Bor, South Sudan, 5 April 2013.

[42] Abraham Mayom Athiaan Deng, letter to Robert Runcie, 26 December 1989.

[43] Daniel Kon Malwal, interview by Zink. Bor, South Sudan, 5 April 2013. It is often reported that Mayol did 12,000 baptisms in three days but in an interview he remembered 1,601 that he had documented in a baptismal register that was subsequently lost during the war.

FIGURE 4.3
The Rev. Peter Bol Arok with members of Christian community in Itang, 1990. Collection of Timothy Biles. Used by permission.

In 1989, he baptized over 2,000 people in a single service.[44] Anecdotal reports give a sense of the size of the growing church. A visitor in 1989 found 1,500 to 1,800 people in church on Sunday.[45] The following year, Bol Arok reported to a visitor that there were 8,000 people attending services on Sundays.[46] In contrast to the church in the SPLA–controlled areas in southern Sudan, in the Ethiopian camps a period of pre-baptismal preparation was maintained, though it was shorter than the multi-year process characteristic of the mission era. Those who were to be baptized still had to learn catechism answers, which they were taught at their local prayer centers. There was an eagerness for the knowledge. In the midst of the hard work of surviving in a poorly resourced refugee camp, Christian activity came as a

[44] Marc Nikkel, *Dinka Christianity: The Origins and Development of Christianity among the Dinka of Sudan with Special Reference to the Songs of Dinka Christians* (Nairobi: Paulines Publications Africa, 2001), 239.

[45] John Boyer, "Assistance to Sudanese Refugees in South West Ethiopia," 7.

[46] Timothy Biles, *Windows on the Sudan: A Story of Pain and Pride,* 3rd ed. (Dorset, UK: self-published, 1994 [1991]), 80.

welcome break. One informant remembered, "we went to the church because we didn't have anything. We didn't have our cattle or anything. The only thing that we were looking for was a school. And before we [had] a school, we were just building our houses. So we go to church so that we can go and dance and sing."[47]

Christian life among Dinka who had fled to Ethiopia differed in some regards from that in southern Sudan. In east- and west-bank communities, Christians encountered well-established religious practices and sacred places. As a result, there was a corresponding emphasis on destroying shrines and burning *jak*. But in Ethiopia, refugees were rebuilding their lives from scratch. There were no cattle camps or shrines to *jak* to be found. The demographics of the camp skewed younger, which meant there were fewer older men around to uphold the religion of the *jak*. Christian conversion in a refugee camp did not have to involve an explicit repudiation of *jak* because the *jak* had not come to Ethiopia. They had been effectively destroyed in the flight from home. Instead, Christianity came to represent a new and helpful identity that was needed in the midst of war, an identity associated with education and a new world of international organizations and foreign institutions.[48]

Informants cite a factor leading to conversion in Ethiopia that is muted in southern Sudan. Many young people remember that a significant moment in their religious change was when they heard that belief in Jesus Christ would lead to eternal life. Eternal life is a classic motive for conversion to evangelical Christianity and it is a theme that recurs in some "Lost Boy" memoirs from religious publishing houses in the United States: "When I heard John 3:16, that God so loved the world that He gave His only Son Jesus Christ to die for my sins, I believed. . . . I desperately needed to know I was loved and that I had a purpose. I was eleven years old when I accepted Jesus as my Lord and Savior."[49] Evangelical publishing houses are no doubt sympathetic to such stories. But similar views are also expressed independently by informants who have not written memoirs or been to the United States. The views are noteworthy in contrast to those who spent the war in southern Sudan.

---

[47] Field notes in Phoenix, Arizona, 26 June 2012.
[48] Marc Nikkel, "Christian Conversion among the Jieng Bor," in *Religion and Conflict in Sudan: Papers from an International Conference at Yale, May 1999*, ed. Yusuf Fadl Hasan and Richard Gray (Nairobi: Paulines Publications Africa, 2002), 167.
[49] Nhial and Mills, *Lost Boy No More*, 37.

For these people, particularly on the east bank of the Nile, the emphasis fell on the need for protection from *jak* and the opportunities provided by Christianity. But in a situation in which one's friends had died while walking to Ethiopia and in which death was an ever-present reality, the promise of eternal life took on a new significance. In a sense, eternal life became seen as one of the protective functions of the new religion.

The impact of conversion was seen in the lives of young people themselves. The church became a focal point of community life. In fact, Christianity became so central that some people began to go just to see what was going on. One informant remembers he first went to a prayer-center meeting because "I see a lot of people going to church so I would just follow them and see what is going on there. . . . So I just go there and dance and that's it."[50] As time went on, worship services grew in size and frequency, and Christianity became a topic of conversation among refugee minors. More significantly, Christianity helped minors interpret the experience of military training and life in the camps more generally. An informant remembers how "the community of the church was very important, very, very important. It brings us together. It [was] counseling us. And it provided education. So we were not looking to our pastor as just a pastor but as a father also. And the [women], we see them like that."[51]

The church became an alternate community to the one the SPLA was trying to establish. The effects of the church were noticed by the international representatives in the camps. In an extensive report on the minors, the Swedish nongovernmental organization Rädda Barnen (Save the Children) was surprised to learn that only 1 percent of minors were classified as "mentally disturbed" and in need of psychological counseling from its staff. Given the devastation of the war, the organization expected a far higher number. This resilience was attributed, in part, to the way in which "churches give direction to the otherwise disturbed pattern of life."[52] The circumstances of war and refuge that had brought the minors to these camps made many look at Christianity in a new way. A Christian church was beginning to take shape among the Dinka and other Nilotic people who found themselves in southwestern Ethiopia.

---

[50] Gabriel Chol Kuany, interview by Zink. Phoenix, Arizona, 27 June 2012.

[51] Abraham Yel Nhial, in-person interview by Jesse Zink. Aweil, South Sudan, 19 July 2011.

[52] Rädda Barnen, "Unaccompanied Minors of Southern Sudan," 8, 45.

It is important not to overstate the significance of this church, however. In the Ethiopian camps, as in southern Sudan in this period, Christian adherence was not as pervasive as some Christians claimed. Christians were not a majority in these camps. Some young people hesitated to embrace the new religion. They worried about the consequences when they went home, and in the late 1980s and 1990, the success of the SPLA made a return home seem an imminent possibility. For those who did seek baptism, it did not always involve a serious commitment to religious change. One informant remembers being nonchalant about his baptism: "I just take it, because others are taking it. I didn't have a goal that I would be going and convert my parents so that they can believe in this. I was indifferent."[53] Baptism was a decision for which new Christians were occasionally mocked. Another informant remembers that some non-Christians derisively called the newly baptized "dreamers."[54] Many Dinka young people were turning to Christianity, but there were some who were not.

The displacement of the civil war and difficult conditions of the refugee camps did not automatically lead to Christian conversion. But the shattering of the microcosm did create a set of conditions in which many young people looked at Christianity from a new perspective. The separation from a home community, the difficulty of refugee life, and the need for greater resources to assert oneself in a situation of weakness all tended to push young people in the direction of Christianity. But the religious change was not permanent, and still reversible.

The Move to Kenya

The events of 1991 that transformed Sudan's civil war had a significant impact on refugee populations in Ethiopia. The fall of Mengistu in May led to the sudden closure of the Ethiopian refugee camps and the rapid return to southern Sudan of the hundreds of thousands of people living in them. It was the closure of these camps that weakened the SPLA, led to the movement's split in August, and ultimately precipitated the so-called Bor Massacre in November. These events had two major impacts on displaced Dinka. First, the refugees in Ethiopia were forced to move to new camps, both in Sudan and outside it. Second, these camps were swelled by the addition of hundreds of thousands of newly displaced

---

[53] Field notes in Phoenix, Arizona, 26 June 2012.
[54] Gabriel Chol Kuany, interview by Zink. Phoenix, Arizona, 27 June 2012.

who fled their homes on the east bank of the Nile River. By 1992, a dominant—indeed, *the* dominant—feature of east-bank Dinka life was displacement. By the end of that year, 70 percent of the east-bank Dinka population had been displaced or killed.[55]

As in the first near-decade of the war, the church both shaped the experience of displacement and was shaped by it. Dinka ended up in camps in northern Uganda, in Kenya, and near Nimule in southern Sudan. This section concentrates on Kakuma Refugee Camp, the camp in northwestern Kenya that opened in 1992. While more Sudanese refugees ended up in Uganda, it was Kakuma that became a central focus for the Dinka church and the place where the religious energy of the Ethiopian camps was mostly clearly continued. The comparative stability provided by the camp allowed the church to consolidate the growth of the early years of the war and so establish itself as an indigenous institution.

The journey that began when the Ethiopian camps were shuttered in April 1991 and that ended when Kakuma opened in June 1992 was difficult, uncertain, and marked by great confusion. Different parts of the refugee population went in different directions, making international assistance difficult. Nonetheless, throughout the journey refugees sought to recreate elements of their life in Ethiopia. When they stopped long enough in one place, they tried to re-start schools. On the long walk into Kenya, one Dinka who accompanied a large population of young people remembered, "We prayed a lot. We prayed every morning at 5 o'clock, all of us. Wherever people were they would gather to pray. . . . The children made up many songs about their difficulties and their faith. There were lots of references to the children of Israel in the desert. That thought was one of things that strengthened them."[56] Among the initial 30,000 refugees at Kakuma's opening in 1992 were approximately 10,000 "unaccompanied minors" from Ethiopia. But they now had a new name. Media reports first began to refer to them as "The Lost Boys of Sudan," attaching a name that would follow some refugees to resettlement in Canada, Australia, and the United States.[57] In Kakuma,

---

[55] Sharon Elaine Hutchinson, "Spiritual Fragments of an Unfinished War," in *Religion and African Civil Wars*, ed. Niels Kastfelt (London: Hurst, 2005), 37.

[56] Mecak Ajang Alaak, quoted in "He Led God's Children across the Desert," *Anglican World* (Advent 1995): 25.

[57] Mark Bixler, *The Lost Boys of Sudan: An American Story of the Refugee Experience* (Atlanta: University of Georgia Press, 2005).

it was noticed that among the few items these young people had been able to carry with them from Ethiopia and through a difficult year in Sudan were "their long wooden crosses and any Bible or hymn book they might possess."[58] It is, again, important not to overstate the role of the church. Studies have documented the isolation and alienation that many Nuer young people, for instance, felt after their expulsion from Ethiopia, and the destructive ways in which it was manifest.[59] But for those who made it to Kakuma, the church was an important social actor in structuring their experience.

Kakuma became a center of activity for the new Dinka diaspora. Several features of the camp allowed this. First, as was the case with the Ethiopian camps, it was outside the borders of Sudan, which meant that it was safe from attack. One informant who was displaced from the Bor area in 1991, first to the west bank of the Nile and then to Kakuma a few years later, remembered that at camps in Sudan, "we were being disturbed by bombardments and many of them [refugees] don't go to church and some of the activities in the church are not alway being practiced because many people are so fearful: maybe if you go to church a plane may come for the bombardment."[60] The large refugee camps near Nimule in Sudan were almost overrun in serious fighting in 1992. By contrast, Kakuma was protected from this direct violence. At the same time, however, Kakuma was close enough to Sudan to allow for a fair degree of movement, including of church leaders, between the camp and southern Sudan.

In contrast to the dominant role the SPLA had taken in the Ethiopian camps, the rebel movement was a weakened force when Kakuma opened. The loss of its supply lines in Ethiopia upended its hitherto successful strategy. The split in the organization meant much of its energy was directed against its erstwhile allies rather than the Khartoum government. It also meant that some of its flaws were exposed to greater scrutiny from international actors. Although the wives and families of many SPLA commanders lived in Kakuma and the SPLA recruited in the

---

[58] Andrew C. Wheeler, "Finding Meaning amid the Chaos: Narratives of Significance in the Sudanese Church," in *Religion and African Civil Wars*, ed. Niels Kastfelt (London: Hurst, 2005), 60.
[59] Hutchinson, "Spiritual Fragments of an Unfinished War"; also Berger, "Southern Sudan's Red Army."
[60] James Nhial Maler, in-person interview by Jesse Zink. Bor, South Sudan, 6 April 2013.

camp, by the mid-1990s the SPLA's reputation had deteriorated among many young southern Sudanese, who no longer saw it as defending their interests.[61] The relative weakness of the SPLA meant greater prominence for other institutions among the Dinka. Dinka looking for a social institution they could trust turned to the church.

Nonetheless, one of the overriding factors of life in Kakuma was insecurity. Kenya itself had only reluctantly allowed the camp to open and made it difficult for refugees to integrate into larger society. Budgetary constraints for international organizations hindered their work and could hamper the delivery of relief supplies. While Nuer and Dinka were physically separated, the effects of the split in the SPLA occasionally manifested in violence between the two groups. Other violence stemmed from Kakuma's location in the territory of the pastoralist Turkana. Some Turkana grew to resent the growing presence of refugees in their midst, not to mention what was perceived to be preferential treatment for the displaced from international organizations. Violence and insecurity was one result.[62] These challenges were compounded by the difficulty of living in a refugee camp. The policies of international organizations call for the gradual reduction of food rations for refugees in an effort to encourage self-sufficiency. But northwestern Kenya is not an environment that allows for much agriculture and animal husbandry was forbidden to curtail the potential for clashes with the Turkana.[63] As a result, refugees remained "almost completely dependent on aid for their survival," even as that aid was gradually reduced.[64] Many refugees would go several days without food, which, in turn, affected their ability to concentrate in school and their susceptibility to disease and illness.

Thus, although Kakuma was more secure and stable than Sudan, life was still fraught. One refugee told interviewers that life in Kakuma "is like you want to fly, but you have no wings. The days in the camp are

[61] Eggers with Deng, *What Is the What*, 419; Jok Madut Jok and Sharon Elaine Hutchinson, "Sudan's Prolonged Second Civil War and the Militarization of Nuer and Dinka Ethnic Identities," *African Studies Review* 42, no. 2 (September 1999): 140. Jeff Crisp offers a contrasting view: "A State of Insecurity: The Political Economy of Violence in Kenya's Refugee Camps," *African Affairs* 99 (2002): 623.

[62] M. Jan Holton, *Building the Resilient Community: Lessons from the Lost Boys of Sudan* (Eugene, Ore.: Cascade, 2011), 77; Linda Bartolomei, Eileen Pittaway, and Emma Elizabeth Pittaway, "Who Am I? Identity and Citizenship in Kakuma Refugee Camp in Northern Kenya," *Development* 46 (September 2003): 88.

[63] Guglielmo Verdirame, "Human Rights and Refugees: The Case of Kenya," *Journal of Refugee Studies* 12, no. 1 (1999): 68.

[64] Verdirame, "Human Rights and Refugees," 62.

horrible. I never dreamt that I would live in such a place. It is hot, dusty, windy. Every day I sit down with my friends in this broken down shelter. We talk, we listen to the radio and in the evening we walk down the street. Every day is the same, but every day is getting worse."[65] The condition of life was expressed in Christian discourse as well. One hymn composed in Kakuma says, "We suffer in the wilderness, we suffer in the forest without homes, enduring thirst and hunger."[66] Even those refugees who graduated from the schools in Kakuma were stuck in limbo. Kenya made it difficult for them to work legally in the country and there was no possibility of employment in Sudan. Instead, they remained in Kakuma, but with no opportunities for further study or work.[67] The particular challenges and obstacles of Kakuma shaped the life of all who lived in it.

The Church in Kakuma

As they arrived in Kakuma, church members began to reconstitute what they had known in the Ethiopian camps. Kakuma was divided into zones, with the Dinka concentrated in three of these, Zones 2, 3, and 4, and with lesser numbers in other zones. Each of the three Dinka zones had a lead church where people in the zone gathered for worship on Sunday and other days of the week. In the earliest years, the churches were open-air gathering places that could accommodate thousands. The American priest Marc Nikkel first visited Kakuma in February 1994, 20 months after the camp was established:

> On our first Sunday morning, I was sobered to find some six thousand people assembling for the 6:00 a.m. . . . service in the largest of three open-air churches. These massive forest chapels are set among the thorn trees and spindly, fine-leafed acacias of the region; their meager shade encourages worship in the cool of early morning. (I later realized that youth are up as early as 4:30 a.m. laying out handkerchiefs to reserve their places.) The pews are long, smoothed loaves of dried mud, occasionally marked with crosses molded in relief. . . . [O]n weekdays I sat among three hundred to five hundred "minors" who gather for prayer at 5:00 a.m.[68]

---

[65] Quoted in Oostland and Berkvens, *Sudanese Life Stories*, 60.
[66] Quoted in Marc Nikkel, "Songs of Hope and Lamentation from Sudan's 'Unaccompanied Minors,'" *Sewanee Theological Review* 40, no. 4 (1997): 490.
[67] Oostland and Berkvens, *Sudanese Life Stories*, 66.
[68] Marc Nikkel, letter to supporters, 15 April 1994, collected in *Why Haven't You Left? Letters from the Sudan*, ed. Grant LeMarquand (New York: Church Publishing, 2006), 108.

FIGURE 4.4
Zone 3 church in Kakuma Refugee Camp, c. 1994. Collection of Marc Nikkel. Used by permission of Durham University Library.

As Kakuma grew, more zones were added and the Dinka population spread. As new zones were created, new churches were added as well.

In addition to these central churches, there were smaller gatherings that met more frequently. As in Ethiopia, these groups met for Bible study, prayer, and, crucially, singing. They were known in Dinka as *luang de guëër* or "gathering places." But as Dinka young people began to identify more closely with the biblical narrative, they used another word to describe them, "synagogue." This name linked the Dinka experience of displacement in northwestern Kenya to the wandering of the Israelites in the desert before they arrived in the promised land. As in Ethiopia, the synagogues were where the actual work of conversion and catechesis happened. Again, songs were a primary form of catechesis. The synagogues became places where hymns were written, collected, shared, learned, and preserved. One informant who was involved in this work recalled:

> Everybody [went] to that [synagogue] at night so you cannot just sit at home. At the church someone is teaching the hymns, every evening, from 7pm to 10pm. . . . We don't have paper in our hands. Just memorize them

in your mind. So when you come back next time and we start singing again and again and over and over, then that's where we learn all the hymns.[69]

The lack of ordained clergy meant that leadership in the synagogues was in the hands of young male evangelists who coordinated services and rotated responsibilities like preaching and leading worship among themselves. As time passed and the population of the camp grew, some of these synagogues grew into churches of their own and held services on Sunday.

Although the structure of the church in Kakuma—made up of central churches and smaller, peripheral meeting places—paralleled that in Ethiopia, the church in Kakuma was on a larger scale. Christians displaced from the east bank of the Nile joined those from Ethiopia and elsewhere to make for a larger institution. The growth of the church was evident in its sacramental ministry. In 1993, Bishop Nathaniel Garang Anyieth confirmed more than 10,000 people over three days, many of whom were people who had been baptized in Ethiopian camps.[70] Young people who may have been baptized in Ethiopia as a result of peer pressure or the belief that it was some kind of game were now consciously committing more fully to Christianity. Confirmation was seen, *inter alia*, as a mature affirmation of faith, distinct from baptism. The changing course of the war made returning home seem much less likely than it had been in Ethiopia. Greater Christian commitment was one result. Having confirmed Christians also meant that the Eucharist became an occasional feature of worship life. This, in turn, required ordained leaders, which Garang also provided.

The confirmations and ordinations also indicate the easier access that Nathaniel Garang and other church leaders had to their people. Garang had been unable to visit the camps in Ethiopia. But Kakuma and other displaced camps were easier for him to access, in part because he and his family had been displaced in the violence of 1991 and worked from a base in Kenya. Bishop Nathaniel's connection to Kakuma was important, but it was not the only link Kakuma had to church hierarchies.

---

[69] Gabriel Chol Kuany, interview by Zink. Phoenix, Arizona, 26 June 2012.

[70] As with reports of mass baptisms in the Ethiopian camps, these claims are unverifiable with any precision. But that such a service took place is attested by a variety of sources. See, for instance, Hugh McCullum, "Ministering during War," *One World* (June 1995): 14 (NSCCA); Nikkel, "Songs of Hope and Lamentation from Sudan's 'Unaccompanied Minors,'" 490.

Church leaders who were confined to government-held areas of Sudan were now able to visit. The Anglican archbishop of Sudan, Benjamina Yugusuk, visited Kakuma on more than one occasion. Archbishop of Canterbury George Carey visited the displaced camps in Nimule. The grassroots revival ethos of the Dinka church within Sudan and in Ethiopia persisted, but the church itself was becoming more closely linked to existing hierarchies. Indeed, Nathaniel Garang in time incorporated Kakuma into the Diocese of Bor as an archdeaconery, appointing a senior cleric to oversee the work in the camp. The ecumenical spirit that had been evident in Ethiopia persisted in the work of the New Sudan Council of Churches and other ecumenical committees, but the time in Kakuma was also a period of deepening denominational ties.

The links with the wider church were important, but the enthusiasm for Christianity continued to turn in large measure on the continued emphasis on education. The events of 1991 had again offered compelling proof of the need Dinka had for new resources to assert themselves in the world. Education, more than anything else, was that resource. The skills that had once led to success for Dinka men in cattle camps were no longer sufficient, particularly now that it was clear that a return to those camps was no longer imminent. In a sense, this was the same realization of the small number of pre-war Dinka converts: in order to have power in the changing world, one needed to be educated. Now, however, that realization was nearly universal. Education had been important in Ethiopia, but several factors in Kakuma intensified interest in it. Because refugees were not able to keep cattle, it was not possible for these young men, some of whom were now reaching marriageable age, to pay a bride price and find status through marriage and family.[71] Without families to rely on, many young men adopted as their slogan, "Education is your mother and your father."[72] In a context of familial breakdown, education was seen as the sole means to improve one's condition. Researchers who interviewed refugees in Kakuma reported their overwhelming desire for education: "These children generally give almost desperate confidence to the virtues of education

---

[71] Sabine Knoedlstorfer, "Kakuma Refugee Camp: A Report" (Berlin: March 1999), 27 (NSCCA).

[72] Martin Masumbuko Muhindi and Kiganzi Nyakato, "Integration of the Sudanese 'Lost Boys' in Boston, Massachusetts, USA, 2002," 7. Available online at https://cis.mit.edu/sites/default/files/documents/IntegrationOfTheSudaneseLostBoys.pdf, accessed 29 January 2018.

which they believe can change their lives."[73] It was the same dynamic that had been present in Ethiopia and earlier in Dinka history, but now it was intensified and widespread. It was no longer a minority of young Dinka men who were seeking education, but virtually all of them. One observer noted: "When it comes to education the young Sudanese are very fanatical. Some even sell food to be able to buy lamp oil, so that they can study at night. Others sell their food in order to be able to buy a school book."[74]

But the desire for education was not matched by its provision. By 1996, for instance, Kakuma had 20 primary schools with over 17,000 students. But there was only a single secondary school with room for 250 students.[75] That meant that each year thousands of students finished primary school only to find there was no path for them to continue their education. There were a handful of vocational opportunities but not enough to meet demand. Still, it was more than what was available in southern Sudan, where virtually all educational opportunities in Dinka areas had disappeared.[76] A further attraction of the school in Kakuma was that it offered education according to the Kenyan curriculum and awarded the Kenya Schools Certificate. In no school in the Ethiopian camps could refugees receive a transferrable, recognized certificate.

At previous points in Dinka religious history, an increased desire for education led to an increased commitment to the church. Becoming Christian was simply what students did. The connection was seen as almost "axiomatic."[77] But in Kakuma, the mismatch between the overwhelming desire for education and its lack of provision intensified this dynamic. If students could not attend a secondary school—and many who wanted to could not—they could at least join the church, share in the creation and learning of hymns, and learn to read the Bible. In contrast to the missionary period when the provision of education met

---

[73] Johannes Zutt, *Les enfants de la guerre: seuls dans la vie au sud du Soudan* (New York: UNICEF, 1994), 30. This sentence translated by Jesse Zink.
[74] Oostland and Berkvens, *Sudanese Life Stories*, 49.
[75] Oostland and Berkvens, *Sudanese Life Stories*, 38.
[76] Marc Sommers, *Islands of Education: Schooling, Civil War and the Southern Sudanese (1983–2004)* (Paris: International Institute for Educational Planning, 2005); Justin Willis, "Who Put the 'Y' in the BYDA? Youth in Sudan's Civil Wars," in *Africa's Young Majority*, ed. Barbara Trudell et al. (Edinburgh: Centre of African Studies, University of Edinburgh, 2002), 100.
[77] African Rights, *Great Expectations: The Civil Roles of the Churches in Southern Sudan* (London: African Rights, April 1995), 24.

or exceeded demand, the converse was now true. The church became a near substitute for the school. Christianity became a way for young people to get ahead in life. And the church began to create institutions that reflected this.

Jo Wo Liec (*JWL*) was the primary church affinity group for young men in Kakuma.[78] Its name is a Dinka phrase that means "turn back on us." The name comes from an idea deeply rooted in Dinka Christian beliefs that God was abandoning the Dinka because they had worshipped the *jak*. Now that Dinka were turning to Christianity, God was beseeched to turn back and remember the Dinka. *JWL* started on the east bank of the Nile in the late 1980s, but it remained a nascent group until the stability of Kakuma allowed it to grow rapidly.

Members of *JWL* were young, unmarried men in their late teens and early twenties, an age range that included the bulk of the young people who had left home as children and come to maturity in refugee camps. They were divided into four loose sub-groups: *aloong*, whose members were responsible for collecting and documenting songs that were being composed; *agayth*, which was responsible for Dinka language learning and literacy education; *luängic*, which translated and taught the Bible; and *lek*, whose members were responsible for evangelism. There was overlap between the sub-groups, but the division shows the priorities of the church. The leaders of the synagogues, for instance, were members of *lek*. As time passed, *JWL* took on responsibility for producing new resources for the church. *Agayth* produced at least one Dinka-language primer, *Lokku Tueng ne Thɔɔngjieng* ("Let us go ahead with the Dinka language"), which was published in 1997. *Aloong* members played a key role in the creation of a new Dinka hymnal, the subject of chapter 5.

In addition to the practical impact on the development of the church, *JWL* was important for the belonging and sense of membership that it gave its members. For many young people who were separated from their families, membership in the church as mediated through *JWL* gave an important sense of community that they were lacking elsewhere. One favorite Bible verse of many *JWL* members was Psalm 27:10: "If my father and mother forsake me, the Lord will take me up." Many *JWL* members frequently rendered this verse without the conditional, as "Your mother and father have deserted you but God will never desert

---

[78] The history of *Jo Wo Liec* in the following paragraphs is rooted in interviews with its members.

you."⁷⁹ Membership in *JWL* came to be highly desired, and people could only belong if they were members of the church in good standing. As a result, church membership and attendance was encouraged, not just in verbal exhortation and evangelism, but in the developing system of social rewards that was being created in Kakuma.

The growth of the church was seen in expanding zonal churches, affinity groups, and new Christian publications. The impact of this growth was seen in the lives of the displaced young people, an impact that was widely noted by those who interacted with them. Kakuma attracted a variety of aid workers with extensive international experience. A consistent theme of their reports is that the refugees they encountered in Kakuma were in a better psychosocial state than their past experience would lead one to believe. Julianne Duncan, who worked for an American Catholic organization interviewing minors prior to their resettlement abroad, recalled that based on her previous experience in refugee camps, "If children have been brutalized and treated badly, they themselves will have psychic wounds that can't be healed. This will come out in antisocial behavior, psychotic behavior. That's a kind of truism." Among the people she worked with in Kakuma, however, "I didn't really see that. I attribute this to the very kindly cadre of caretakers who were guiding them through Christianity."⁸⁰ Later, when Duncan worked with some of these same refugees after they had been resettled in the United States, she concluded that "the population had considerable strength and resiliency. The major protective factors were belief in God, desire for and success in education, [and a] desire to be helpful to society in the future."⁸¹ Although these refugees did exhibit signs of mental-health distress, it was less severe than Duncan's experience would have led her to believe.⁸² She roots this in their Christian commitment. Nonreligious observers noted these trends as well. UNHCR workers found the

---

⁷⁹ Public talk by Marc Nikkel, Rochester, New York, USA, 25 April 1997. Video recording held privately by Nancy Frank.

⁸⁰ Julianne Duncan, telephonic interview by Jesse Zink. 27 March 2013.

⁸¹ Julianne Duncan, "Sudanese 'Lost Boys' in the United States: Adjustment after Six Months," United States Catholic Conference/Migration and Refugee Services, 30 May 2001, 2. Available online at http://www.brycs.org/documents/upload/lostboys.pdf, accessed 23 November 2017.

⁸² On this question, see also the work of Jan Holton, who has made an extensive study of the question of resilience among "Lost Boys": Holton, *Building the Resilient Community*, 110.

minors—to their surprise—to be "cheerful, patient, cooperative, sensitive and . . . courageous."[83]

The ways in which Dinka appropriated Christian theology are a subject of later chapters. What is important to note here, however, is how the young people found, in Christian narratives, resources that allowed them to hope for the future. The Christian narrative gave refugees a sense of status that living in a refugee camp might have taken away. One resident of Kakuma said that refugees "have the feeling that God is supporting us. . . . It is also God who will take care of us in our future because we call his name."[84] The Christian faith became a coping mechanism for people who were losing hope. As one said, "Our religion is strengthening us, otherwise I would have mentally broken down. God knows what he is doing. We are leaving everything in his hands. He is the only one who knows the cause of everything."[85] For those who had experienced combat and the brutalizing impact of SPLA training, Christianity gave converts a new moral universe that allowed them to question their past behavior.[86] Yet the impact of Christian conversion should not be overstated. The church was not a panacea for the problems many young refugees faced. "Lost Boys" may have been more resilient than other refugee populations, but many suffered psychosocial distress. The church in Kakuma waxed and waned at various points. Still, of those who wound up in Kakuma, the church became an institution of central importance, one to which many young refugees turned at a time of need.

Kakuma intensified and deepened the trends that were apparent in Ethiopia. The young refugees recreated the pattern of Dinka social life in these refugee camps. The changed circumstances of the war made many of them look at Christianity in a new way. It gave them new resources (or the *hope* of new resources) not only in education but also in a system of social rewards and a way to interpret their experience of the war. The result was a shift in religious identity that was a consequence of the displacement to Ethiopia and then Kenya. These Dinka young people were

---

[83] UNHCR Programme and Technical Support Section, "Kenya: Registration and Needs Assessment of Southern Sudanese Minors, 15 July–3 September 1992," PTSS Mission Report 92/32, vii (UNHCRA).

[84] E. Linnemeyer, "The Religious Experience of Sudanese Refugees: Kakuma Refugee Camp, October/November 1996," paper presented at "Sudan Church Study Seminar," February 1997, Limuru Kenya, 19 (NSCCA).

[85] Quoted in Oostland and Berkvens, *Sudanese Life Stories*, 57.

[86] Hutchinson, "Spiritual Fragments of an Unfinished War," 37.

now more likely to identify as Christian, even if that faith played a varying role in their life and as a tool to cope with the challenges of displacement. The widely apparent impact of Christian conversion became noted with some irony. The SPLA's intention of creating an army of youth who could fight the war—the *jiech amer*—had been subverted by the refugees themselves. Rather than creating a military army, the children who had left home in the 1980s were now a Christian army—a church.[87]

Returning Home

In the late 1990s and early 2000s, a small minority of unaccompanied minors were resettled in the United States, Canada, Australia, and elsewhere, where their story became widely known as a result of intense media coverage and the ability of many "Lost Boys" to tell their stories in compelling fashion. But most remained in East Africa. Even before the end of the war came into view in the early 2000s, their movement and migration continued. This had implications for the spread of Christianity, which are seen most clearly in the growth of Dinka Anglicanism in the former Catholic mission sphere.

One result of dividing southern Sudan into spheres for missionary activity was the expectation that if Dinka came from the area around Aweil and Wau and were Christian, they were Catholic. In the early 1990s, there were few Christians. One of the few Dinka Catholic priests, Rudolph Deng, estimated in 1992 that one quarter of the population in the former Catholic sphere would call themselves Christians.[88] Jok Madut Jok, who conducted anthropological fieldwork at this time, reported that about 15 percent of western Dinka were Christian, largely those who had attended school at some point. In his fieldwork survey of the village of Akon among the Rek Dinka east of Aweil, Jok found only 4 percent of households had members who were Christian.[89] Some of the young refugees in Ethiopia were from this area, however, and some were baptized as Anglicans. When the refugees were expelled from Ethiopia in 1991, not all of them ended up in Kakuma or another camp for the displaced. In the confusion of war, going home was for some people an option that seemed to provide the most safety. For instance, one young

---

[87] Wheeler, "Finding Meaning amid the Chaos," 60.
[88] Wheeler, "Finding Meaning amid the Chaos," 64.
[89] Jok Madut Jok, *Militarization, Gender and Reproductive Health in South Sudan* (Lampeter, UK: Edwin Mellen, 1998), 112.

baptized refugee, Santino Bol, had an uncle who was a commander in the SPLA and based in their home region around Aweil. Bol found he could live in relative safety under his protection.[90] The initial Anglican presence in Aweil came simply from the ongoing displacement of the war.

But there was also a deliberate Anglican missionary effort. In the early years of the war, Wilson Garang had fled his home near Aweil and sought refuge in Ethiopia, where he became connected to the growing Christian movement. In 1991 he returned to southern Sudan and sought permission from Abraham Mayom and Nathaniel Garang to evangelize northern Bahr el Ghazal.[91] The Sudan Armed Forces controlled a handful of towns like Aweil and Wau, but, as elsewhere, the vast rural areas were largely under the control of the SPLA. In May 1992 Wilson Garang and a handful of others returned to their home region. Working with people like Santino Bol, this small group of people acted as evangelists in the area around Aweil, where they could work with relative freedom. In 1993, Nathaniel Garang ordained Wilson Garang with almost no training and sent him back to organize official Anglican churches.

In many ways, this preaching was largely consistent with the developing Anglican ethos. Converts were told they needed to burn their *jak* and seek baptism to confront the spiritual dangers the war had created. Wilson Garang and others had a healing ministry that generated support for their leadership. There was a strong sense of spiritual warfare, as he recalled, in relation to destroying traditional religious items:

> I told the people who were with me that we should not be with these idols and so we started breaking them and then we took and we burned them. The idols threw one man down and took him to a palm tree because that idol was from a palm tree. . . . So I went there and I prayed for that man and that man woke up so we finished the work. When we went to the house it started to attack me and when it started to attack me it would make me unconscious and when I started praying it moved away but when I stop praying it came. . . . So I have been praying for the whole day and night and I was disturbed by it for two days and after two days it left. I prayed for the people and I baptised them. Then I left and now they are okay.[92]

---

[90] Santino Bol, in-person interview by Jesse Zink. Nakuru, Kenya, 26 September 2013.

[91] Wilson Garang, in-person interview by Andrew Wheeler. Location uncertain, 22 May 1997 (transcript in papers of Marc Nikkel).

[92] Wilson Garang, in-person interview by Andrew Wheeler. Location uncertain, 22 May 1997.

FIGURE 4.5
Ordination of Anglican clergy by Bishop Nathaniel Garang Anyieth at Adoor, Sudan, outside Aweil, April 1998. Collection of Marc Nikkel. Used by permission of Durham University Library.

As was true elsewhere, women and young people were among the first to convert to Christianity. Between 1993 and 1994, Wilson Garang claimed to have baptized 5,000 people.[93] Even allowing for the exaggeration of self-reporting, it still represents a significant accomplishment in a region in which there had previously been no Anglicans. It was this activity that Ezekiel Diing, the Anglican archdeacon of Wau, was becoming aware of in the 1990s.

The people at the forefront of the growth of Anglicanism in this area were those who had left their homes in the turmoil and disruption of the early years of the war. They returned as Christians, which they had not been when they left. They received support from Nathaniel Garang, who was officially appointed as caretaker bishop in 1996, as the region had no resident Anglican bishop. In this role, Bishop Nathaniel visited in April 1998 and conducted the first Anglican ordinations in the Aweil area. Many others were consecrated as lay readers or commissioned

[93] Wilson Garang, in-person interview by Michael Medley. Dhiaukuei, South Sudan, 27 December 1994 (transcript provided by Michael Medley).

evangelists. Of the 21 men ordained then, 11 had spent time in Ethiopia or Kakuma and saw themselves as members of *Jo Wo Liec*.[94] Even as the church took root in Aweil, the continued movement of people allowed it to maintain its links with the larger Dinka diaspora. For instance, Stephen Mou was a young Christian who had been in Ethiopia and Kakuma. In 1997 he returned to his home in the Aweil area, bringing with him knowledge of the nascent Dinka hymnal. He was assigned to teach pastors and evangelists the hymns that were motivating church members in Kakuma and elsewhere. In this way, knowledge in one part of the church spread to another, furthering the growth of the Christian movement.

Although ecumenical feeling had been strong in the Ethiopian camps, when refugees began returning home this began to dissipate. The Catholic church in the region was concentrated in a network of parishes centered on towns. Outlying stations were served on a sporadic basis by "pastoral safaris" in which a priest visited two or three times a year to offer a limited sacramental ministry.[95] The leadership of the church was provided largely by expatriate clergy, who maintained important international connections and focused the church's work on humanitarian relief. There was also clear Catholic teaching regarding Dinka traditional religion: catechists and priests were to "create awareness of the dubious nature of some of the religious practices. . . . However, this should never lead to taking drastic measures with their beliefs and religious symbols, such as burning or destroying their symbols with disrespect." Moreover, they were instructed to "endeavour to absorb some of their sound religious rites and symbols into the Christian rites and values."[96]

The contrast with the Anglican approach could hardly have been more stark. The war meant that the young Anglican evangelists were largely unable to access the towns, where Catholic churches were. Differing approaches to ordination meant that there were few Dinka Catholic clergy. Within a few years, there were seven Anglican clergy in the region, all of whom were native to the region and stationed there, compared to five Catholic Sudanese clergy, not all of whom were native Dinka speakers and only three of whom were actually stationed

---

[94] Marc Nikkel, letter to supporters, 31 May 1998, in *Why Haven't You Left?*, 168–69.
[95] *The Diocese of Rumbek at a Glance, 1998*, 5 (NSCCA).
[96] Diocese of Rumbek, "Pastoral Guidelines," rev. ed., 14 September 1999 (NSCCA).

FIGURE 4.6
Anglican clergy outside Aweil, c. April 1998. Collection of Marc Nikkel.
Used by permission of Durham University Library.

in southern Sudan.[97] Baptismal preparation differed. Catholics continued to require a catechumenate process whereas Anglicans under the influence of Nathaniel Garang were much more willing to baptize with little or no preparation. During the colonial period, there had been far more Catholic than Anglican missionaries in southern Sudan. The balance was now reversed: there were more Anglican lay evangelists and clergy in the region than there were Catholic.

These differing approaches meant that the Anglicans found converts relatively quickly. The resulting growth is testified by the ire it raised among Catholics. Some derided Anglicans as the "church of Bor," a mistaken indication of where they thought the energy for the movement was coming from.[98] It was people native to Aweil who were the

[97] The statistics for the Anglican clergy are taken from letter of Wilson Garang Chan to Daniel Zindo, 30 September 1996, in the papers of Nathaniel Garang. The statistics for the Catholic clergy are taken from "List of Diocese of Rumbek Church Personnel in South Sudan and Kenya, 24 Sept. 1999" (NSCCA).
[98] Quoted in Nikkel, letter to supporters, 31 May 1998, in *Why Haven't You Left?*, 169.

evangelists. The report of the Catholic diocese's annual assembly in February 1999 records that "there have [sic] been infiltration of foreign protestant brothers and sisters, who through gift-giving try to obtain apostasy of young and old from the catholic faith to some protestant denomination." The report concludes that it is necessary to ask "for the intervention of the civil authorities to dispel this christian or non-christian intrusions and respect the traditional religious affiliation of the people."[99] In this case, "traditional religious affiliation" referred to the historic spheres established during the Condominium period. In a further reversal of that period, it was now the Catholics who thought the Anglicans were infringing on their territory.

Further study could helpfully illuminate other aspects of the growth of Anglicanism in Bahr el Ghazal. In particular, the role of the SPLA in facilitating the travel and protection of these evangelists needs further study, as does the relatively weak role of education in Christian conversion there in contrast to other areas of the country. But the larger point is the impact of the continued movement of Dinka young people on the growth of the Anglican church in southern Sudan. Migrants who had moved first to Ethiopia and Kenya returned home as Christian evangelists and planted a new church. There are now several Anglican dioceses in the former Catholic mission sphere. As the bishop of one of these dioceses says, "The fruit of Kakuma is seen today in Aweil."[100]

Conclusion

This chapter and the previous one have followed parallel paths in describing the movement of religious change that took place among some Dinka during Sudan's civil war. In the former Anglican mission sphere within southern Sudan, many Dinka communities turned to Christianity. In refugee camps outside of the country, young Dinka led a movement toward Christianity as well, which some then brought back to southern Sudan when they returned. The energy and passion for Christian conversion is seen in the growth of preaching centers, the writing of new hymns, the formation of Christian affinity groups, and the numbers of baptisms, confirmations, and ordinations. Religious belief and practice among

---

[99] Diocese of Rumbek, "Annual Assembly Report, Nairobi, February 1–6, 1999," 5 (NSCCA).
[100] Abraham Yel Nhial, interview by Zink. Aweil, South Sudan, 19 July 2011.

many Dinka by the year 2000 was substantially different from what had been the case when the war began nearly 20 years earlier.[101]

But Dinka experience within and outside of southern Sudan also highlights differences in religious change. In an influential argument, J. D. Y. Peel has argued that two broad criteria for religious change are a religion's truth-value and its identity-value. Potential converts "must feel that its [the new religion's] message expresses the reality of things: what we may call its truth value." Second, the converts "must regard the identity conferred by joining the new religion to be compatible with what they feel or want themselves to be . . . what we may call its identity value."[102] These shifts can be gradual, in which case truth and identity evolve in tandem, or sudden, as in moments of crisis, when the evolutions of the two diverge. In the east- and west-bank communities in southern Sudan, the war caused a shift in the relative truth-values of the religion of the *jak* and Christianity that led to a shift in identity. But among the displaced community of unaccompanied minors, the conditions of religious change were different. Here, the identity-value of religion shifted first. The civil war shattered the microcosmic life of these young people by bringing about a transition from a life centered on villages and cattle camps to one centered on large refugee camps connected to a world of international organizations, rebel movements, and foreign governments. Such a situation demanded a new identity, which was found in Christianity. In the education offered by Christianity and the promise it held for future assertiveness, many young Dinka men found a religious identity and community that helped them navigate and make sense of the war that was taking place around them. They were freer to adopt this new religious identity because the displacement of the war had removed obstacles to conversion that had previously been presented by older men and other authority figures in society. The truth-value of religion also shifted so that Christianity became a more logical choice but it was the identity needs produced by the displacement of the war that drove conversion.

---

[101] In addition to the displacement within southern Sudan and to neighboring countries, a third stream of displacement was toward the north. Large settlements of southerners began to grow around Khartoum and other northern cities and religious change took place in these communities as well. A close study of this population is beyond the scope of the present book.

[102] J. D. Y. Peel, "Postsocialism, Postcolonialism, Pentecostalism," in *Conversion after Socialism: Disruptions, Modernisms and Technologies of Faith in the Former Soviet Union*, ed. Mathijs Pelkmans (Oxford: Berghahn, 2009), 191.

Refugees are frequently depicted as passive, immobile recipients of aid who bide their time through the good graces of others until they can return home.[103] The trajectory of the unaccompanied minors challenges this view. The Dinka who left their homes in the 1980s, first for Ethiopia and then for Kenya and elsewhere, sought Christian conversion and used that conversion as a motive force toward education and evangelism. The refugee camps of Pinyudu, Itang, Kakuma, and elsewhere were not places where they simply went to wait. They were, instead, staging grounds for further church growth and development. In Christianity, refugees found mutual aid, education, community, and a set of beliefs that allowed them to understand their time of "exile." If the study of unaccompanied minors demonstrates anything, it is the need to examine more closely the social life of refugees and see it as equally dynamic as any other social life regardless of location. War-time displacement can lead to religious change, something that has been documented anecdotally but needs further study.[104]

The unaccompanied minors were not the only Dinka who were displaced. Among the large refugee populations in Ethiopia and elsewhere were a large number of women, who were also finding new opportunities in Christianity. It is this population to which this book now turns.

---

[103]Roger Zetter, "Labelling Refugees: Forming and Transforming a Bureaucratic Identity," *Journal of Refugee Studies* 4, no. 1 (1991).

[104]See, for instance, Adrian Hastings, *African Christianity: An Essay in Interpretation* (London: Geoffrey Chapman, 1976), 29, 34. Jason K. Stearns, *Dancing in the Glory of Monsters: The Collapse of the Congo and the Great War of Africa* (New York: Public Affairs, 2011), 182.

5

Singing through Civil War
Women's Leadership and Theological Reflection in a Growing Church

The tumult of the civil war in Sudan and the rapid growth of the church created many new opportunities for leadership. Young men in the SPLA–controlled areas in southern Sudan and in refugee camps abroad came to new positions of prominence. Many women were included in this number as well. Martha Kuei Marier was one of many women who became leaders of local Christian congregations in southern Sudan, in her case in her home village of Titagok on the west bank of the Nile. In that role, she led worship and music, preached, and prepared people for baptism. In the context of Dinka culture, she recalled the role as something of an innovation: "God says people are equal, whether men or women they are all equal in the Lord. And we are free in the church. We can even stand in front of people and talk about the kingdom of God. But in the Jieng community tradition, women are not allowed to stand, even when there is family discussion."[1] The religious change that took place among many Dinka during the second civil war had significant impacts on gender roles and relations. The church of the missionary period had been primarily composed of male converts. One indication of the way in which Dinka were transcending that mission heritage during the civil war was the new roles that women came to occupy.

This chapter complements the previous one and points toward the themes of the remaining chapters. In addition to changing generational relations, Sudan's second civil war also led to changes in gender relations. These

---

[1] Martha Kuei Marier, in-person interview by Jesse Zink. Rumbek, South Sudan, 19 September 2013.

changes were expressed in church life and institutions. Women rose to new positions of leadership in the church both within southern Sudan and in refugee camps abroad. They founded new congregations and established an affinity group that paralleled *Jo Wo Liec* and structured their experience in refugee camps. At the same time, women were composing many of the hymns that the movement of religious change was bringing forth. When a new Dinka hymnal was put together in the 1990s, it contained a substantial contribution from women. Through hymns and other innovations, women shaped the theology of Dinka Christianity. This is particularly true in regard to the political theology of the civil war that Dinka put forth. In studying women's theological contributions to Dinka Anglicanism, the ideational resources that Christianity provided to Dinka become clear and set the stage for consideration in later chapters of the ways Dinka appropriated the Christian message. Christianity helped make sense of the civil war— and women played a large role in developing that understanding.

A WEAK, MALE MISSION CHURCH

Missionary activity in southern Sudan had tended to produce mostly male converts. This was in part due to the belief that only women missionaries could work with Dinka women, as well as the strong educational focus of missionary activity. Leonard Sharland, the senior missionary among the Dinka after Archibald Shaw's retirement, reported in 1946, "A primary weakness in our Dinka work has been the lag so far as girls and women are concerned. We have had a predominance of bachelors in Dinka work and that has partly been responsible for no organised work. Also we have so far not found women educationists for the Dinka work although we urgently need them."[2] This created problems. Christian conversion took male converts out of Dinka cycles of production, which made it difficult for them to pay a bride price in cows. Sharland reported on one wedding involving a Dinka Christian man working for the government and a woman from a Dinka village. It was almost called off when the brother of the bride protested that the groom could not pay the required bride price. It took the intervention of the district commissioner to ensure the wedding went ahead.[3] In general, women were largely left out of the small Dinka Anglican church of the mission period.

---

[2] Leonard Sharland, "Annual Letter," 1946 (Sudan Archive, Durham [hereafter SAD] 865/2/15).
[3] Leonard Sharland, circular letter from Akot, 20 May 1947 (SAD 865/2/17).

The Akot-area revival in the late 1930s and its spillover effects in Kongor and elsewhere began to transcend these gender barriers. Around Kongor in the 1940s, a young woman named Mary Nyanroor Duoot Chol was baptized and began to compose hymns. The lack of support for these new Christians, however, meant that Nyanroor and others eventually drifted away from the church. The economic and ecological factors of the early 1960s that led many young men to leave Dinka territory did not have as strong an impact on women. Still, a small number migrated north and became part of the same religious change that was affecting men. One of the most important for the later church was Mary Achol Deng. In the late 1960s, she left her home near Kongor on the east bank and spent time in Khartoum between 1968 and 1974 where she was baptized.[4] When she returned to the east bank, she was one of the first women to be licensed as a lay reader by the Dinka archdeacon, Khedekia Barac Mabior.

In rural Dinka territory, some families were coming to see that having a family member who was educated—and therefore Christian—could be useful. But this only applied to men. Women brought value to a family by being attractive for marriage and the bride wealth that would bring. As late as the 1970s, families were concerned that Christian conversion of their young women would make them less attractive in marriage. Mary Alueel Garang, who would later become an important hymn writer, spent a short period in the town of Malakal as a child in the 1970s and briefly attended school. "But I was taken, snatched from the town, to be taken home. At that time, the Dinka say, 'Our girls cannot be in towns. We need our girls to be in the cattle camps.'"[5] For women who did become Anglican, baptismal requirements made it a lengthy process. One female informant became engaged to a Christian man and so sought baptism. Because of her struggles to learn to read, the baptismal preparation process took seven years, rather than the usual two for a male student.[6] When the war began in 1983, the Dinka Anglican church had poor representation from women. Relatively speaking, it was easier for men to surmount the obstacles, chiefly literacy, to church membership than it was for women.

---

[4] Mary Achol Deng, in-person interview by Jesse Zink. Juba, South Sudan, 28 April 2013.
[5] Mary Alueel Garang, in-person interview by Jesse Zink. Bor, South Sudan, 14 April 2013.
[6] Martha Kuei Marier, in-person interview by Jesse Zink. Rumbek, South Sudan, 19 September 2013.

The Emergence of Female Leadership

Women were among the first people who attended worship services at the new preaching centers in SPLA–controlled areas in the 1980s. There were multiple reasons for this. Women were primary caregivers and were concerned about the health and welfare of their families, particularly their children who would carry on the family name. Christianity offered religious rituals for protection and healing that were cheaper than those offered by the ritual experts who sacrificed to *jak*. Mary Achol Deng, the female lay reader, recalled that "[w]omen came to church because they wanted to protect their children so the *jak* wouldn't kill their children. When children fall sick, and the woman came to church and prayed, the children got better."[7] Rather than having to provide animals for sacrifice—a high cost to pay in the middle of a war—Christian healing prayer was free and quickly took on a centrality in worship. As one woman recalled, "Those who worship [a] *jɔk*, the leader of that *jɔk*, when another person get sick, he used to say, 'OK, if you don't bring a bull or a cow or whatever, this person will die.' . . . But with people in the church, a person get sick, the church leaders they just come, they pray, they touch him, and that is all."[8] As was true of other conversion movements in sub-Saharan Africa, the appeal of inexpensive healing rituals was significant in attracting female converts.[9]

Preaching centers and Christian gatherings also provided new avenues for female sociality. Existing patterns of Dinka life meant that many women, particularly married women, stayed close to their home villages. It was young men who traveled far afield with cattle. Women bore primary responsibility for agriculture and so were tied to a particular place. While ritual in the religion of the *jak* would bring women together and afford them a role in worship, this was often only in a limited and sporadic fashion. By contrast, in the church women found new roles available to them. They could lead worship, speak publicly, and testify to their faith on a regular and recurring basis. One male informant recalled his realization during the war that, for women, church had become "an avenue for which they could come for socialization. They meet with

---

[7] Mary Achol Deng, interview by Zink. Juba, South Sudan, 28 April 2013.

[8] Mary Aruay Majak, in-person interview by Jesse Zink. Rumbek, South Sudan, 13 September 2013.

[9] J. D. Y. Peel, *Religious Encounter and the Making of the Yoruba* (Bloomington: Indiana University Press, 2000), 234.

other women and pray to the Lord together, they sing together in the church."[10] As Martha Kuei Marier discovered, the freedom to speak publicly that was found in the church was unusual in the context of existing Dinka practices. The Dinka experience echoes that of other East African pastoralists. Studies of the Maasai, for instance, have documented how conversion to Christianity allowed women to create a new kind of community that was beyond the control of men. In coming together to learn, to pray, and to talk to one another, these Maasai women found that it was "the spirit, not the structure, of the church that appealed to them."[11] Something similar was happening among some Dinka women.

Yet neither the appeal of healing prayer nor the new avenues for sociality would have led to enduring conversion were it not for the freedom that some male church leaders felt in reinterpreting church membership practices. The surge of interest in Christianity combined with the lack of print resources and the distance from the church hierarchy led to a weakening of the connection between literacy and baptism. Church leaders like Nathaniel Garang Anyieth and Benjamin Mangar Mamur were willing to offer baptism with virtually no preparation and certainly no literacy requirements. This did not mean that Christian catechesis was abandoned, however. The civil war led to an outpouring of hymn composition that explained, articulated, and appropriated the Christian faith in the context of civil war. To learn about Christianity through song rather than a book was a much more familiar cultural practice for women and so made conversion to Christianity easier. One church leader in this period remembered, "[For] those who cannot read, they hear God through the music. Because when the songs are being sung, people can hear them and people can feel the importance of that song. . . . So the songs attracted the people because it's saying that God can help us, God has done this for us."[12] The freedom in church practice that the civil war permitted allowed many women to escape "the discipline of literacy" and become Christian regardless of their educational background.[13]

---

[10] Stephen Mathiang Kuc, in-person interview by Jesse Zink. Juba, South Sudan, 10 April 2013.

[11] Dorothy L. Hodgson, *The Church of Women: Gendered Encounters between Maasai and Missionaries* (Bloomington: Indiana University Press, 2005), 187.

[12] Ezekiel Diing, in-person interview by Jesse Zink. Bor, South Sudan, 5 April 2013.

[13] Wendy James, "Uduk Faith in a Five-note Scale: Mission Music and the Spread of the Gospel," in *Vernacular Christianity: Essays in the Social Anthropology of*

The participation of women in the church challenged societal expectations. This was particularly noted of young women who joined in public Christian worship in contrast to the expectation that they remain close to home until marriage. The content of this worship could also scandalize. In one song composed by a woman, for instance, the singer exhorts her hearers to burn their shrines: "A girl who has not been called / to burn [a shrine] / is like one who has been refused by God."[14] In a male-dominated religious environment, it was an astonishing claim. Such exuberance led to concern that the church was "corrupting" young women. Some older men feared that their daughters would never find a suitable husband after joining the church. It was not only young women who encountered this opposition. Mary Achol Deng was married when she returned to the east bank as an evangelist. She remembered that "people thought we had gone mad. The people insulted us because they did not understand."[15] In the church, women were creating new social bonds that allowed them to challenge the expectation that they stay close to home.

The intrinsic appeal of Christian practices and the new openness to Christian initiation explains some of the movement of women toward the church. But it must also be seen in the context of a changing demography. Many men went or were sent to SPLA training camps in southwestern Ethiopia in the 1980s. The refugee camps there, closely linked to the SPLA, had a greater percentage of men than would be expected in the population as a whole. The older men who remained in villages in southern Sudan maintained control over the religion of the *jak* and saw little need to change. But new preaching centers needed leadership and many congregations turned to women. In a 1991 interview, Abraham Mayom Athiaan, one of the few educated church leaders on the west bank noted how individual congregations selected their own leaders: "If the mother [i.e. woman] is senior to the evangelist then we put that lady to be responsible for that church. And then we put evangelists under her."[16] Allowing women leadership roles like this was an innovation in

---

Religion Presented to Godfrey Lienhardt, ed. Wendy James and Douglas H. Johnson (Oxford: JASO, 1988), 134.

[14] Marc Nikkel, *Dinka Christianity: The Origins and Development of Christianity among the Dinka of Sudan, with Special Reference to the Songs of Dinka Christians* (Nairobi: Paulines Publications Africa, 2001), 313.

[15] Mary Achol Deng, interview by Zink. Juba, South Sudan, 28 April 2013.

[16] Abraham Mayom Athiaan Deng, in-person interview by Andrew Wheeler and Roger Schrock. Location uncertain, 14 September 1991 (NSCCA).

comparison to the religion of the *jak*. When the New Sudan Council of Churches (NSCC) was founded in 1991 as an ecumenical organization to serve Christians in the SPLA–controlled areas, one of its key priorities was theological education for new church leaders. It was noted at the NSCC's first general assembly that this effort should focus equally on women since "women are already involved in all of these areas and would be expected to participate fully."[17] The changing demographics brought about by the war make the Dinka somewhat different from other experiences across Africa. Other studies of Christianity among pastoralists have argued that men retained positions of church leadership and that women were largely uninterested in such authority.[18] Yet for the Dinka, the war created a situation in which women were needed to provide leadership in the absence of men.

This leadership often extended beyond the confines of an individual preaching center. In the west-bank church, one of the leading evangelists, regardless of gender, was a woman named Mary Aruay Majak. As an unmarried and childless woman who neither generated cows for her male relations through marriage nor produced sons who could carry forward their father's name, she occupied a wholly peripheral position in Dinka culture. The spur for her conversion to Christianity came in the mid-1970s when she saw how the Rumbek congregation handled the funeral of a Christian woman whose only relation was a son in Khartoum. Aruay Majak remembers how Reuben Maciir Makoi, then pastor of the Rumbek church, told the members of the congregation, "This is your mother in Christ. She has died. We have to take care of her. Even if there is no person from her family who is around her, we will be responsible for it."[19] The church, Aruay Majak realized, could alleviate the weakness of her social position.

Like many other people, Aruay Majak was forced to leave Rumbek because of the war. She returned to her home region of Maper, north of Rumbek. There, she began evangelizing her family members and others nearby using familiar methods: beating a drum to gather people, singing songs, and explaining them. The opposition that she encountered was different from concerns about the "spoiling" of young women who

[17] Ginni Cook, "Summary Report to ESP on First General Assembly of NSCC," April 1991, 2 (NSCCA).
[18] Hodgson, *Church of Women*, 187, 197.
[19] Mary Aruay Majak, interview by Zink. Rumbek, South Sudan, 13 September 2013.

turned to Christianity. Instead, she recalled that people said of her, "this woman who has never given birth to any child, she is now trying to misuse our women. She might come with some unique faith which is against our tradition."[20] But as was happening in other places in the region, many young people and other women were attracted to her message. Over the course of the war, she founded 23 new congregations in an area that had previously had none. While she had assistance from some men, including some young men who converted in the cattle camps, and one or two who had been educated and began classes with the new Christian converts, the growth was initiated and driven by a woman who never married and had no children. From a socially marginal position, she found new social status through the church. Aruay Majak is noteworthy for the number of churches she founded. But there were many other women who played a similar role, not only providing leadership to preaching centers but also founding them and so extending the reach of the church.

The extent of women's leadership is quantified in church documents. A 1991 report from the Diocese of Bor, which covered the whole of the east bank, listed 62 male clergy and 72 male evangelists. But it also listed 30 Mothers' Union staff and 101 "Women Workers with Badges," that is women consecrated for leadership in the church. The breakdown by parish is also revealing. In Duk Faiwil parish, for instance, a larger community in the northern reaches of east-bank Dinka territory, there was one male priest, three deacons, five evangelists, and nine consecrated female leaders.[21] In a 1992 report from Rumbek Diocese, covering much of the west bank, women's names feature prominently in a list of the person in charge of each of over 200 congregations. Around Akot, for instance, 2 of 5 parishes were led by women and 11 of 25 sub-parishes were. In Maper, where Mary Aruay Majak worked, 2 of 6 parishes and 4 of 19 sub-parishes were led by women.[22] These statistics do not show gender parity and women were not able to be ordained in the Episcopal Church of the Sudan until the early 2000s. The leading positions in church affairs continued to be occupied by men. But the significance of these statistics should not be underestimated. For many Dinka who were turning to Christianity for the first time in a local preaching center,

---

[20] Mary Aruay Majak, interview by Zink. Rumbek, South Sudan, 13 September 2013.

[21] Nathaniel Garang, "Diocese of Bor 1991 Report" (NSCCA).

[22] "Statistics of the Church in the Diocese of Rumbek," 17 January 1992 (NSCCA).

their introduction to the faith was mediated by a woman who would direct their catechesis and preparation for baptism. It was a situation that stood in contrast to the marginal religious position of women prior to the outbreak of civil war.

WOMEN IN A REFUGEE CHURCH

Young boys were not the only people who sought refugee in camps in southwestern Ethiopia in the late 1980s. There were also women among the hundreds of thousands of refugees. At the same time as the displaced young men turned to the church and rose to leadership positions, a parallel movement occurred among women that demonstrated the way in which Christianity was coming to structure social life during the war. And, just as the religious change that took place among young men in refugee camps led to the emergence of a new affinity group, *Jo Wo Liec*, so too did the women create their own group, which channeled their church activity into new forms of association and activity.

In the Ethiopian refugee camps, women took a leading role in responding to the needs of refugees. After the difficult journey across southern Sudan and at a time when international agencies struggled to provide aid, the early years in the refugee camps were marked by many sick and suffering refugees and inadequate resources to meet their needs. Victoria Adhar Arop, who arrived in Dimma from the west bank, remembered her first impression: "When I arrived it was in terrible condition. There were no latrines, and the feces were all over the ground. . . . So I and the other women began digging latrines, and teaching the children how to use them." The role expanded beyond immediate relief as well: "We trained them [the boys] how to make bricks for building. They were taught how to make dressings, give injections and cook for themselves."[23] Some unaccompanied minors were on their own for the first time and separated from family members. Women began to fill this gap in a way that, for some, was mediated through the church. Mary Achol Deng, the east-bank evangelist, was among those who fled to Ethiopia in the late 1980s. She recalled how, on her arrival, she organized women in the church to care for the young boys and their physical health needs. But they also preached to them and taught them Christian

---

[23] Lydia Stone, "'We Were All Soldiers': Female Combatants in South Sudan's Civil War," in *Hope, Pain and Patience: The Lives of Women in South Sudan*, ed. Friederike Bubenzer and Orly Stern (Johannesburg, South Africa: Fanele, 2011), 36.

hymns.[24] Dominic Matong, one of the few Catholic priests who worked in the camps at this time, later recalled how he was always "so encouraged by the Dinka Bor women. They are positive in their message. If someone is sick they say, 'Do not only ask for medicines, but call on the one who knows how to heal.' When someone is healed they go to the Church to offer thanks." In a situation of great need, Christians were at the forefront of the response and it was women who were primarily involved in this work. Matong also contrasted the religious life in Ethiopia with what he knew from southern Sudan: "Here people are praying that God will protect their people. . . . It is a very serious sort of prayer. The faith grows deeper. . . . sometimes when the women pour out their prayers it is long."[25] Christianity was giving women new ways of accessing *Nhialic*.

Like the population of young people, many women were forced to flee Ethiopia when the camps were abruptly closed in 1991. Some ended up in refugee camps around Nimule in southern Sudan. Others ended up in Kakuma in northwestern Kenya where they encountered many of the same problems that the unaccompanied minors did as well: challenging relations between Dinka and Nuer and between residents of the camp and local Turkana; difficulty finding legal status in Kenya; and diminishing rations that led to health and educational problems. One particular moment of stress came in 1997. In April, a cholera outbreak in the camp led to over 100 deaths in five weeks. In August, there was an increase in interethnic violence. Among those killed was one of the senior Anglican priests in Kakuma, John Majok Tuil, who was shot in his home at night. In September, political unrest in Mombasa meant that food deliveries could not make it to Kakuma and rations were sharply curtailed. It was an upsetting, frustrating, and challenging time. Women responded through the church.

The medium of response was a group known as *Thiec Nhialic*, a Dinka phrase that means "to ask (beseech) God." *Thiec Nhialic* was an explicitly Christian group whose membership was restricted to women. Branches of it existed in Kakuma as well as other refugee camps within and outside of southern Sudan. The group had been formed in the early 1990s and, like *Jo Wo Liec*, it was divided into sub-sections. One group

---

[24] Mary Achol Deng, interview by Zink. Bor, South Sudan, 28 April 2013.

[25] Dominic Matong, interview by Marc Nikkel. Rome, Italy, 11 October 1989 (transcript in NSCCA).

focused on evangelism and teaching Christian practices to other Dinka. Another, known in Dinka as *Tuk Yinhiɔl* ("Bow down"), but often referred to in English as "prayer warriors," was responsible for active, engaged, and ongoing intercessory prayer for peace, for the world, and for the needs of church members. A final group focused on planning and logistics for various events.[26] In April 1997, during the cholera outbreak, members of *Thiec Nhialic* marched around the hospital in Kakuma and prayed for those who had cholera. These were Christian prayers, and they were performative as well. As they marched, women carried long, thin crosses that they lifted up in the air, making an explicit comparison with the bronze serpent that Moses lifted up in the wilderness, and which Jesus invoked when he said that he also needed to be lifted up (Numbers 21:8-9; John 3:14-15).[27] At a time when other actors in society seemed to be impotent, these women turned to the Christian God for assistance.

In September, after the death of Majok Tuil and the cutting of rations, members of *Thiec Nhialic* returned with a prayer campaign that this time targeted not the hospital but the compound containing the headquarters of aid agencies and the United Nations. For four days in early September, they surrounded the camp with their prayers, marching, and singing. The American priest, Marc Nikkel, observed this and left a lengthy description:

> At 6am on September 10, 171 determined women put on "sackcloth" (their most ragged old clothes), wrapped themselves in dark rags, and gathered in Zone 1, at the southernmost point of the camp. They determined to act with one heart crying out for God's salvation, offering their petitions, first, for an end to the killings, secondly, for an improvement in health care in the camp, and, finally for the restoration of food rations. After initial prayers they divided into three groups, one walking along the *khor*, the dry riverbed bordering the west side of the camp, another following the *khor* which forms Kakuma's eastern perimeter, and the third, walking down the central road, all to converge at the camp's northern tip, some five miles away. For four days, from 6am until 1pm, they encompassed the camp with their "weeping prayers." . . . On September 11 the women took their lamentations before the double iron gates and

---

[26] Nathaniel Athian Deng Mayen, *Christian Faith among the Jieeng: The Shift in Values, the Stages of Faith, and the Cultural and Religious Experiences of Jieeng Believers in the Episcopal Diocese of Bor* (Denver: Outskirts, 2015), 100–101.

[27] Marc Nikkel, letter to supporters, 1 November 1997, collected in *Why Haven't You Left? Letters from the Sudan*, ed. Grant LeMarquand (New York: Church Publishing, 2006), 160.

razor-wired fences of the UN compound, there casting themselves on the ground, rolling in the dirt (knowing, as they recall, that some thought they were mad).... They implored God with song.[28]

The songs that were sung were ones that had been composed during the course of the war. One hymn they sang contained the refrain: "Look upon us, O Creator who made us. God of all peoples, we are yearning for our land that we may pray to you in freedom."[29] Many of the expatriate aid staff were not aware of the religious life of the refugees, but camp administrators did at one point invite three women, including Mary Achol Deng, to meet with them. Achol Deng told camp staff: "We have fled from war, believing we would be protected in a refugee camp. We have no way to obtain food in this desert but through the provision of the UN. Now we are being killed and are near starvation. Since the UN does not help us, we cast ourselves on God."[30] Later, the protest and prayer march moved from the UN compound to the camp's cemetery, praying that no one else would be added. The prayers were long and extemporaneous. Nikkel recorded some of them, including one that included the petition, "Pray for those who kill their own brothers. Pray for those who are sick, and those whose legs have been cut off, and for the aged, and for the fetus still unborn. We are dying because of the laws our brothers are trying to impose on us! They have killed our pastors with the bullet. Jesus Christ, hear me, hear me, hear me. I am a feeble person, and I am being killed by one who is powerful."[31]

The 1997 activities in Kakuma are one demonstration of the work of *Thiec Nhialic* and capture several important aspects of the role women were taking in the growing church. Public prayers and demonstrations were directed by women and were composed almost exclusively of women. These activities brought the resources of the church—hymns, prayers for healing and intercession—directly to bear on the situations Dinka were encountering. They directly invoked the Christian cross and appropriated its message to the context.[32] *Thiec Nhialic* also had

---

[28] Marc Nikkel, letter to supporters, 1 November 1997, 161–62.
[29] Marc Nikkel, letter to supporters, 1 November 1997, 162.
[30] Marc Nikkel, letter to supporters, 1 November 1997, 162.
[31] Marc Nikkel, letter to supporters, 1 November 1997, 158.
[32] Marc Nikkel, "The Cross of Bor Dinka Christians: A Working Christology in the Face of Displacement and Death," *Studies in World Christianity* 1, no. 2 (1996): 160–85.

several important impacts on the life of the church. As an affinity group, it served as a "networking" opportunity for women and built links between women in different refugee camps. Mary Achol Deng had been living in one of the refugee camps near Nimule in southern Sudan but was asked to come to Kakuma to help lead the 1997 prayer marches. At a time of continued turmoil and displacement, women found in the church a way to connect with one another and sustain their social existence. Moreover, the women who participated in these demonstrations believed they were effective. The cholera epidemic ended and rations were restored after the 1997 actions. More broadly, members of *Thiec Nhialic* came to believe that their activity created the conditions for the end of the war. As Mary Achol Deng later recalled, "So many things changed [as a result of their prayer]. People were not getting killed. And the Machakos peace process started. We believe that is because of our prayer. We will not get our country through guns but through talk. God is the one who organized [the peace process]."[33] Sentiments such as these are not uncommon. Many Dinka women had turned to Christianity during the war. Now, this new faith was providing the prayers and the direct access to God necessary to bring an end to the war.

A New Dinka Hymnal

The story of women marching and singing in front of the UN compound in Kakuma is only one of many indications that music was important to Dinka religious activity. Previous chapters have highlighted the role of music in religious change. To spend time in a Dinka church today is to be inside a packed church building nearly bursting with the energy of exuberant song, most sung by memory by the congregants. This is not surprising. The Dinka have historically had a relatively weak material culture, which has led to an emphasis on singing as a central cultural activity. Dinka composed and sang songs in honor of a particular ox, about romantic relationships, and in competition in cattle camps.[34] In the religion of the *jak*, singing was part of animal sacrifices and other significant ritual moments. This made song composition a highly prized skill. Leading songwriters were widely known and feted. But it was also the preserve of men. In their studies of the Dinka, Godfrey Lienhardt

---

[33] Mary Achol Deng, interview by Zink. Juba, South Sudan, 28 April 2013.
[34] Francis Mading Deng, *The Dinka and Their Songs* (Oxford: Clarendon, 1973).

and Francis Mading Deng both associate religious song composition with men.[35] As one Dinka author noted, "Composing and singing songs was [in the male] sphere. It is not that women never composed or sang songs at all, but the fact is that men did it most of the time."[36] To understand how Dinka Anglican women came to be composing and singing hymns in their worship and protest, it is necessary to first understand the background of music in the Anglican church and the creation of a new hymnal during the second civil war.

For the first several generations of the Anglican church, the amount of Dinka-language music was limited. CMS missionaries translated some hymns from the popular hymnal *Golden Bells*. But there were no hymn compositions by Dinka Christians until the flourishing of interest in Christianity around the mission station at Akot in 1939. John Collison, the missionary at Akot, recalled how Ater Bai, a workman, composed several choruses that replaced "the old, badly sung English hymns. They were accepted with great enthusiasm and the singing of them was inspiring and much used by the Holy Spirit."[37] A more prolific composer of music was Daniel Ayup, who had previously had little contact with the mission station. His hymns were "completely indigenous—the message, the idiom, the rhythm and tune are entirely their own so that here we have quite a new departure from western ideas."[38] Their popularity among new converts meant that their content formed the basis of many people's understanding of Christianity, even as some missionaries raised concerns about the limits of orthodoxy. In 1956, a Dinka hymnal of 118 hymns was published. In the early 1980s, Dinka Christians in Juba produced a small mimeographed book of hymns and made about 1,000 copies.[39]

Whatever the merits of this existing hymnody, it was rapidly dwarfed by the compositions that came forth during the civil war. One fact that many informants attest to is the scale of the songwriting that occurred during the war. Young men in cattle camps who converted to Christianity would start writing songs about the Christian God. Women would

---

[35] Godfrey Lienhardt, *Divinity and Experience: The Religion of the Dinka* (Oxford: Clarendon, 1961), 18–19; Deng, *Dinka and Their Songs*, 81.

[36] Isaiah Majok Dau, *Suffering and God: A Theological Reflection on the War in Sudan* (Nairobi: Paulines Publications Africa, 2002), 77.

[37] John Collison, "The Christian Church on the West Bank of the Nile, 1938–1940," 1 April 1981, 3 (NSCCA).

[38] "A Dinka Song-Maker," *Southern Sudan Mail Bag* 1, no. 10 (1949): 21.

[39] Rhys Hall, letter to Marc Nikkel, 28 October 1992 (NSCCA).

do the same. These songs circulated through the new congregations, forming the basis of the worship and catechesis. In a church that no longer placed the same emphasis on literacy, music became an important way to transmit the Christian message. When Bishop Nathaniel Garang wrote to supporters outside of Sudan in 1989 after several years out of contact, one of the first things he asked for was more paper and exercise books to record the songs that were being written.[40] When Garang attend the first general assembly of the New Sudan Council of Churches in 1991, he carried with him more than a thousand new hymns that had been written in east-bank communities during the previous few years.[41]

The reestablishment of communication between the Dinka church in the SPLA–controlled areas and foreign supporters, formalized in the creation of the NSCC in the early 1990s, allowed east-bank church leaders to think about creating a new hymnal. With an initial grant from the Church Missionary Society, work began on publishing a new collection to replace the one from before the war. The war created many logistical problems, but in 1992 and 1993 a hymnal committee met in Gulu, Uganda. The central figures were Stephen Dit Makok, an Anglican priest who was widely noted for his songwriting ability when he lived in the north, and Reuben Akurdit Ngong, a graduate of Bishop Gwynne College who was then serving as the secretary of the Diocese of Bor. The group reduced the number of hymns by eliminating duplicates and screening out those hymns that did not meet their theological criteria. Prior to this meeting, virtually all Dinka-language written material had been directed and overseen by missionaries or government officials, that is, by non-native speakers of the language. The hymnal project was almost certainly the first time a committee of Dinka had collaborated to produce a written document of such length.

By 1993, 100 copies of a trial edition of a hymnal were printed. It was titled *Bung de Diɛt ke Duɔ̈ɔ̈r* (*Book of Songs for Worship*; abbreviated *BDD*) and *Jo Wo Liec* members in Kakuma were involved in testing it and using it in worship. As people in Kakuma went further afield, they took it with them. Although the hymnal was written in the Bor dialect, it was used throughout the Dinka Anglican church. Stephen Mou brought a copy with him from Kakuma to Bahr el Ghazal and used it to educate the new Anglican converts in the region. In 1998, 6,000 copies

---

[40] Nathaniel Garang, letter to Marc Nikkel, 30 June 1989 (NSCCA).
[41] Andrew Wheeler, letter to Marc Nikkel, 1 May 1991 (NSCCA).

of the hymnal were published, followed by 7,500 in 1999, and smaller numbers as needed in subsequent years. In the context of the total population of the Dinka and the size of the church, these numbers are not overwhelming. Oral transmission continued to be one of the primary means of sharing hymns. But a new Dinka hymnal, created by Dinka with assistance from international supporters, was now in use. It was an achievement without parallel in Dinka religious history.

WOMEN AND HYMN COMPOSITION

The editors and compilers of *BDD* were largely male. But the material on which they drew had been significantly shaped by women. In contrast to the religion of the *jak*, Dinka Anglican women took a significant role in composing many of the new hymns. *BDD* includes an index of authors, which allows the influence of women to be quantified.[42]

The 660 hymns are divided into two sections: 164 "long hymns" and 496 "choruses." Generally, these latter compositions are shorter and designed to be repeated while the former have multiple stanzas and develop more complex theological themes. Of the 164 long hymns, 82 are composed in Dinka, 75 are translated from English or other languages, and 7 have an unknown derivation. The translated hymns are mostly carried over from the mission period. It is the 82 vernacular compositions that are of particular interest. Male composers wrote 47 of them (57 percent) and female composers 35 (43 percent). There is no way of comparing this data with Dinka music composed before the second civil war. But given the apparent consensus on the limited role of women in musical composition, 43 percent authored by women is a strikingly high figure. There are 19 different female composers of long hymns, but the most prominent are Mary Alueel Garang, who has 9 to her credit, and Doruka Akuek Makuac, with 7. A total of 35 men are listed as composers of the 47 long hymns, and no individual has more than 4 compositions to his name. The prominent female voice in the hymnal is channeled through a relatively small number of individuals.

The choruses are more clearly Dinka compositions. Of the 496 choruses, 458 are composed in the vernacular, only 5 are translated, and a further 33 are of uncertain or unknown derivation. Of the 458 vernacular choruses, 292 (64 percent) are by men, and 159 (35 percent) are by

---

[42] What follows is based on the index in *Bung de Diɛt ke Duɔ̈ɔ̈r* (Nairobi: Sudan Literature Centre for the Episcopal Church of Sudan, 8th printing, 2007).

women. (For a further 7 choruses, it was not possible to determine the gender of the composer.) This initially appears to show a lesser role for women in the choruses than in the long hymns. But two further issues must be considered. Fourteen choruses are attributed to Daniel Ayup, and a further 54—the greatest by any single author—are by Stephen Dit Makok, the hymnal editor. If Ayup's and Dit Makok's choruses are discounted, the total composed by women is close to 41 percent, a figure that is more in line with the figure for the long hymns. There are 78 different female composers of choruses and 106 different male composers. Some women have as many as a dozen choruses attributed to them, though these are generally different women from those who composed the long hymns.

To date, only the Dinka Bor hymnal has been produced. Efforts to produce a similar hymnal for west-bank communities have faltered, which means there are no equivalent data to assess the role of women in hymn composition in those communities. But the available data demonstrate a roughly 60/40 split between men and women in composing hymns. This is not parity but it is a more significant role for women than would have been expected in the religion of the *jak*. Moreover, women have a more pronounced role in the composition of the long hymns. It is these hymns that have done so much to shape the theology of Dinka Christianity and which are sung with such fervor by Dinka Christians today. That claim can be further supplemented with qualitative observations. In interviews, several informants pointed independently to the influence of hymn 144 as being a crucial moment in their process of conversion. Hymn 144 is one of the long hymns written by Doruka Akuek Makuac, and stresses the change that God is bringing in the world through the civil war and how God seeks to bring people into God's presence. Another popular hymn among many Dinka, still sung loudly and with great energy in congregations, is hymn 4, composed by Mary Alueel Garang. The opening stanza calls on its singers to "give thanks to the Lord in the day of devastation and in day of contentment.... When we beseech the Lord and unite our hearts and have hope then the *jɔk* has no power. *Nhialic* has not forgotten us. Evil is departing and holiness is advancing, these are the things that shake the earth."[43] Rather remarkably, Dinka are enjoined to praise God in the middle of civil war. In the same way that Charles Wesley used hymnody to shape

---

[43] Nikkel, *Dinka Christianity*, 314.

the theology of the early Wesleyan movement, it is possible to identify a small number of Dinka women who have had an outsize influence on Dinka Anglican theology. The popularity of these two hymns gives some indication of the way in which music has both shaped and expressed the grassroots theology of the Dinka Anglican church—and the important influence of women on this process.

The other noteworthy aspect of these hymns is the background of the composers. Biographical details are not available for all of the notable female composers, but Mary Alueel Garang is a noteworthy example. Like the west-bank evangelist Mary Aruay Majak she came from a socially marginal position. When Alueel Garang converted to Christianity, she was divorced, and her only child had died. This put her in an unusual and almost powerless position in Dinka society. Today, however, she is widely recognized in the Dinka church and beyond. Her music is played on radios in the market of the town of Bor, for instance. Like Mary Aruay Majak, she is widely known by an honorific, Nongdit. Both Alueel Garang and Aruay Majak found in Christianity a way to alleviate the weakness of their social position and challenge their marginality.

Vernacular hymnody has been a vital part of Christian conversion movements elsewhere in Africa.[44] The creation of a Dinka Bor hymnal is an indication both of the increasing institutionalization of the church as well as the prominent role that women took in the growing church. Women composed many of the hymns they then used as part of their religious-political expression, in the way for instance that members of *Thiec Nhialic* did in Kakuma. Music pervaded (and pervades) the Dinka Anglican church, both as a spur to conversion and as the centerpiece of worship and action. It is women who are composing this music and then using it in their religious life. The hymns shape not only the activity of women, however, but the life of the entire church.

A Christian Theology of War

Women turned to Christianity because it offered them new avenues of sociality and new opportunities for leadership. But Christianity also offered answers to the questions that were being raised by the war, answers that were then expressed in hymns. By studying these hymns,

---

[44] James, "Uduk Faith in a Five-note Scale"; Bengt Sundkler, "African Church History in a New Key," in *Religion, Development and African Identity*, ed. Kirsten Holst Petersen (Uppsala, Sweden: Scandinavian Institute of African Studies, 1987), 80.

it is possible to see the outlines of a Dinka theology that accounted for the war in religious terms. It is particularly appropriate to consider this theology in the context of the role of women in the church, given the major contribution of women in shaping it.

Dinka Christian theology began with a particular understanding of God. In an interview, Mary Alueel Garang, one of the leading composers of long hymns and, as a result, a leading theologian of Dinka Christianity, was asked what words she would use to describe God. She began with familiar concepts, including describing God as loving and forgiving. She added: "When we ignore him . . . he can cause a problem, like a punishment. He rebukes his people." She drew a parallel between God's action and that of a Dinka father: "In our culture, if you love your child and he is doing bad things, you can beat him." The Western interviewer responded that some people might have a hard time reconciling the idea of God as loving with the idea of God as someone who beats his children. Alueel Garang replied that she could understand this view but that in the book of Hosea in the Old Testament, God was portrayed in the way she was describing. Alueel Garang's comments reflect a basic understanding of God: the Christian God is a loving God but also one who wants all people to follow him. Therefore, the Christian God acts to bring about that obedience, through punishment if necessary. Alueel used an Old Testament phrase to describe the Dinka as "stiff-necked": they refused to follow the Christian God and instead relied on the *jak*.[45] God is the Creator and source of life while also being a God whose judgment brings destruction.

This doctrine of God is reflected in many hymns. One of Alueel's most popular hymns was composed in 1992, not long after the devastating violence that followed the split in the SPLA, and quoted earlier. Its chorus affirms that Dinka can give thanks "in the day of devastation / and in the day of contentment." The fifth verse explores the reasons for the war: "It is not that God / does not have power to deliver us, / but we had to endure our punishment / because of our foolishness / of worshipping wood and animals. / So God thrashed out sin / from within humankind / and then he called us / to come with purity into his presence."[46] The hymn presents an image of God as both a figure

---

[45] Mary Alueel Garang, interview by Zink. Bor, South Sudan, 14 April 2013.
[46] Hymn 4, *Bung de Diɛt ke Duɔ̈ɔ̈r*, translation taken from Nikkel, *Dinka Christianity*, 314–16.

of punishment but also one of love. The two are different sides of the same coin. It is through punishment that God will lead the Dinka to repentance, in this case a true turning again to God and away from the *jak*. In another hymn, this one composed by an unaccompanied minor in a refugee camp in Ethiopia, the hymn begins with a verse from God's perspective: "You, people of the entire earth, I call you / but you don't listen that you might come. / You say you will not die, but the things of the earth are like drying heads of grass. / You are the people of the blessed Lord. / You are the people of the Lord Christ. / You who've gone astray, come to me, / so I can give you the Holy Spirit."[47] Again, the image is of a God who is calling back a people who have lost their way.

Understanding God in this way leads to a further question: if God was using the war to induce the Dinka to worship God, did God cause the war? Interviews reveal no consistent answer to this question. Mary Alueel Garang said that the war "is an example of [God's] love." Only a God who loved the Dinka would take the time to discipline them with a war.[48] Mary Aruay Majak, the leading female evangelist on the west bank, asserted otherwise: "God cannot bring about bad things. The *jak* caused the war."[49] In this interpretation, it is the vindictiveness and destructiveness of the *jak* that are at the root of the war. The answers point to a divergence in popular theology and emphasize the non-systematic nature of wartime theological reflection. Regardless of the answer to the question of who caused the war, the solution was still the same: reject the *jak* and turn to God.

Aruay Majak's answer indicates the way in which the role of the *jak* in Dinka religious belief was changing. The nature of the *jak* in Dinka religion had been the subject of debate since the arrival of CMS missionaries. Previously, Dinka saw lesser divinities like *jak* on a continuum with various gradations of good and evil. *Jɔngrac* was the word for malevolent spirits. The missionaries, however, referred to all non-Christian spirits as evil or of the devil. For them, *jak* came to refer exclusively to evil spirits.[50] At the same time, CMS missionaries created a new phrase—*Jɔngdit Lajik* ("Great and Pure Spirit")—to refer to the Holy

---

[47] Translated in Nikkel, "Songs of Hope and Lamentation," 494–95.
[48] Mary Alueel Garang, interview by Zink. Bor, South Sudan, 14 April 2013.
[49] Mary Aruay Majak, interview by Zink. Rumbek, South Sudan, 13 September 2013.
[50] Nikkel, *Dinka Christianity*, 288; and Nikkel, "Songs of Suffering," 227.

Spirit. Neither had precedent in the Dinka language but were used by missionaries to set the Christian spirit in opposition to the *jak*.[51]

The CMS belief that all *jak* were agents of evil carried over to the post-mission church. By the time Christian conversion began on a major scale among the Dinka, it was commonplace among Dinka Christians to regard all *jak* as capricious and untrustworthy. In interviews in English, informants would frequently refer to "devils" and indicate that that was their English translation of *jak*. The transition in understanding is illustrated by a comment from Bishop Nathaniel Garang: "In Dinka, the satan is *jɔk*. *Jɔk* is the satan. They call him Satan in English, then they call him *jɔk* [in Dinka]. . . . Before [the] missionaries, there were good *jɔk* and bad *jɔk* from the Dinka people. But this time the Christians believe that there is no good spirit, only the Holy Spirit." Even *Lierpiou*, formerly the premier *jɔk* among the Bor Dinka, had for Garang become evil: "this bad spirit is the same spirit who fought Jesus in the forest [wilderness], tempted Jesus. So people know that this is the bad spirit."[52] Christians read the Bible and saw the presence of evil spirits. They translated this experience to their own cultural understandings of *jak*. *Jak* were now uniformly identified as sources and forces of ill. In his intellectualist theory of conversion, Robin Horton predicted that precisely this would happen: as more people found themselves outside of the microcosm, they would interpret social change by assuming that the lesser spirits were retreating and that the single, supreme deity was gaining greater power. "Hence they come to regard the lesser spirits as irrelevant or downright evil. Hence, too, they develop a far more elaborate theory of the supreme being and his ways of working in the world."[53]

While it is clear how *jak* were uniformly identified in this way, it is harder to see what was believed to have led to this change. Some evidence suggests that what had changed was the Dinka perception of the *jak*. Under this account, the *jak* had always been untrustworthy but Dinka had historically failed to recognize this. As Christians, however, they were able to see the *jak* for what they truly were. Other evidence, however, indicates that it was the *jak* who changed. Rather than protecting the Dinka, as they had for so long, the *jak* were now revealing their

---

[51] Nikkel, "Aspects of Contemporary Religious Change among the Dinka," 85.

[52] Nathaniel Garang Anyieth, in-person interview by Marc Nikkel. London, England, March 1990 (transcript in NSCCA).

[53] Robin Horton, "African Conversion," *Africa* 41, no. 2 (1971): 102.

capricious nature and turning on the Dinka, causing the war. Pinning down a popular theology when it is diffused among a wide array of believers is not an easy task. No doubt, both approaches were believed at different times by different groups of people. Nonetheless, there was broad consensus on the view that God was acting in the midst of the war and therefore that Dinka could find hope in the midst of the devastation. As one lay woman prayed in a displaced camp near the border with Uganda in 1994, "Those sins have bypassed the generations and awaited my coming. Those sins have waited for me, but your word has also come to me amid this death and poverty, amid hunger and nakedness. I am able to rejoice because the Lord has blessed me. Your word has come to me during this time of death."[54] Whatever the reason, evidence for the maliciousness of the *jak* was amply provided by the war. One hymn written during the CMS period by a Dinka convert but popular during the war spoke of how "*Jɔk* jumped into the kraal, / and scattered the people like animals! . . . / It is *jɔk* who is responsible; / *jɔk* caused enmity, / evil *jɔk* plays havoc with guests, / Sheep of Christ the Son, / *jɔk* makes them all disperse."[55] The reasons for the popularity of this hymn are clear: the war was the culmination of the destructiveness of the *jak*. To repudiate the *jak* and turn to the God of Jesus Christ, therefore, made sense as a protective measure against the depredations of the *jak*.

By changing their understanding of the *jak*, Dinka Christians could affirm new religious beliefs while also taking account of their existing commitments. Birgit Meyer has demonstrated how as part of Christian conversion it is necessary to "diabolize" the pre-existing religion. Religious belief must address the cosmological world as new converts understand it.[56] CMS missionaries had begun the process of turning *jak* into demons, but it was in the war that many Dinka found the evidence they needed to affirm this belief themselves. In doing so, they narrowed the distance between Christianity and the existing beliefs: Christian baptism would provide protection from the malicious *jak*. To create a world in which differing religious beliefs so clearly spoke to each other and addressed similar concerns removed obstacles to conversion.

[54] Marc Nikkel, letter to supporters, 1 December 1994, collected in *Why Haven't You Left?*, 125–26.
[55] Translated in Nikkel, *Dinka Christianity*, 292.
[56] Birgit Meyer, *Translating the Devil: Religion and Modernity among the Ewe in Ghana* (Edinburgh: Edinburgh University Press, 1999).

Seeing God as both loving and punishing and the *jak* as capricious and untrustworthy provided the basis for what could be called a political theology of the war. For many Dinka, the spiritual victory over the *jak* symbolized by Christian conversion came to be intertwined with the political and military victory needed in the civil war. Because the suffering of the civil war was, in part, the result of cosmological forces, it was only when these cosmological questions were resolved that the civil war would end. To see these themes, it is necessary to look beyond Christian hymns and to other musical compositions from this period. Some composers who wrote Christian hymns also wrote songs supportive of the SPLA, encouraging the rebels in their fight. Some compositions linked religious and political themes. A song composed by a young man in 1988, for instance, said: "You will lead our land, Jehovah, together with John [Garang] so that we taste freedom. / We are suffering double slavery. / We are enslaved by *jɔk*, enslaved by man as well."[57] Here, the joint causes of the war—human and divine—are clearly identified, as well as the two remedies—the Christian God and John Garang, the leader of the SPLA. In another composition, Mary Alueel Garang provided a spiritual justification for the SPLA to reclaim land from the Khartoum government: "SPLA, raise up your left hand and take the land by force. / Our own land God has given us, the black land, and planted us in it. . . . / Lead us, O God, so that we have victory in our land."[58] The concern here is not slavery so much as it is the loss of land. God has given the Dinka the land, and it is the SPLA who must reclaim it. Relations between SPLA leaders and church leaders were contentious at times during the war. But on a local level, Dinka Christians were part of the base of support on which the SPLA drew. Their Christianity gave them new ways to think both about the war and the rebel group that was fighting on their behalf and for which, in some cases, they themselves were fighting.

Popular theologies are not systematic theologies, and there were inconsistencies in this political theology of the war. In some instances, the war was seen as the result of the Dinka's own sin. The war was God's way of "thrashing" out sin and leading the Dinka to repentance. Such a belief could be a source of hope. For instance, rather than simply

---

[57] Quoted in Marc Nikkel, "Jieng 'Songs of Suffering' and the Nature of God," *Anglican and Episcopal History* 71, no. 2 (2002): 236.

[58] Quoted in Bartholomayo Bol Deng, "Different Routes, but One God: Dialogue between Muslims and Christians in Sudan in the Postwar Era" (M.T.S. thesis, Virginia Theological Seminary, May 2006), 45.

being forgotten refugees in an under-resourced camp, refugees could see themselves engaged in a spiritual battle against not only their own sin but the forces of the *jak* as represented on earth.[59] In other instances, however, the Dinka appealed to God not to forget them and to save them from the destruction of the war. This is the force of the phrases *thiec Nhialic*—"beseech God"—and *jo wo liec*—"turn back on us"—which were so important to the developing Christian self-understanding of women and young people. God needed to be implored to look again with favor on the Dinka. The divergence in popular theology is probably best seen as complementary rather than contradictory. The destruction of the war required an "all hands on deck" approach to theology. Any explanation that could be mustered to explain what was happening was heeded. That the explanations that were heeded—even in songs that praised the ostensibly secular SPLA—were couched in Christian terms is a significant indication of the traction that Christian discourse was gaining among Dinka during the war, even if those explanations were occasionally at odds with one another.

There is a notable silence in Dinka theology: Islam is almost entirely absent from the cosmological landscape. In the songs that gained popularity during the war, neither Islam nor Mohammed nor any other facet of the Muslim faith receives significant mention. In the political theology of the civil war, Islam is scarcely a factor. The closest references are tangential references to the role of the Sudan Armed Forces (SAF). But these are divorced from religious content. For instance, one hymn composed in Kakuma in 1994 reads, "evil has thrust in its hand in the form of human beings, / so that everyone has been scattered and children suffer in the forest / bereft of mother and father."[60] The evil of the *jak* has found its agents in the form of "human beings" who could be interpreted as the SAF but could also be the Nuer faction of the SPLA. In seeing the SAF's activity as part of a larger spiritual battle, Islam, if it is recognized at all, is a part of this military activity. The religious battle is between Christians and *jak*.[61] The civil war in Sudan has often been reduced in a shorthand reference to a Christian-Muslim conflict. In fact, however, from the perspective of Dinka Christians, Islam as a religion had little to do with it.

---

[59] Nikkel, "Songs of Hope and Lamentation," 493.
[60] Quoted in Nikkel, "Songs of Hope and Lamentation," 490.
[61] Nikkel, "Songs of Suffering," 239.

The new understanding of God and the role of the *jak* helped Dinka understand why the war was happening. It demonstrated that the civil war taking place on earth was paralleled by a battle taking place in heaven between God and the *jak*. These theological moves helped narrow the distance between Christian culture and Dinka culture. As Christianity came to help shape Dinka self-understanding, to become Christian no longer seemed like such a radical break from existing norms. The process was driven further forward by new understandings of the Bible, particularly the sacrificial nature of Christ.

Sacrifice was a familiar concept to Dinka, given the emphasis on animal sacrifice in existing religious practice. To apply these concepts to Christ was not difficult. As Nathaniel Garang recalled about the religious practices of his family, "My father brought us a very big bull and then we lay our hands in order to take our whole sins and then die for us. . . . Then it is easy for a Dinka to know that Christ came to save people like that. . . . There is no other tribe who knows sacrifice like the Dinka people. They really know sacrifice. They are close to the Jews."[62] Garang combined images of Christ as the sacrifice for sin with the sacrificial practice of the Jewish people to demonstrate that Christianity was a natural next step from Dinka religious practice. The language Garang uses is not so different from that used in other African Christian communities in which both the existing religion and Christianity were taken seriously and interpreted in such a way as to highlight continuities between the two and downplay the novelty of Christianity.[63] Emphasizing continuity makes conversion seem an easier prospect, a point that will be addressed in greater detail in chapter 7.

Christ's sacrifice was also important because of the purposes of the sacrifice. Although the *jak* were repudiated in Christian conversion, the need for atonement—a Christian concept—and cleansing of moral guilt remained. Such cleansing could be found in Christ's sacrifice. As a result, many of the hymns of the church emphasized sin, guilt, and confession. Such themes appeared in the chorus of a hymn written by a young refugee in Ethiopia: "Bring the Holy Spirit to abide in my heart. / I am only a husk, a husk driven by the wind. / I am a slave of sin who has been

---

[62] Nathaniel Garang Anyieth, interview by Nikkel. London, England, March 1990.

[63] Kevin Ward, "Africa," in *A World History of Christianity*, ed. Adrian Hastings (London: Cassell, 1999), 232.

FIGURE 5.1
Mary Achol Deng, April 2013.
Collection of Jesse Zink.

lost on distant paths. / Come back to me, O Great Lord, to cleanse me with the blood that flowed."[64] In addition to individual atonement, there was also a sense that Dinka needed to make corporate atonement for their disobedience to God. In the same hymn, the people listening are reminded that "You, people of the entire earth, I call you, but you don't listen that you might come. / You say you will not die, but the things of the earth are like drying heads of grass. . . . / You are the people of the Lord Christ. / You who've gone astray, come to me, so I can give you the Holy Spirit."[65] Such language of atonement and expiation is not unexpected in the evangelical milieu that shaped Dinka Anglicanism. What is noteworthy, however, is the way in which the traditional evangelical emphasis on Christ's blood and atonement is seen to parallel preexisting religious language for the Dinka. Beliefs about sacrifice and its effects were transposed onto the person of Christ.

The emphasis on sacrifice is evident in practice as well. Hymns were often sung as part of an active movement of prayer, such as the women who marched and sang in front of the UN compound in Kakuma in

[64] Nikkel, "Songs of Hope and Lamentation," 495.
[65] Nikkel, "Songs of Hope and Lamentation," 494–95.

FIGURE 5.2
Women in procession with crosses at Kakuma Refugee Camp, Kenya, c. 1996. Collection of Marc Nikkel. Used by permission of Durham University Library.

1997. In undertaking these physical activities and demonstrations, women often relied on long, narrow crosses. Indeed, it is not just in public demonstrations that women carry such crosses. During church services, it is often the case that women arrive at church carrying crosses of varying sizes, as totems of their faith and as tools to wave in the air while singing. The cross pointed to many theological truths. It was linked to the sacrificial death of Christ. To hold a cross is to remember the way in which one's sins—the cause of the war, according to one line of thought—have been forgiven. Christ's sacrifice is made present in the life of the believer by holding the cross.[66] The cross was also referred to as a *mën*, the word for the solid central post that supported a *luak*, the traditional cattle byre.[67] By holding it upright, women were indicating its centrality in their lives and the support it provided.

[66] Marc Nikkel, "The Cross as a Symbol of Regeneration in Jieng Bor Society," in *Land of Promise: Church Growth in a Sudan at War*, ed. Andrew C. Wheeler (Nairobi: Paulines Publications Africa, 1997), 86–114; see also Nikkel, "Cross of Bor Dinka Christians," 177.

[67] Mayen, *Christian Faith among the Jieeng*, 14.

FIGURE 5.3
Youth "attacking" a *jɔk* with crosses, Kakuma Refugee Camp, Kenya, c. 1996. Collection of Marc Nikkel. Used by permission of Durham University Library.

The cross was also interpreted in ways that made sense of the violence. It was a transformation of the spear, the traditional Dinka instrument of war. Used in this way, the cross was not just a reminder of a sacrificial death but a weapon to be used against the *jak* that continued to afflict the Dinka. For the spiritual battle whose outcome would determine the outcome of the political and military battles of the war, the cross-as-spear was the perfectly designed weapon.[68] This is part of the reason why women carried crosses with them. The connection between cross and spear was also dramatized in Kakuma. One youth drama, for instance, consisted of several young Christians attacking a figure dressed as a *jɔk* with crosses that functioned as spears. Christ's sacrifice defeated the *jak* in the same way a spear defeated the Dinka's other enemies.

In his study of religious change among the Yoruba, J. D. Y. Peel writes, "Once Christianity could be plausibly seen . . . as affiliated to the community's past as well as to its presumptive future, then conversion

[68] Roland Werner, William Anderson, and Andrew Wheeler, eds., *Day of Devastation, Day of Contentment: The History of the Sudanese Church across 2000 Years* (Nairobi: Paulines Publications Africa, 2000), 557–58.

became less a matter of many individual decisions, more a mass movement which swept people along with it."[69] The study of Dinka theology, rooted in an understanding of God, a changing understanding of the *jak*, and a clear understanding of the nature of sacrifice makes clear how this process of identification took place. Rather than seeing Christianity as a new cultural addition for the future, it was seen as something that had been missed by earlier generations and to which Dinka Christians were now returning. As the Dinka began to identify elements of Christianity in their past, they were more likely to be open to religious change.

Conclusion

This chapter and the two prior ones have offered a close study of religious change among Dinka communities, both within parts of southern Sudan and among communities that were displaced internationally. The religious change that took place during Sudan's second civil war transformed aspects of Dinka society. Young men came to new positions of prominence and self-assertion as a result of their conversion to Christianity. The new faith provided them a new identity to cope with the changing times. But much of this identity was created and provided by women, not necessarily their biological mothers but women who were creating their own new religious space and from there challenging and transforming the church. Women took leadership roles in preaching centers and refugee camps. They formed *Thiec Nhialic* to structure their relationships and create networks of support. They wrote many of the hymns that provided the catechetical basis for young male converts and other new Christians. Their influence is written into one of the most important documents produced during the war, the Dinka Bor hymnal. In these hymns it is possible to see the ways in which Dinka women were adopting and adapting Christianity in ways that affirmed a new faith while also asserting continuity with what had gone before—in a new understanding of the *jak*, for instance, or a changed understanding of sacrifice. Without understanding the contributions of women, it is impossible to fully understand how the Dinka conversion movement unfolded.

In one sense, this study of religious change is unexceptional in the history of African Christianity. The role of education and healing, the appeal of Christianity to young people and to women, and the

---

[69] Peel, *Religious Encounter and the Making of the Yoruba*, 246–47.

connection between migration and change have all been highlighted in other works. What these chapters have shown is the way in which these processes of conversion were set in motion by a uniquely postcolonial event, namely an African civil war. Christianity offered the truth claims and identity needed to survive in the new, destructive context of civil war. The study is all the more important in the context of the Dinka, an agropastoralist people who were historically averse to Christianity. At the outbreak of the war in 1983, there was a gradual trend of religious change toward Christianity. As seen at that point, it seems likely that such change would have continued, allowing Christianity to establish a clear but minority position within the Dinka religious landscape. The war dramatically accelerated those dynamics of change such that massive, widespread religious change was the result.

The Episcopal Church of the Sudan began ordaining women in the early 2000s, and there are a handful of female cathedral deans and archdeacons across the country. Formal sacramental leadership for these women is simply an extension and continuation of the leadership role that many women took during the war. *Thiec Nhialic* continues its prayer activities within South Sudan and large congregations of Dinka continue to sing with fervor songs that were composed by women. On a trip to a rural community in his diocese, the current Anglican bishop of Bor was greeted by a lengthy procession of women walking in formation, waving crosses, and singing loudly. The energy with which they greeted his arrival hardly abated as the bishop led a worship service in their church. Although men were present, it was clear that it was women who were at the center of the community's activity. This community was no exception. As the bishop later told a visitor: "Christianity is strong in Dinka communities because of women. Because they are the ones really who are inspired more than men."[70] Among this bishop's people, one result of the civil war was that Christianity had displaced the religion of the *jak* and was now a sizable—indeed, likely a majority—faith among Dinka, and among Dinka women most of all.

---

[70] Reuben Akurdit Ngong, in-person interview by Jesse Zink. Bor, South Sudan, 12 April 2013.

6

Prophets of Judgment and Change

Isaiah, Archibald Shaw, and the Evolution of Nilotic Prophecy

In 1994, Wilson Garang was a newly ordained Anglican priest who had been sent to his home region around Aweil in the far west of Dinka territory to begin the work of evangelism and church planting in areas that had once been part of the Roman Catholic mission sphere. In an interview with a foreign visitor, he was asked why so many Dinka were turning to Christianity. After all, the interviewer asked, the Dinka continue to suffer: how is the suffering understood? Garang responded, "There is something in the Bible which said that Sudan should be punished." The interviewer asked, "Do you have any idea why Sudan should be punished?" Garang responded, "This punishment should bring us to him." The interviewer asked, "Why is it that people should come to Christianity in the time of war?" Garang responded, "This is the time arranged by God. It is for the people of Sudan to offer him a gift and to worship him, as it says in Isaiah chapter 18."[1]

The previous chapter showed how Dinka began to turn to Christianity when many saw that it provided answers to questions that the catastrophe of the civil war posed. Christian theology offered an answer to the violence of the civil war by reinterpreting the nature of the *jak* and providing insight into the nature of God. Garang's answers to his interviewer are in this vein. But his responses also introduce a new theme, the invocation of the eighteenth chapter of the prophet Isaiah in

---

[1] Wilson Garang Chan, in-person interview by Michael Medley. Dhiaukuei, South Sudan, 27 December 1994 (transcript provided by Michael Medley).

the Old Testament. The answers that Dinka found in Christianity were not only intelligible in terms of the cosmological framework of Dinka communities. They were also intelligible in terms of existing religious institutions, particularly the long-standing tradition of Nilotic prophecy. New Dinka Christians came to understand their religious change as having been foretold by prophets of an earlier generation. But these were not traditional Nilotic prophets. Instead, they were prophets that Christianity brought to the Dinka: Isaiah, in the Old Testament, and Archibald Shaw, the pioneer European missionary in the early twentieth century. Using the material generated by these two prophets, set within a context of a larger understanding of Christian and missionary history, Dinka Anglicans were able to see the wartime religious change as a long-foreseen transition. Such a view lessened the social significance of religious change and made conversion seem a more logical step. The figure of prophet and the institution of prophecy served as a bridge between traditional beliefs and Christianity. Rather than being a moment of rupture, the process of religious change maintained continuities with existing religious practices.

Dinka Prophets and Religion

The Nilotic peoples of southern Sudan have a long-established history of religious leadership by inspired individuals. The anthropologist E. E. Evans-Pritchard drew on an Old Testament parallel in his famous study of the Nuer to christen these figures "prophets."[2] Similar figures have been active in Dinka communities, where they are known as *ran Nhialic*. Across tribal barriers, prophets are people—generally male—who claim inspiration by a divinity and the ability to channel that divinity to exert power over the life of a community to safeguard security and work toward peace.[3] While a prophet may have a mobile and flexible ministry, his work is closely linked with a particular moral or religious community

---

[2] E. E. Evans-Pritchard, *Nuer Religion* (Oxford: Oxford University Press, 1956), 287–310.

[3] Godfrey Lienhardt, *Divinity and Experience: The Religion of the Dinka* (Oxford: Clarendon, 1961), 73–74; Douglas H. Johnson, *Nuer Prophets: A History of Prophecy from the Upper Nile in the Nineteenth and Twentieth Centuries* (Oxford: Clarendon, 1994), 35; Douglas H. Johnson and David M. Anderson, "Revealing Prophets," in *Revealing Prophets: Prophecy in Eastern African History*, ed. David M. Anderson and Douglas H. Johnson (London: James Currey, 1995), 17–24.

and the enhancement of that community's well being. Evans-Pritchard and others saw overlap with the Old Testament role, but Nilotic prophets have a deep history and a robust "cultural infrastructure of legitimacy" that has been built up in the generations since the emergence of the first prophets in the nineteenth century.[4] The first (and the archetype) of Nilotic prophets is Ngundeng Bong, the late-nineteenth-century Nuer figure who emerged as a leader around the time Anglo-Egyptian rule was beginning to make itself felt in southern Sudan. Among the Dinka, the prophet Ariandhit from the Bahr el Ghazal region sought to create a Dinka community separate from British colonial rule in the 1920s and was suppressed by the British as a result.

The memory of a prophet frequently long outlasts whatever leadership he may have offered during his lifetime. It is at this point that prophets begin to turn from religious leaders concerned with contemporary communities to figures who have the ability to foretell the future. During their lifetimes, prophets produce a corpus of material—sayings, predictions, songs—that is vital to their ministries. But this material often outlasts them and takes on great importance to later generations. The material produced by Ngundeng Bong, for instance, has had a lengthy and varied afterlife. During Sudan's first civil war in the 1960s, phrases from Ngundeng's songs composed 60 years earlier began to be applied to specific events in the war. Ngundeng was believed to have predicted various aspects of that civil war. The practice was so widespread that by the end of the first war, Ngundeng and his songs were better known throughout Nilotic territory than they were at the time of his death.[5] Ngundeng's material continued to be used in the 1970s and into the second civil war. New readings of Ngundeng's corpus of songs provided a framework of meaning and interpretation for new events. As the circumstances changed, succeeding generations looked to different sayings or offered new interpretations of material that had already been used in different contexts.[6] Prophets are important for what happens during

---

[4] Sharon E. Hutchinson and Naomi R. Pendle, "Violence, Legitimacy, and Prophecy: Nuer Struggles with Uncertainty in South Sudan," *American Ethnologist* 42, no. 3 (2015): 416.

[5] Johnson, *Nuer Prophets*, 337–38.

[6] Johnson, *Nuer Prophets*, 339–53; Sharon Hutchinson, "A Curse from God? Religious and Political Dimensions of the Post-1991 Rise of Ethnic Violence in South Sudan," *The Journal of Modern African Studies* 39, no. 2 (2001): 326.

their life, but "what is done with the words of the prophet is historically more important than what those words might actually have been."[7]

The example of Ngundeng indicates the importance of studying religious interaction at the level of cultural inheritance and ideas. Religious change is not simply about what provides the best answers to the pressing concerns of the moment. Rather, it is rooted in the existing history and traditions of a people. Prophecy and prophetic legacy provide insight into how Nilotic people think about and respond to new events and new contexts in specifically religious terms. As many Dinka turned to Christianity, they did not abandon prophecy. Instead, many Dinka came to realize that Christianity offered a new corpus of prophetic material that helped explain and make sense of the war. This interpretive step opened the way to Christian conversion.

Isaiah: Prophet of Judgment

Church Missionary Society (CMS) missionaries published a Dinka Bor translation of the New Testament in 1940. Their only published effort at Old Testament translation was a collection of 100 stories that came out in 1935. To this day, the Hebrew Scriptures have not been completely translated into Dinka Bor, although the initial collection of stories remains in wide circulation and was republished in the 1990s in a revised orthography.[8] The Old Testament material that was translated was mostly stories, such as those of the patriarchs, heroes of the faith such as Samson and David, and warnings to figures such as Job or Jonah. There are only a limited number of prophetic passages in the volume. Nonetheless, Dinka Anglicanism places the Bible, and particularly the Old Testament, at its center. Two related claims are made. First, the experience of the Dinka parallels that of the Jewish people in exile. Second, Sudan and the Dinka appear in the Old Testament. What is written in the Old Testament therefore can be seen as a corpus of prophetic material that applies directly to the experience of the Dinka in the middle of the *riäk* of civil war.

---

[7] Johnson and Anderson, "Revealing Prophets," 23.
[8] *Pïööc de Lëk Theer (Lessons from the Old Testament, in the Words of the Bible, in Dinka, Bor Dialect)* (London: SPCK, 1996/1950/1935). The Old Testament has been translated into Dinka Padang, the northernmost dialect of Dinka, and this translation is in limited use among some Dinka farther south. A translation of the Old Testament into Dinka Bor is ongoing.

Some parallels between the Old Testament and the life of the Dinka are obvious. Stories of semi-nomadic cattle-keepers who sacrificed animals to God have a clear parallel with Dinka agropastoralism. But the parallels that mattered to many Dinka were religious in nature. One of the earliest articulations of these themes came in the writings of John Malou Ater, who in the 1970s became the first Dinka Anglican priest to go on to further degree-level study abroad. In a graduate dissertation, Malou made multiple comparisons of religious practice. He argued, for instance, that Dinka are monotheistic, "despite references which are often made to secondary gods or spirits—such beings are simply understood as the messengers of the one supreme God . . . these sub-deities hardly play a role of greater importance than that of patron saints in the Christian world."[9] Malou also argued that both Dinka and the Israelites believed in a life after death.[10] These claims are open to serious contestation. Compared to Lienhardt's treatment of Dinka religion, for instance, Malou seems to deliberately underplay the *jak* and other divinities in arguing for a Dinka monotheism. He also creates a belief in an afterlife which neither Lienhardt nor any other anthropologist had detected. But such concerns are beside the point. In an interpretive move made by many other Christian intellectuals across Africa, Malou recognized something familiar in the Old Testament and reinterpreted Dinka religious practice to bring it more in line with a putative Old Testament monotheism. His argument is representative of the general belief among many Dinka Anglican leaders: Dinka religion and the religion of the Old Testament had much in common. Therefore, it was not a huge step for Dinka to adopt the religion that the people of Israel were, in time, believed to have adopted in Jesus Christ.

The identification of the Dinka as God's chosen people was given further impetus by a translation decision made by CMS. In the New Testament, the word *Gentile* was translated into Dinka as *jur*, the word that Dinka used to refer to foreigners and non-Dinka. The connotations of *jur* are inferiority and uncleanliness. By implication, therefore, the Dinka were identified with the Jewish people chosen by God. While the apostle Paul's New Testament teaching on relations between Jewish people

---

[9] John Malou Ater, "The Dinka Priesthood: A Study against the Background of Native Religious Belief and Cult, Leading to a Comparison with Biblical Concepts of Priesthood, and an Evaluation of Missionary Strategies" (M. A. thesis, Near East School of Theology, Beirut, 1976), 1–2.

[10] Malou Ater, "Dinka Priesthood," 15.

and Gentiles works to break down barriers between the two groups, *jur* retains a potency in translation. Rather than encouraging Christians to think of a new synthesis in the people of God, it led to an attitude of "superiority of one group above all ethnic groups, tribes and nations."[11]

These readings offered Dinka ways to see their own experience and identity in light of the stories told in the Bible. The civil war offered a new point of comparison: the displacement of the war was a clear parallel with the exile of the Israelites. Exile came to be an idea that shaped how Dinka Anglicans understood the war. When asked what stories of the Bible were highlighted in preaching during the war, one informant pointed to verses concerning exile: "With this displacement [Dinka] move from their own homeland where they cultivate, they cross the land. They are there, but they do not feel good; they are not cultivating, they have no cattle. . . . So the verses they use are those of [the] Israelites, because their land has been occupied by people they don't know. Like Jerusalem was under siege and captured, so the same like Bor, like Yirol."[12] The importance of a homeland became a theme in many Dinka musical compositions. One song written in Kakuma Refugee Camp expressed the sense of loss: "Away from your homeland, your integrity is ruined. / Away from your homeland, people see you as useless. . . . / Away from your homeland, you're like a baby that's been weaned too soon."[13] The Israelites had lost their land. In the war, so too had the Dinka. One could only hope, as an informant said, that the dispossession would not endure in the same way: "We hope that it is not long like Israel. It may be tens of years, not hundreds."[14] Although exile and displacement was a harsh and difficult experience, seeing the parallel between Israel and the Dinka meant that Dinka Christians could have confidence in the knowledge that God had redeemed God's people in the past. There was no reason it could not happen again now. In identifying themselves in the Old Testament, Dinka Anglicans shortened the

---

[11] Marc Nikkel, "The Outcast, the Stranger, and the Enemy in Dinka Tradition Contrasted with Attitudes of Contemporary Dinka Christians" (S.T.M. thesis, The General Theological Seminary, April 1988), 138.

[12] Mark Akuein Gak, in-person interview by Marc Nikkel. Location uncertain, 16 June 1992 (transcript in NSCCA).

[13] Quoted in Marc Nikkel, "Songs of Hope and Lamentation from Sudan's 'Unaccompanied Minors,'" *Sewanee Theological Review* 40, no. 4 (1997), 492.

[14] Abraham Mayom Athiaan, in-person interview by Michael Medley. Dhiaukuei, South Sudan, 26 December 1994 (transcript provided by Michael Medley).

distance between Christianity and existing Dinka religious beliefs and so made conversion an easier, shorter step.

These readings of the Bible made it a valuable document for many Dinka, and one worth consulting. But what made it especially valuable was the belief that Sudan is mentioned in the Bible. This argument turns on the translation of the word "Cush." As used by Old Testament authors, Cush most frequently refers to the kingdom of Nubia, a location that overlaps with contemporary Sudan. But biblical authors are not consistent and at times use Cush to refer to Babylon or Midian.[15] The Authorized Version frequently translates Cush as Ethiopia, following the lead of the Septuagint which did the same. Psalm 68:31, for instance— "Ethiopia [Cush] shall soon stretch out her hands unto God"—has been invoked by other African Christian communities and was a key verse in the pan-African movement of the late nineteenth and early twentieth centuries.[16] But this wide variety of potential translations for Cush can be easily overlooked. Every appearance of Cush can be taken to refer to Sudan. At a lecture in a seminary of the Episcopal Church of the Sudan in Juba, the lecturer spent the entire class identifying no fewer than 13 times in which Sudanese appeared in the Old Testament. His lesson for the students was simple: "You are among the people of God that has been mentioned in the holy word of God."[17] The argument can be taken further: not only are the people of Sudan in the Bible, the arrival of Christianity in Sudan is as well. One wartime convert who went on to write a master's thesis argued that the encounter between Philip and the African court official often called the Ethiopian eunuch in Acts 8 is in fact the beginning of Christianity in Sudan. As a result, he argues, "Christianity should be described as older than Islam in Sudan."[18] Not only is this a

---

[15] Bruce M. Metzger and Michael D. Coogan, ed. *The Oxford Companion to the Bible* (Oxford: Oxford University Press, 1993), 145.

[16] James T. Campbell, *Songs of Zion: The African Methodist Episcopal Church in the United States and in South Africa* (New York: Oxford University Press, 1995), 119; John Pobee, "Let Ethiopia Hasten to Stretch Out Its Hands to God," *Ecumenical Review* 49, no. 4 (1997).

[17] Field notes at Bishop Gwynne College, Juba, 15 September 2010. The passages cited were Psalm 87:4; Isaiah 18, 20:3, 43:3, 45:14; Zephaniah 3:10; Esther 1:1, 8:9; Jeremiah 46:9; Ezekiel 30:4-5, 9; 38:5; Daniel 11:43; Amos 9:7. This is not an exhaustive list of the mentions of Cush in the Hebrew Scriptures.

[18] Bartholomayo Bol Deng, "Different Routes, but One God: Dialogue between Muslims and Christians in Sudan in the Postwar Era" (M.T.S. thesis, 2006, Virginia Theological Seminary), 19–20.

claim with political overtones, it indicates the way in which many Dinka approached the Christian Bible.

The most significant apparent appearance of Sudan in the Bible is the eighteenth chapter of Isaiah, a chapter devoted entirely to Cush. It begins by invoking a "land of whirring wings beyond the rivers of Ethiopia [Cush], sending ambassadors by the Nile in vessels of papyrus on the waters! Go you swift messengers, to a nation tall and smooth, to a people feared near and far, a nation mighty and conquering, whose land the rivers divide" (Isa 18:1-2 NRSV). CMS missionaries had seen the parallels between these verses and the Dinka: many Dinka are tall, believed to be warlike, and live in a land shaped by rivers. One missionary speculated in the 1930s that the peoples of southern Sudan must have been known in biblical times because "it would not have been possible for anyone to have written such a good, brief description of the country and people as Isaiah does without such knowledge."[19] (Despite acknowledging these parallels, CMS did not include chapter 18 in the 100 Old Testament passages it translated.) As the church grew in southern Sudan, Sudanese clergy adopted this view as well. In a report introducing the Sudanese church to Anglicans around the world, Archbishop Benjamina Yugusuk wrote in 1988 that the "history of Christianity in the Sudan goes back to Biblical times, Isaiah 18:1-2."[20] Old Testament scholars from the Euro-Atlantic world are not in agreement that the entirety of the seven-verse chapter refers to Cush. As one notes, the chapter is "exceedingly obscure ... [and] has defied the understanding of commentators."[21] But these exegetical issues are easy to disregard. For many Dinka, all of chapter 18 is believed to concern them. To believe that one's people appears in the Old Testament makes the Bible a book about oneself rather than a foreign importation. Dinka could look at the Bible and make the powerful claim that they actually appeared in its story. By identifying with the story, whether actually or analogically, the Dinka came to think in terms laid out by the Old Testament, that is, in proto-Christian terms.

The civil war gave new prominence to the Isaiah passage. Rather than merely describing the Dinka, chapter 18 was believed to predict the

---

[19] Untitled and undated draft article from the 1930s in papers of G. H. Martin (Sudan Archive Durham [hereafter SAD] 47/8/4).

[20] Benjamina Yugusuk, letter to bishops at Lambeth Conference 1988 (NSCCA).

[21] Walter Brueggemann, *Isaiah 1–39* (Louisville: Westminster John Knox, 1998), 152. See also Joseph Blenkinsopp, *Isaiah 1–39: A New Translation with Introduction and Commentary* (New Haven: Yale University Press, 2000), 309.

suffering of the war and the attendant religious change. It was not a stretch to think the Isaiah text could be making claims about the future: Christians call him a prophet and chapter 18 comes in the midst of a series of chapters that consists of prophecies against Israel's neighboring countries. The link between chapter 18 and the war was given additional impetus by early editions of Today's English Version, a translation first published under the title *Good News Bible* in 1976 and designed to present "the Biblical content and message in a standard, everyday, natural English" for all people, native-speakers or not, "who use English as a means of communication."[22] The translation principle was one of "dynamic equivalence," in which translators sought to render into English the putative meaning of the original text rather than the exact words.[23]

In the Good News translation, Isaiah 18 is given a heading that is not in the Hebrew text: "God Will Punish Sudan." The middle verses of the chapter are very loosely paraphrased in a way that could not but bring out resonances with the experience of war: "Before the grapes are gathered, when the blossoms have all fallen and the grapes are ripening, the enemy will destroy the Sudanese as easily as a knife cuts branches from a vine. The corpses of their soldiers will be left exposed to the birds and the wild animals. In summer the birds will feed on them, and in winter, the animals" (18:5-6).[24] The original Hebrew does not mention corpses, soldiers, or enemies, but this paraphrase allowed the text to have obvious parallels with the war. (The NRSV, which is more faithful to the original Hebrew, translates those same verses as: "For before the harvest, when the blossom is over and the flower becomes a ripening grape, he will cut off the shoots with pruning hooks, and the spreading branches he will hew away. They shall all be left to the birds of prey of the mountains and to the animals of the earth.") Seen in this way, Isaiah was now a prophet who had predicted the suffering of the Sudanese civil war. Further confirmation of this view came from the fact that chapters 17 and 19 of Isaiah refer to Egypt and Syria. In 2013, some informants said that ongoing unrest in both countries was an indication of Isaiah's prophetic ability. The prophecies merely came true for Sudan first.[25]

---

[22] "Foreword," *Good News Bible: Today's English Version*, first British usage edition (The Bible Societies, 1976).
[23] John Fea, *The Bible Cause: A History of the American Bible Society* (Oxford: Oxford University Press, 2016), 255.
[24] *Good News Bible* (The Bible Societies, 1976).
[25] Field notes in Bor, South Sudan, 12 April 2013.

Chapter 18 concludes with a verse that was definitive in turning the text into a prophetic one: "At that time gifts will be brought to the Lord of hosts from a people tall and smooth, from a people feared near and far, a nation mighty and conquering, whose land the rivers divide, to Mount Zion, the place of the name of the Lord of hosts" (18:7 NRSV). Following the punishment of the war, this verse was believed to predict that the same Dinka people referenced in the early verses would bring gifts to the Christian God at Mount Zion. In other words, Dinka would convert to Christianity. Isaiah had foretold that.

The *Good News Bible* was a major publishing success, and millions of copies were sold. The means by which it came to southern Sudan are not clear. But by the time of the second civil war, some church leaders were using English translations of the Old Testament in their spontaneous retelling of the biblical material.[26] The importance of orality to the transmission of the Christian faith is again made clear. Although Christianity's growing influence had brought with it a new emphasis on literacy, the Isaiah material was being transmitted primarily through oral means. As has happened elsewhere in Africa, in a context in which literacy was not widespread, church leaders were able to appropriate written material and turn it into oral communication suitable—both in medium and content—for their audiences.[27]

In this oral form, the prophecy of Isaiah was one more confirmation of the political theology of the war that many Dinka were developing. The war was God's punishment on the Dinka for the worship of the *jak* and other divinities. God did this because God wanted to draw people to the true worship of God through Jesus Christ. The war, therefore, served as a call for Dinka to abandon these divinities and come to worship the God of Jesus Christ. In one of the rare letters he wrote from SPLA-controlled areas in the 1980s, Nathaniel Garang asked Benjamina Yugusuk to "Pass our greetings to all the Bishops and the family of God. Tell them to remember the book of the Prophet Isaiah. Isaiah 18. Tell them

---

[26] Marc Nikkel, "ECS Worship and Music: Isolation and Innovation," in *"But God Is Not Defeated!" Celebrating the Centenary of The Episcopal Church of the Sudan, 1899–1999*, ed. Samuel E. Kayanga and Andrew Wheeler (Nairobi: Paulines Publications Africa, 1999), 145.

[27] Bengt G. M. Sundkler, *Bantu Prophets in South Africa*, 2nd ed. (Oxford: Oxford University Press, 1961), 191, 275; Tibebe Eshete, *The Evangelical Movement in Ethiopia: Resistance and Resilience* (Waco, Tex.: Baylor University Press, 2009), 128–29.

to pray very much and sincerely. This Prophecy is for the whole Sudan. It is going to come very soon."[28] From the refugee settlements in Ethiopia, Abraham Mayom Athiaan wrote that the church was "focus[ed] on Isaiah 18. This suffering is being preached always to all our people wherever they are. And this objective of suffering is what obliged most of our people to believe Jesus Christ as the Savior of the world."[29] The influence of the Isaiah passage is particularly evident in its frequent invocation in hymns. Sometimes, the reference is a direct one. One hymn composed by a young Christian convert in a refugee camp in Kenya asserts: "We are roaming about in the bush enduring the life of homeless people, / and we keep our hearts turned toward the word once spoken through the mouth of Isaiah concerning our land / . . . your salvation will finally come / according to the word you have spoken."[30] Other times, it is the text of the biblical verses that is quoted and transformed. In a lengthy hymn offered in a church service in a refugee camp in 1997, one woman addressed God: "We call upon you, God of all peoples: Who has created us? Isn't it you who created us? You have said that the land of Sudan will be clawed to shreds by birds flapping their wings."[31] The imagery of Isaiah, as mediated through the *Good News Bible*, was shaping the popular theological understanding of the war.

The punishment predicted by Isaiah and enacted in the civil war was not necessarily reason for despair. Instead, it could be reason for hope. Nathaniel Garang Anyieth explained during the war that although God's punishment of Sudan was predicted in Isaiah 18 and that the war is in "the planning of God," there was still hope for the Dinka: "when God is doing something, there must be a reason why he did that. . . . He will help his people, he will get good people there. He will get those who have faith."[32] Similarly, Abraham Mayom wrote, "Though we are in the middle of [a] sea of suffering as prophesied by the prophet Isaiah,

---

[28] Nathaniel Garang Anyieth, letter to Benjamina Wani Yugusuk, 21 October 1988 (ACOA ACC/CH/Prov/21/3 folder (a)).

[29] Abraham Mayom Athiaan, letter to Marc Nikkel, 13 August 1989 (NSCCA).

[30] Quoted in Marc Nikkel, letter to supporters, 10 October 1995, collected in *Why Haven't You Left? Letters from the Sudan*, ed. Grant LeMarquand (New York: Church Publishing, 2006), 138.

[31] Quoted in Marc Nikkel, letter to supporters, 1 November 1997, in *Why Haven't You Left?*, 161–62.

[32] Nathaniel Garang Anyieth, in-person interview by Marc Nikkel. London, England, March 1990 (transcript in NSCCA).

we hope that our Lord will save us like Noah in the world flood."[33] This was not a far-fetched belief. God was, after all, believed to be acting to protect Christian communities. Indeed, readings of the Bible offered an explanation for the punishment. Second Chronicles describes an attack by a Cushite commander against an Israelite king (2 Chron 14:9-15). While the Cushite commander and his million-man army are defeated, some Dinka argued that since "the Sudanese plotted to destroy [the] people of God, God directed punishment against Sudan as a result of that invasion." It is not clear that this was a widely held view, but it provides an example of the kind of reasoning with which some Christians approached the Bible. Above all, Dinka could have hope because Isaiah 18 concludes with a prediction of people worshipping God: "the Sudanese people found themselves in the Bible as part of God's people who would continue to worship him despite punishment."[34] God was simultaneously punishing the Dinka and welcoming new converts.

The interpretations may have differed but the uses of the Old Testament material, particularly that found in Isaiah, show widespread agreement on one central fact: here was a corpus of prophetic material that could reliably be used to interpret events taking place during the war. The role the Isaiah material played in Dinka religious discourse was little different than that played by Ngundeng's corpus of songs and stories. That the Isaiah material was clearly associated with Christianity made conversion seem a more appealing step. It was conversion that brought access to this new corpus of material.

Isaiah 18 and other uses of Cush in the Old Testament came to be so widely believed to be in reference to the Dinka that they ceased to be the exclusive domain of Christians. The rebel army, the Sudan People's Liberation Army (SPLA), had at times a difficult and contentious relationship with the burgeoning Christian movement in its midst. But that did not prevent SPLA leaders from adopting the biblical material as well. At a 1996 conference between the SPLA and nascent civil society organizations in southern Sudan, both John Garang, the SPLA leader, and Kuol Manyang, a senior deputy, cited biblical passages as explanations for events. Kuol used the Isaiah passage to explain the inter-ethnic violence that had followed the 1991 split in the SPLA: "When we read Isaiah 18 about God punishing the Sudan it was Upper Nile that was meant. . . . There is no law

---

[33] Abraham Mayom Athiaan, letter to Nikkel, 13 August 1989 (NSCCA).
[34] Bol Deng, "Different Routes, but One God," 18, 19.

and order in many parts of the Upper Nile. . . . God is still punishing the people."³⁵ In his speech, John Garang went on at length about the number of times Sudan appeared in the Bible, citing not only the Isaiah passage but several other mentions of Cush as well. He reverses the identification in the Second Chronicles 14 passage, in which a Cushite general raises an army of a million men but is defeated by 300,000 people of Judah under King Asa: "[W]hen General Bashir threatens us with raising an army of one million men. . . . I want to tell him that he was not the first Sudanese to raise an army of one million men."³⁶ The Sudanese in the Bible are now those in Khartoum; southern Sudanese are analogized to the people of Israel. Here, the Biblical material proves itself to be particularly supple in its applicability. That Garang could draw on it so confidently shows its widespread influence. Biblical narratives were coming to shape how Dinka understood events.

The embrace of Isaiah 18 was not universal. In general, Anglicans and other Protestant Christians were more enthusiastic in their embrace than Roman Catholics.³⁷ The strong interpretative focus on judgment did not sit well with some educated Christians. Paride Taban, Catholic bishop of Torit and a leader of the New Sudan Council of Churches, frequently argued that to understand Isaiah 18 as referring to Sudan's civil war was to deny Jesus' redemptive work.³⁸ Isaiah Majok Dau, leader of the Sudan Pentecostal Churches and himself a Dinka from the east bank, concluded an exegetical study of the chapter by arguing that emphasizing judgment and ignoring "the message of hope and restoration must be regarded as biblically and theologically one-sided and deficient."³⁹ Yet the central point remains: for large numbers of Dinka, material from the Hebrew Scriptures, still not entirely translated into Dinka, had become a potent tool of political and religious prophecy. Biblical narratives in primarily oral form were coming to shape Dinka understanding

---

³⁵ Speech by Kuol Manyang at SPLM's Conference on Civil Society and the Organisation of Civil Authority of the New Sudan, 1 May 1996 (SAD 306/8/53).

³⁶ Speech by John Garang at SPLM's Conference on Civil Society and the Organisation of Civil Authority of the New Sudan, 30 April 1996 (SAD 306/8/39).

³⁷ Sharon Hutchinson documents similar interpretations of Isaiah 18 among Nuer Presbyterian communities in *Nuer Dilemmas: Coping with Money, War, and the State* (Berkeley: University of California Press, 1996), 316–17.

³⁸ Field notes of Michael Medley from NSCC Fifth General Assembly, Yambio, South Sudan, 18 March 1995.

³⁹ Isaiah Majok Dau, *Suffering and God: A Theological Reflection on the War in Sudan* (Nairobi: Paulines Publications Africa, 2002), 64.

of events as they were added to existing prophetic material. Conversion to Christianity seemed the next logical step.

Archibald Shaw: Prophet of Conversion

Isaiah 18 was important in helping Dinka converts understand themselves as Christian. But one persistent feature of the movement of religious change among Dinka on the east and west banks of the Nile is the emphasis new Christians placed on their identity as Anglicans. This emphasis was rooted in part in a further body of prophetic material produced by the early CMS missionaries.

In some African contexts, the legacy of European missionaries was deeply contested and subject to postcolonial and nationalist critiques from early leaders of independent African countries. But in southern Sudan and especially among the Dinka, the penetration of both colonial rule and missionary influence was relatively weak and inconsistent. When the last CMS missionary left Dinka territory in 1959 and was not replaced it only confirmed what had already largely been the case, namely that the Dinka church was operating under its own leadership and direction. A generation after the end of the mission period, early CMS missionaries were remembered by some Dinka Anglicans as flawed and imperfect. One lay informant remembered that missionaries "dismissed the existing religious background. . . . Instead, they brought a foreign soil with them to the Dinka territory. They started their mission with the European situation in mind."[40] Other Dinka Christians shared this view, citing the hostility missionaries showed to Dinka customs such as polygamy and dancing, their close linking of spiritual and secular authority, and their insufficient support for native clergy as reasons why CMS struggled with the Dinka.[41] In spite of these shortcomings, the early CMS missionaries could also be remembered as heroes of the faith who were to be remembered for their efforts, imperfect as they may have been, to bring the gospel to Sudan. In the early 1980s in the diocese of Rumbek, which contained all of Dinka territory, Bishop Benjamina Yugusuk put great effort into building a church near the site where missionary bishop Guy Bullen had died in a plane crash in 1937. On the first visit to the site in May 1981, Yugusuk and others erected a pillar to remember Bullen on which they wrote, "The path of duty was the path of glory." The church, which was never finished

---

[40] Nathaniel Anai Kur, quoted in Malou Ater, "Dinka Priesthood," 135.
[41] Malou Ater, "Dinka Priesthood," 135–37.

because of the war, was named St. Bullen Church and built one hundred yards from the site of the crash.[42]

During the civil war, church leaders in SPLA–controlled areas frequently recalled what CMS had done. Abraham Mayom Athiaan, for instance, emphasized in his reports how the church aimed to establish a school, church, and dispensary in each area: "There is a saying which says, 'A cooking point must stand on three legs (i.e. stones) for making good food for the household.' Likewise the church, school and dispensary symbolized the three stones to obtain [a] good standard of living for our people."[43] That CMS' missionary strategy had been similarly three-pronged was not missed. The church in the SPLA–controlled areas was, in its activities, presenting itself as the natural inheritor of CMS' efforts. Bishop Nathaniel Garang Anyieth made this connection to CMS explicit: "We have to set up CMS. We don't destroy it. . . . Because it is not our work. It is [the] work of Archdeacon [Archibald] Shaw. He prayed, he prayed until he died. So God heard him. . . . So this is their fruits. It is not ours."[44] The importance of CMS was acknowledged at the grass-roots level as well. When Diana Witts, the then-head of CMS, travelled into SPLA–controlled territory on the east bank in February 1992, she described being overwhelmed by the reception she received at Malek, the site of the first CMS mission station: "A speech of welcome had been prepared that included a CMS history of Bor. . . . I was welcomed as being the first person from CMS to be in Bor Diocese since the last missionary left in 1956 [sic.]. In one of the most isolated and devastated parts of the world that I have ever been in I found myself being welcomed as a long-lost member of the family."[45] On a visit a year later to the former west-bank mission station at Akot, she recalled, "The drama of our welcome was meticulously planned. As we approached the church compound at Akot, the entire church community was lining the route. Bishop Nathaniel [Garang] led the way with his hand on my shoulder—clearly the arrival of CMS was seen as being of historic significance."[46]

---

[42] Benjamina W. Yugusuk, "Aliab Visit," 21 May 1981 (NSCCA).

[43] Abraham Mayom Athiaan, "Report for ECS Dioceses of Rumbek and Wau, 1991," 14 November 1991 (NSCCA).

[44] Nathaniel Garang Anyieth, in-person interview by Andrew Wheeler and Roger Schrock. Location uncertain, September 1991 (transcript in NSCCA).

[45] Diana Witts, "Report of Visit to Sudan: February 1992" (ACOA ACC/CH/PROV/21/3, folder (b)).

[46] Diana Witts, *Springs of Hope* (Stanhope, UK: The Memoir Club, 2005), 164.

The emphasis on CMS by church leaders is not surprising. Nathaniel Garang and other leaders had been educated in mission schools in the 1940s and 1950s. The last generation of CMS missionaries was personally known to them, and they heard stories of the early missionaries from a young age. Moreover, with the scarcity of resources brought on by the war, any connection to international assistance was beneficial. To remind a CMS leader of her connection to the region is an implicit claim for further resources. For Garang to put his hand on Witts' shoulder is full of symbolism, both in the transfer of authority from missionary to indigenous leadership and the physical connection between a putative provider of aid and a local church leader. Indeed, the historic connections served as the basis of appeal for assistance. In an earlier letter to Witts requesting aid, Abraham Mayom wrote, "we need CMS as the real Mother Church to be solely involved with the Young Emerging Christian Churches of the ECS in this crucial time of suffering in the Sudan."[47] Garang, in a letter to Archbishop of Canterbury Robert Runcie, made a similar claim based on a shared heritage: "The Church in exile and the Church in the Government controlled towns are all under your leadership, and they need your assistance irrespective of where they are."[48] Such appeals—and CMS' perceived failure to respond adequately—contributed to tensions between CMS and ECS in the later years of the civil war. It was a tension that only existed because of the perception of a long-standing relationship. In other African contexts the critique of missionaries has centered on how they suppressed or failed to make room for African leadership. Among the Dinka, by contrast, there was little legacy of missionary paternalism to rebel against. During the civil war, no such suppression took place and Dinka leadership flourished.

But it was not just at an elite level that Dinka Christians highlighted their Anglican identity. The specifically Anglican understanding of Christianity flourished at a grassroots level as well, and it did so because of the deep-rooted importance of prophecy. Archibald Shaw, the longest-tenured of the CMS missionaries, was believed to be a prophet who had foretold the religious change that occurred during the war. Shaw was the preeminent CMS missionary in southern Sudan. Although he worked among a variety of ethnic groups, the fact that he remained at Malek after his other early companions left gave him particular credibility

---

[47] Abraham Mayom Athiaan, letter to Diana Witts, 3 June 1990 (NSCCA).
[48] Nathaniel Garang Anyieth, letter to Robert Runcie, 27 March 1990 (NSCCA).

among the Dinka. Shaw had also worked in unconventional ways to make himself known among the Dinka. He kept a cattle herd so that he could relate to other Dinka men. He visited Dinka cattle camps and took part in wrestling matches. Once he learned the language, he reveled in the articulate and argumentative debating styles of Dinka men. Shaw's prickly personality made him a difficult colleague for other missionaries and colonial officials. But he established a profile for himself among Dinka communities, who gave him a cattle name, Macuor, by which he is still remembered.[49]

Shaw's knowledge of the Dinka led him to realize that the task of evangelization would be a long one. In a report written after five years at Malek, he wrote, "The people are very primitive and ignorant with deep tribal prejudices against foreigners of any kind. Unlimited patience and years of labour are, humanly speaking, necessary before these people can be won for Christ."[50] While the task would be long, Shaw saw a clear way forward: "We must learn this much then from Islam's methods of advance and our experience at Malek, that the Christianising of these Jieng tribes must be done by Jieng missionaries. . . . I am strongly of the opinion that wisdom lies in the course of not multiplying European-manned stations, but of having one or two well equipped stations from which converts may be won, trained, and organised as native missionaries."[51] This was a conventional Protestant missionary view. Shaw describes what, in broad outline, was the policy of CMS and other mission organizations across Africa: young people would be educated at mission stations and return to their home communities as evangelists. Among other people groups in southern Sudan, focusing on young people led to success. Among the Dinka, it did so much less.

Shaw may have been frustrated at his lack of success among Dinka communities. But the words he had written remained. In the hands of Dinka Christians during the second civil war, these words were turned from the report of an exhausted and frustrated missionary into the inspired declaration of a prophet. One young Dinka who converted

---

[49] Marc Nikkel, "Archibald Shaw 'Machuor': 'The Only White Man with the Heart of the Jieng,'" in *Gateway to Africa: Missionary Pioneers in Sudan*, ed. F. Pierli, M. T. Ratti, and A. C. Wheeler (Nairobi: Paulines Publications Africa, 1998), 106–10.

[50] Archibald Shaw, "General Report on the British Mission Sphere of Anglo-Egyptian Sudan," no date, no page numbers, c. 1911 (CMSA ACC111 F1/1).

[51] Archibald Shaw, "General Report on the British Mission Sphere of Anglo-Egyptian Sudan" (CMSA ACC111 F1/1).

during the war remembered Shaw's words in a thesis he began on Dinka Christianity: "Shaw . . . made his prophesy stating that, '***Christianizing of the [Jieng] tribe must be done by [Jieng] missionaries.***' He pronounced his prophesy after having tried tirelessly all efforts to share the gospel with the Jieng."⁵² In the oral culture of Dinka society, the words began to change somewhat as well. Shaw had written both that it would take a long time to evangelize the Dinka and that it would be young people who would lead the way. This added a time element to the prophecy. An informant summarized his understanding of Shaw's prophecy in this way: "If these people don't listen to me, to the word of God, their children will one day preach the gospel."⁵³ Another recalled the prophecy in these terms: "[N]o other people could teach the word of God among the Jieng apart from their own children."⁵⁴

This prophecy began to be fulfilled during the civil war in at least two ways. First, young Dinka were at the forefront of the religious change. People noticed that it was young people who were converting in cattle camps and then becoming evangelists of the new religious message. In the SPLA–controlled areas in southern Sudan and in refugee camps in Ethiopia and Kenya, it was young people who were taking a leading role in the emerging church, leading worship services and evangelistic events and seeking baptism in large numbers. Shaw's idea that young people could become conveyors of a religious message was now coming to pass. That it was so unusual—and had been predicted by Shaw—was yet one more piece of evidence that God was truly at work among the Dinka.

---

⁵² John Chol Daau, unpublished research on the life of Nathaniel Garang Anyieth, 37. Emphases in original.

⁵³ Ezekiel Diing, in-person interview by Jesse Zink. Bor, South Sudan, 5 April 2013. An interesting parallel with the Anglican treatment of Shaw is provided by the case of Eduardo Mason, Catholic bishop of Wau from 1947. As the Sandersons write, "[F]or some Raik schoolboys at least, Bishop Mason seemed to have filled the traditional role of a Dinka prophet. Like Ariandhit in the early 1920s, he was seen as a 'man of God' with supernatural power to deliver the Dinka from adversity and hostile pressure, and to re-order Dinka society—to 'put the land in order.'" *Education, Religion and Politics in Southern Sudan 1899–1964* (London: Ithaca, 1981), 405. Shaw's transformation into a prophet engaged the entire Dinka community, an indication of the growing spread of Christianity as compared to its more limited reach during Mason's time.

⁵⁴ Nathaniel Athian Deng Mayen, *Christian Faith among the Jieeng: The Shift in Values, the Stages of Faith, and the Cultural and Religious Experiences of Jieeng Believers in the Episcopal Diocese of Bor* (Denver: Outskirts, 2015), 31.

A second confirmation of Shaw's prophecy was the people in charge of the church. The growth of Dinka Christianity thrust many individuals with ties to CMS into new leadership roles. On the west bank Reuben Maciir Makoi had been educated at mission schools and so served as a link with the last generation of CMS missionaries before independence. Others were at a slightly further remove: Benjamin Mangar Mamur's father was baptized by Archibald Shaw. On the east bank Nathaniel Garang Anyieth could remember interacting with Shaw as a child. (Shaw made frequent visits to southern Sudan following his retirement to Kenya in 1939.) Garang had a further connection to Shaw. His mother's brother was Alier Bol, a *tiët* on the east bank when Shaw arrived in 1906. Bol had befriended Shaw even as he distanced himself from the religious innovations Shaw put forward. The success of the ministries of people like Garang, Maciir, Mangar, and others combined with the astonishing growth of the church became a kind of "retroactive confirmation" of Shaw's own ministry.[55] Not only had Shaw's prophecy that the Dinka would be converted by their children come true, the people at the head of the church were, in one way or another, people whom Shaw had taught and prepared for this ministry.

As with the Isaiah material, the influence of Shaw's prophecy is seen in the way it entered new Dinka hymn compositions. One hymn, written by a female convert, drew on both Isaiah and Shaw:

> The Father spoke to us through the prophets, / Isaiah spoke of the suffering we now face. Was it / not long ago that he spoke these things? Yet they / are now being fulfilled and we are suddenly surprised. / Behold! Behold! Behold! The suffering that has come upon us / is the beginning of the greater judgement still to come.... Holy Spirit, you have fulfilled your work, the truth you spoke through / Archdeacon Archibald Shaw when we refused to hear him. He said / Our own children will teach us the Words of God. What he said has now come / to pass and we must pay attention to it.[56]

The frustrated Macuor had foreseen what was now taking place.

The prophecy about young people was not the only prophecy attributed to Shaw. When Shaw opened a new station at Lau in 1912 on the west bank, he planted a banyan tree. It is remembered that he said when

---

[55] Marc Nikkel, "Aspects of Contemporary Religious Change among the Dinka," *Journal of Religion in Africa* 22, no. 1 (February 1992): 84–85.

[56] Dau, *Suffering and God*, 68–69.

it was planted, "If this tree dies, Christianity will die in this place. But if it grows big, by then Christianity will have flourished."[57] The prophecy is multivalent. Either the tree could wither, a sign of the death of Christianity. Or it could be interpreted to mean that only when the tree grew large would Christianity flourish. In the event, CMS closed the station at Lau in 1920, but the tree remained. By the time of the war, it was large and vibrant.[58] The prophecy had been fulfilled.

It is not surprising that Dinka would remember Shaw. Significant figures are remembered across generations by Dinka, and to be able to trace one's lineage back through generations is something that all Dinka learn how to do. In one sense, then, Shaw had become a kind of ancestor for a new Dinka lineage, an explicitly Christian one.[59] It was a lineage that started small and weak but grew to great prominence. This coincided with the growing sense that Christianity created a new kind of age group for the Dinka. The Christian lineage did not replace blood lineages; instead, it functioned in a similar but parallel manner. CMS was not seen as an agent of the exploitative colonial state or subject to nationalist critique. Rather, the memory of the mission was embraced. Elsewhere in Africa, local converts have created myths around the work of missionaries that diverge from the actual intentions and actions of the missionaries themselves.[60] For the Dinka, this process was helped by the fact that the most recent missionaries had departed a generation prior to widespread religious change. They were safely in the past.

Understanding Shaw as a prophet offered the Dinka a way to understand the religious change taking place. If it had been prophesied, then what was happening must be right. That belief, in turn, encouraged more Dinka to consider religious change and added momentum to the conversion movement. Moreover, the apparent confirmation of Shaw's words gave him a new stature in the church long after his death. In

---

[57] Benjamin Mangar Mamur, in-person interview by Jesse Zink. Rumbek, South Sudan, 11 September 2013.

[58] Samuel E. Kayanga and Andrew C. Wheeler, *"But God Is Not Defeated!" Celebrating the Centenary of the Episcopal Church of the Sudan, 1899–1999* (Nairobi: Paulines Publications Africa, 1999), 65.

[59] Roland Werner, William Anderson, and Andrew Wheeler, *Day of Devastation, Day of Contentment: The History of the Sudanese Church across 2000 Years* (Nairobi: Paulines Publications Africa, 2000), 557.

[60] Tomas Sundnes Drønen, *Communication and Conversion in Northern Cameroon: The Dii People and Norwegian Missionaries, 1934–1960* (Leiden: Brill, 2009), 113–14.

the late 1980s and early 1990s, divisions became apparent in the westbank church over baptism and charismatic practice, proxies for a larger struggle between Benjamin Mangar Mamur and later Abraham Mayom Athiaan on the one hand and Reuben Maciir Makoi on the other. Schism was avoided in part by appealing to Shaw's legacy and the nature of Anglicanism. Abraham Mayom argued against schism by telling people, "We have to follow the steps of Macuor when he came here. . . . We have to promote the Word of God in unity, to follow what Macuor did in Rumbek, in Yirol, and Bor."[61] At various points it was thought that Benjamin Mangar would leave the Anglican church during the conflict to establish his own church. He, however, declined to depart in recognition of the fact that it was important to preserve, if also change, the Anglican church: "My people are here [in ECS]. If I move out, they will not all move out. . . . The Anglican church is the tradition they are keeping on."[62] Five decades after his retirement, Shaw's legacy and the Anglicanism he had bequeathed were sufficiently strong that church leaders could appeal to it as a determining factor. The initial hostility to Christianity that Shaw had encountered among some Dinka had faded. Now, in the sweep of time, they could see that God had been working through Macuor to bring about their own religious change. It is an approach to missionary forebears that is neither one of unquestioning embrace nor unquestioning rejection but rather one of critical reverence. Shaw was a prophet and a vernacular saint, a figure who had predicted the conversion of the Dinka, and who had worked for it. He was to be admired, heeded, and emulated—so long as he remained safely in the past, unable to interfere in the contemporary running of the church.

Religious Encounter and Orality

In his study of Nuer religion, Evans-Pritchard suggested that the development of prophets among the Nilotic peoples in the nineteenth century was in part a response to social change and historical circumstance. The institution of prophecy was both "a development of potentialities in their traditional religion and a change in its character."[63] A similar combina-

---

[61] Abraham Mayom Athiaan, interview by Nikkel. Location uncertain, September 1991.
[62] Benjamin Mangar Mamur, interview by Zink. Rumbek, South Sudan, 11 September 2013.
[63] Evans-Pritchard, *Nuer Religion*, 310.

tion of development and change took place during a later period of social change. For Dinka in the 1980s and 1990s, existing patterns of religious communication and belief did not so much shift as develop by the addition of new material. This development gave added impetus to significant religious change that was taking place, but did so in a way that was intelligible to many Dinka and continuous with their religious practice. This combination of development and change is illustrated by one hymn composed by a young Christian woman in the 1980s. The first verse begins in Christian fashion: "War was prophesied by Isaiah; and so it has come among us. . . . It is just as in the days of the ark of Noah once told to us, but we could not believe." By the third verse, however, the source of prophetic authority has shifted: "The destruction of the land was foretold by Ngundeng, who said, 'The youth who will come will have bad times.'"[64] The material from Isaiah and the material from Ngundeng are of equal weight in making sense of the war. Conversion to Christianity allowed for an expansion of the range of available material but it did so within the confines of existing religious practice.

The institution of prophecy offers a helpful reminder about the nature of religious encounter. CMS missionaries focused on literacy and education: if Dinka could be brought to schools on mission stations and taught to read, they could become Christian and then become evangelists to their own people. The vast amount of energy missionaries invested in building and maintaining mission stations and translating hymns, the prayer book, and the Bible testify to their commitment to this approach. But by their own measures, CMS had little success. Few Dinka were able to or interested in meeting the standards CMS set for biblical literacy and comprehension prior to baptism. Yet the departure of the missionaries began to free Christianity from its associations with literacy and allowed Dinka to transmit the religious message by other means, particularly those most familiar to many Dinka. Hymns are one example. This chapter has offered another: the oral transmission of a corpus of sayings. While the ideal of literacy remained central to Dinka Christianity and great weight was placed on education, functional illiteracy remained the lot of many of these converts, particularly women. For Christianity to grow, it had to be transmitted orally. It was unwritten

---

[64] Marc Nikkel, *Dinka Christianity: The Origins and Development of Christianity among the Dinka of Sudan, with Special Reference to the Songs of Dinka Christians* (Nairobi: Paulines Publications Africa, 2001), 335–36.

sources that took on the most important formative role in the development of Dinka Anglicanism. The nature of religious interaction did not change so much as it added new material to existing patterns of transmission and development.

Many mission organizations across sub-Saharan African pursued similar strategies as CMS in emphasizing education. As a result, literacy is often seen as paramount in the study of African Christianity, and many studies of African Christian movements have focused on written material, much of it generated by African Christians themselves.[65] In part, this is what survives. But the study of the Dinka, aided as it is by being a relatively recent case, suggests that it is necessary to be aware of what people are saying and singing as well as what they are writing. Even as a society shifts toward literacy, the central assumptions of communication can remain grounded in orality. It is these assumptions that shape how texts are received.[66]

In South Sudan today there is a large and active Dinka Anglican church, which continues to expand and consolidate the growth that took place during the civil war. This would have shocked Archibald Shaw and the other missionaries. The institution of prophecy was one of the key sites of the religious interaction that led to religious change. Isaiah's prophecy helped Dinka see themselves as Christian. Shaw's prophecy helped them see themselves as Anglicans.

---

[65] E.g., J. D. Y. Peel, *Religious Encounter and the Making of the Yoruba* (Bloomington: Indiana University Press, 2000); Derek Peterson, *Ethnic Patriotism and the East African Revival: A History of Dissent, c. 1935–1972* (Cambridge: Cambridge University Press, 2012); Joel Cabrita, *Text and Authority in the South African Nazaretha Church* (Cambridge: Cambridge University Press, 2014).

[66] Emma Wild-Wood, "Powerful Words: Reading the Diary of a Ganda Priest," *Studies in World Christianity* 18, no. 2 (2012): 137–38.

7

Prophet and Place
Continuity and Change in Dinka Anglicanism

For a few months toward the end of 1990, the Sudan People's Liberation Army (SPLA) recaptured the town of Bor from the Sudan Armed Forces (SAF). Many Dinka who had been living in the rural hinterland of the east bank of the Nile began to return and reestablish the homes they had been forced to flee from five years earlier. Among those who returned were two emerging leaders of the church. One was Reuben Akurdit Ngong, who became the priest in charge of the Anglican congregation in Bor. Akurdit's story was typical of a Christian convert of his generation. In the 1970s, as a young adult, he left his rural cattle camp behind when it became clear there would not be sufficient cattle in his family for him to marry. He moved to Juba to seek work, joined an evening club and school, and, in time, converted to Christianity and was baptized. In the early 1980s, he attended Bishop Gwynne College, the training institution for clergy of the Episcopal Church of the Sudan. He befriended the American missionary Marc Nikkel, who helped him raise the necessary funds to pay the bride price so he could wed. His wife was the daughter of Khedekia Barac, the senior Dinka clergyman in Juba. When he returned to Bor in 1990, Akurdit represented the way in which the Anglican mission heritage expanded via urban education centers to include former cattle camp youth.

The other Christian leader had a less typical path to conversion. His name was Paul Kon Ajith and he had converted to Christianity and been baptized by Nathaniel Garang Anyieth in 1986. Rather than an urban center, his conversion and baptism had occurred in a rural village outside Bor in the SPLA–controlled areas of the east bank of the Nile. Prior to his baptism,

FIGURE 7.1
Kon Ajith, Reuben Akurdit Ngong, and others outside church in Bor, September 1990. Collection of Reuben Akurdit Ngong. Used by permission.

Kon had received no Western education, and he never received any formal theological training. But he was a Christian minister nonetheless. After his baptism, he became an itinerant evangelist, traveling the region and urging people to reject their local divinities and seek Christian baptism.

When Kon's travels took him to Bor in 1990, Akurdit welcomed him to the church and insisted they pose for a photograph, together with a woman who is likely Kon's wife. The photograph shows a stark contrast. Akurdit is dressed in a collared shirt, trousers, and black shoes, clothing that would not be out of place in a gathering of clergy in England or the United States. Kon, by contrast, has a blanket draped around his body. His shoulders are bare, and he is wearing sandals. He holds a walking stick in his hands. Apparently, he has dressed up to attend church; many stories about Kon told how he frequently went naked, not uncommon for a Dinka man, but not allowed in the church. In his dress and his personal history, Akurdit represents the legacy of mission involvement in the founding of ECS: a Christian leader who became Christian when he went to school in a town and whose dress and customs changed as a result of his conversion. Kon Ajith, by contrast, embodies the emerging Christianity: a man who was raised in a Dinka village, never attended school, and spent much of his time in a cattle camp. At the time of their meeting in Bor, it was arguably Kon who was the more significant Christian leader among Dinka on the east bank of the Nile River. One no longer had to be educated and live in a town to be Christian. Christianity was now potentially open to all Dinka in the very center of their traditional culture and way of life.

One theme of the study of the encounter between European missionaries and Dinka was the way in which the strategies the missionaries pursued created a social, cultural, and physical distance that converts needed to cross in order to join the church. To become Christian converts needed to reject completely many cultural practices and leave the Dinka heartland of cattle camps and villages to move to a town or mission station. Previous chapters have used a broad perspective to study the way in which that distance began to close during the civil war, leading to religious change among the Dinka. In addition to adopting prophetic material, as the last chapter demonstrated, particular individuals and places also became central to Dinka Christianity. Together, this chapter and the previous one demonstrate how Christianity and Dinka cultural practice came to have significant overlap during the civil war.

Kon Ajith is a good example of this trend. With the highest profile of the several Christian prophets who emerged during the war, his life and ministry demonstrate how the emerging Dinka Christian identity drew on the new religious discourse offered by the church but could contain it within an existing cultural form, that of a Nilotic prophet. Dinka Christianity could be congruent with the religion that preceded it. At the same time, Dinka Christians retained a profound commitment to the traditional Dinka landscape. Kon Ajith reclaimed a cattle camp to build an important Christian shrine. More significantly, Anglicans on the west bank created a new Christian village, Dhiaukuei, located in the heart of the *toc* and at the center of Dinka seasonal practices. The lesson of both the ministry of Kon Ajith and the creation of Dhiaukuei is that the distance between Christianity and Dinka culture had narrowed almost to nothing. These developments both indicated the extent of wartime religious change and drove it forward.

The Ministry of Kon Ajith

Kon Ajith stands in the tradition of Nilotic prophets introduced in the previous chapter. Unlike Ngundeng, the prophet Isaiah, or Archibald

Shaw, however, his ministry took place during the second civil war. Rather than studying him retrospectively and examining how his prophetic material was repurposed, Kon Ajith can be studied for the significance of his life, not his afterlife. Yet this is not an easy task. There is no contemporaneous written documentation that survived the civil war.[1] The research for this chapter is based primarily on approximately a dozen interviews with informants who knew Kon and were active in the church during his lifetime. As many of these sources have some connection to the church, the analysis is correspondingly limited by this particular viewpoint. Given the 20 years that elapsed between Kon's death and these interviews, it can be difficult to determine dates and sequences of events with certainty. The passage of time has also changed memories. With Kon safely in the past, it appears likely that some informants have modified their views to ensure that their own role appears in a more positive light. Nonetheless, it is still possible to draw a picture of Kon's life and ministry that fits the pattern of a Nilotic prophet.

A combination of ecologic, economic, and political factors led to a serious famine on the east bank in 1986 when Kon Ajith was in his late 20s. East-bank Dinka remember this as *yang apar*, a famine year. To this point in his life, there was no indication that Kon Ajith was destined for anything unusual. He had grown up near the village of Der in Bor County. His family was associated with the *jɔk* known as Akoor, which was believed to be more powerful than other local *jak*, creating a modest source of income for the family as neighbors came to sacrifice to it. A near contemporary of his in Der, Stephen Mathiang Kuc, remembers that as a young man, "he was . . . just like anybody. There was nothing unique about him."[2] When Kon first became known more widely on the east bank, the one fact that was known for sure about him was that he was simply "a person who looked after cows."[3] In other words, for a Dinka, he was nothing exceptional.

---

[1] The American missionary Marc Nikkel visited the east bank in 1994, two years after Kon's death, and took several pages of notes, which have been useful in the following description of Kon's life. The Dinka priest Paul Majer Mac has taken extensive notes on Kon Ajith's life, which he has gathered in interviews conducted over the last several years. He shared these with me in translation during our interview.

[2] Stephen Mathiang Kuc, in-person interview by Jesse Zink. Bor, South Sudan, 9 April 2013.

[3] David Magot Ngong, in-person interview by Jesse Zink. Bor, South Sudan, 11 April 2013.

But the *yang apar* changed Kon's course. Around August, the point in the growing season when the extent of the crop failure was becoming clear, Kon and a friend crossed the Nile River to the territory of the Dinka Aliab. Two unusual things happened. First, they encountered a man who was cursing some young women who were singing Christian hymns. Kon intervened to tell him to stop. Second, in the middle of a rainstorm, Kon stayed dry while others around him became wet.[4] After their return home, Kon had a dream in which he believed he was told he should remove whatever items to the *jɔk* were in his compound and burn them. If he failed to do so, he would be punished. In the morning, Kon did as the dream commanded. He assembled the items of the *jɔk* in the middle of his compound and set them on fire. Kon's brother, Gordon Aboi Ajith, had spent time in Juba in the 1970s and was one of the many educated Christians who had fled to the rural areas at the outbreak of the war in 1983 and now lived near Kon again. When Aboi Ajith realized what Kon was doing, he wondered if his brother had gone mad. But Kon told him the story, about how he defended the church women, how he had stayed dry in the rain, and how he had a dream commanding him to burn the *jɔk*. Aboi offered to pray with him and, although it was not a Sunday, took him to a place where a small Anglican congregation had begun to pray together in the few years prior to these events.

So unusual was the decision to burn the *jɔk* that word of Kon's actions spread among other Dinka. He was dismissed as either crazy for destroying a *jɔk* that generated income or dangerous for threatening to incur its wrath. As people traveled in search of food, the story spread. Before long, the news reached Bishop Nathaniel Garang Anyieth. When Garang next was near Der, he sought out Kon and baptized him toward the end of 1986. Following the common practice of taking a biblical name on baptism, Kon became Paul Kon Ajith, but he was widely known then and now simply as Kon Ajith. It is unclear who chose the name, but the resonance with the biblical Paul, who also had a sudden conversion experience, is strong.

Kon was not the only one who was baptized by Garang. Several surrounding families sought baptism as a precautionary measure. It

---

[4] It is not unusual for rain to fall in one place and not another. Lienhardt records how on the west bank of the Nile, religious leaders could boast that rain had fallen on their garden but not on that of neighbors (Godfrey Lienhardt, *Divinity and Experience: The Religion of the Dinka* [Oxford: Clarendon, 1961], 209). Control of the rain is a critical power in a society such as that of the Dinka.

was commonly believed that the destruction of a *jɔk*'s shrine enraged the divinity and led to retribution. The neighbors were concerned that although Kon's baptism would protect him from retribution from the *jɔk*, it might direct the *jɔk*'s anger at Kon's neighbors. With the small community of Christians now present, Garang established a church in the village so they would not have to travel to the more distant congregation that Kon had visited shortly after his vision. Kon had joined the group of Dinka on the east bank of the Nile who had repudiated the religion of the *jak*. What came next, however, was unexpected.[5]

Evangelism was an important component of the faith that Dinka Anglicans professed in the 1980s. Christians wanted to tell others about the church they had joined. It is not surprising, therefore, that Kon Ajith became an evangelist after his baptism. What is surprising, however, is one of his first targets: Kuol Manyang, the regional SPLA commander. While Nathaniel Garang appeared to have good relations with SPLA leaders, the SPLA remained a secular, ostensibly Marxist organization intent on controlling the loyalties of east-bank Dinka. The church provided a potentially competing source of loyalty, generating tensions that were to recur throughout the civil war. Neither pastors nor evangelists were in the habit of seeking out Kuol Manyang. But Kon went directly to Kuol at his headquarters in Baidit and asked him to order the collection of the items of the religion of the *jak* and their destruction.[6] Kon said that the SPLA would not succeed if it allowed the *jak* to remain. If Kuol did not order the destruction of the *jak*, Kon predicted that disaster would come. Indeed, he claimed, in words that were widely reported, that Baidit itself would be turned to ash. Kuol dismissed Kon without acting on his demands. Not long afterward, the course of the war changed, the SAF advanced on Baidit, Kuol was forced to flee, and the community was burned to the ground.[7] Kon's powers of prediction and foresight became more widely known.

The encounter with Kuol begins to reveal Kon as a prophet. Kon deliberately targeted the locus of authority in SPLA–controlled areas

[5] The account of Kon's conversion is based on an in-person interview with Gordon Aboi Ajith by Jesse Zink. Bor, South Sudan, 13 April 2013.

[6] Paul Majer Mac, in-person interview by Jesse Zink. Juba, South Sudan, 18 April 2013.

[7] In the course of my research, I sought to interview Kuol Manyang, who has lately been governor of Jonglei state and South Sudan's Minister of Defense, without success.

and offered a religious message concerning the destruction of the *jak* that was tied to the future of the community through military victory. Kon then further developed the prophetic role by beginning an itinerant preaching career that focused on east-bank Dinka but took in both banks of the Nile. He is reported to have traveled as far west as Rumbek and to the northern edge of Dinka territory in Duk. Kon stood out for several reasons. He often went naked. He carried a drum, a bell, and a flag with a cross on it. None of this was unusual among the Dinka. Drums and bells were used to draw attention and flags to mark particular areas. What was unusual was that Kon embraced these items to promote a Christian message. His lack of clothing in particular marked him out from other Christians, for whom clothing had traditionally been an important marker. But the nakedness was a part of his message. When Dinka accused Kon of being crazy, informants remember him responding, "God told me not to wear clothes. God told me 'I have sent those who have the clothes to the people but they did not listen. You go now without clothes because people will come to see you and you will preach the word of God.'"[8] Kon the prophet was carving out a distinct space at the intersection of Dinka and Christian cultures, borrowing from each and challenging each.

Throughout his travels Kon's basic message remained the same: the Dinka needed to repent of their failure to follow the God of Jesus Christ and demonstrate this repentance by destroying their shrines. If they did not do so, punishment and destruction would follow. Whether he made this link explicit or not, the story of Kon's dream commanding him to be baptized was widely known. Kon was a prophet: someone believed to be inspired by a divinity and offering a message concerning the "moral community," the group of people sustained by a common set of religious beliefs and practices. But his prophetic message was similar to that offered by Christian pastors. Kon had culturally appropriate metaphors to draw on. The Dinka are "loose and moving like a cow out of control," he preached. "But my preaching will tie the Dinka down again."[9] In another variation, the message was remembered as, "Burn all the *jak*. . . . [I]f they are burnt, the confusion will cease."[10] At a time of the

---

[8] Mary Achol Deng, in-person interview by Jesse Zink. Bor, South Sudan, 28 April 2013.
[9] Paul Majer Mac, interview by Zink. Juba, South Sudan, 18 April 2013.
[10] Marc Nikkel, "Notes on Zion," c. May 1994 (personal papers of Marc Nikkel).

unsettlement of war, this was a message of stability and certainty, that is, a message of peace.

Yet in the comparatively stable years of the late 1980s on the east bank, the message of religious change was largely rejected. On a few occasions, however, Kon's message was strengthened by a perceived correspondence between his preaching and events of the war. In the period when the SPLA took control of Bor, Kon preached to people there, a visit documented in the photograph with Akurdit Ngong. He told them that if they listened to him, they would learn how to follow God in the right way. But if they ignored him, rain—representing flooding and thus destruction—would fall. Many people dismissed him as mad and a disturber of the peace, and Kon left Bor. When the SAF later bombed Bor and subsequently retook the city, the events were interpreted as the falling of the metaphorical rain on those who had rejected Kon. His stature as a prophet grew.

Nilotic prophets have often been associated with a particular place. Ngundeng Bong had a mound, which transcended political divisions in the region and became a place at which his followers gathered.[11] Kon, too, began preaching about a place, but it was understood in Christian terms. Not only did the Dinka have to repudiate the *jak*, Kon said, they had to mark this conversion with the construction of a church at a place he called Zion. The inspiration for this claim came from the final verse of Isaiah 18, which speaks of the people of Cush bringing gifts to "Mount Zion, the place of the name of the Lord of hosts" (18:7 NRSV). Kon's Zion church would be the place at which this gift-giving took place. Kon often illustrated his plans for the church by drawing a sketch in the dirt. Unlike other churches that were rectangular and oriented on an east-west axis, Zion was to be made of four rectangles, each pointing in the cardinal directions of the compass. This had a double meaning. On the one hand, it meant that all people were welcome to Zion. The four doors were entrances, not just for the Dinka but also for the Nuer (who lived to the north), the Murle (east), the Mandari (south), and Dinka from the west bank of the Nile. But the four doors were exits as well. Evangelists would leave from Zion and go to all those places to preach the message of Jesus Christ. It was both an enactment of the evangelical Christian imperative and an apparent embodiment of intercommunal harmony.

---

[11] Douglas H. Johnson, *Nuer Prophets: A History of Prophecy from the Upper Nile in the Nineteenth and Twentieth Centuries* (Oxford: Clarendon, 1994), 90.

One of the most challenging retrospective questions to ask of Kon concerns his relationship with both the church and the SPLA. Church leaders had obvious grounds for common work in that Kon's call to repudiate the *jak* was not substantially different from what many ECS pastors and evangelists were preaching at the same time. But the dominant tone of the relationship seems to have been one of suspicion. Reuben Akurdit, who later had his picture taken with Kon, recalled how he did not agree with Kon's teaching at first: "He was somebody who had his own way of seeing things. . . . A number of people disagreed with him."[12] Kon offended church sensibilities: he was not educated and could neither read nor write, but was claiming to be preaching from the Bible. ECS leaders were also suspicious of Kon because of their belief that Jesus Christ was the final revelation and that no prophets could come after him. But the picture is muddied by contrasting recollections. For instance, several informants recalled that John Kelei, one of the most senior ECS pastors on the east bank, "thoroughly" opposed Kon Ajith from the beginning.[13] But Kelei himself says he saw Kon as sharing a mission with ECS and that he did not oppose him.[14] Short of contemporaneous documentation, this is likely not something that can be known with certainty. Suffice it to say, however, Kon's ministry generated, at the minimum, suspicion from ECS pastors, and possibly even hostility and opposition. Kon replied in kind, at times preaching against church leaders. He is remembered as saying of ECS pastors that they were like cows who had been led to water but were not drinking. He said the pillars that supported the church were being eaten away, as ants eat away the wood that supports a house.

The key figure in this contention was the bishop, Nathaniel Garang Anyieth, who had baptized Kon and must have tacitly approved of his ministry. There is, at any rate, no recollection of any intervention. Instead, people remember how Garang reminded his clergy of a moment when Jesus' apostles told him about some people who were preaching the gospel without his authorization. Jesus encouraged his followers to allow them to preach, for "whoever is not against you is for you" (Luke 9:49-50; cf. Mark 9:38-41). Kon, Garang said, was similar. In an echo of the

---

[12] Reuben Akurdit Ngong, in-person interview by Jesse Zink. Bor, South Sudan, 12 April 2013.

[13] Paul Majer Mac, interview by Zink. Juba, South Sudan, 18 April 2013.

[14] John Kelei, in-person interview by Jesse Zink. Bor, South Sudan, 16 April 2013.

counsel of Gamaliel in the Acts of the Apostles (5:34-39), Garang counseled patience and humility. If Kon's message was from God, it would be successful; if not, it would fail. Because Kon did not baptize anyone, people who burned their *jak* as a result of his teaching turned to ECS pastors for baptism and formation. One priest informant recalls how he did not accept Kon at first but allowed Kon to continue his evangelism while the priest stayed with the organized congregations: "And when he went and preached over there, people came and joined us in the churches."[15] The fact that Reuben Akurdit would have posed with Kon Ajith is an indication of the increased prominence of Kon and his acceptance by mainstream church leaders. Akurdit even came up with a rationale: "Those evangelists [in the Bible], prophets like Isaiah, Jeremiah, everybody did not agree with them."[16] The same could be said of Kon. Gradually, Kon came to be seen as an ally of ECS and not as an opponent.

Kon targeted the SPLA from the beginning of his ministry, but its leaders seem to have dismissed him. They disliked the ferment he was creating among Dinka and the challenges he posed to societal leaders, on whom the SPLA initially relied for support.[17] It does not appear as if they actively opposed him or sought to suppress him and his message, but neither did SPLA leaders actively support him. Their lack of support is likely rooted, in part, in the secular nature of the rebel movement in the 1980s. More significantly, the SPLA's lack of support demonstrates the political nature of Kon's message. Kon's attempt to reframe the nature of Dinka community in Christian terms and so provide peace clashed with the SPLA's search for peace in military terms.

In spite of the stridency of his message and perhaps because of the significance of the opposition, Kon Ajith appears to have had little success in the years between his baptism and the critical year of 1991. He was noteworthy—the fact that he had destroyed his *jɔk* was widely known—but in these early years it is not even clear that Kon was continually on the move. Some east-bank Dinka were becoming Christian, but it was not yet a genuinely mass movement, nor was Kon Ajith at its head.

---

[15] Andrew Mayol Ajak, in-person interview by Jesse Zink. Bor, South Sudan, 25 April 2013.

[16] Reuben Akurdit Ngong, interview by Zink. Bor, South Sudan, 12 April 2013.

[17] Marc Nikkel, "Christian Conversion among the Jieng Bor," in *Religion and Conflict in Sudan*, ed. Yusuf Fadl Hasan and Richard Gray (Nairobi: Paulines Publications Africa, 2002), 166.

East-Bank Crisis and New Opportunity for Kon

A consistent theme of Kon Ajith's preaching had been that disaster would follow if people did not destroy their *jak*. This belief cohered with the larger belief among Christians that the war was part of God's punishment. Kon's prediction had been confirmed in localized instances, such as the destruction of the SPLA headquarters in Baidit or the reconquest of Bor by the SAF. But the cataclysmic events of 1991, and especially the so-called Bor Massacre in November when a breakaway faction of the SPLA attacked Bor and its surrounding area, made people consider Kon Ajith's message again. The widespread displacement and destruction was interpreted by some as the fulfillment of Kon's prophecy. Kon encouraged this link, preaching, "The Nuer has come and done his will. But did they take the *jak*? They took the cows, but they left the *jak*. They burned the villages. But did they take the *jak*? No. The Dinka have to do that for themselves."[18] If the *jak* had value, Kon argued, the Nuer would have taken them. Since they had not, it was up to the Dinka to rid themselves of them. Kon also said that if the *jak* were destroyed, the Dinka would find protection in the God of Jesus Christ. In particular, they would find protection from hunger and famine, from the "Arabs" (i.e., the SAF), and from the Mandari, the Nuer, and the Murle, the other major people groups on the east bank.

Kon's preaching resonated at a moment of crisis in east-bank communities. Their vulnerable position encouraged many people to look for new answers to provide security and stability. The credibility of existing religious leaders collapsed. People who had previously opposed the church now looked at it anew. Bishop Nathaniel Garang Anyieth and his family had been among those displaced by the 1991 violence. The senior Anglican priest remaining on the east bank was John Kelei, who is remembered as having opposed Kon Ajith. Kelei himself remembers of this time: "It was only [Christian] priests who were in the position of *tit*. Those priests, they don't require anything that you can give them, like the *tit*. You don't need a cow [to be a Christian]."[19] Without the cattle necessary to sustain the religion of the *jak*, even people who had once been opposed to Christianity sought baptism and Christian conversion.

But another significant change took place as well. Kuol Manyang and the now-weakened Dinka SPLA began to listen afresh to Kon Ajith.

---

[18] Paul Majer Mac, interview by Zink. Juba, South Sudan, 18 April 2013.
[19] John Kelei, interview by Zink. Bor, South Sudan, 16 April 2013.

In part, this must have been because of the decidedly militaristic tone of Kon's preaching. He promised that if his Zion was built, Kon himself would be able to lead 49 soldiers on Bor and the SAF would be unable to resist.[20] Kuol Manyang ordered compliance with the teachings of Kon. He is remembered as saying: "Let Kon Ajith do whatever he wants because we don't know what is going on. If Kon Ajith is insisting with his god, let it be done in the way he likes it. Let us see the consequences of this."[21] At a time when the SPLA was militarily weak, Kon's teachings seemed to be worth the effort. Informants related stories of the SPLA ordering the seizure of *jak* by force. Working closely with Christians, *jak* were seized and gathered at a place called Pakeo, a cattle camp that was not far from where Kon Ajith grew up, and the site of his long-predicted Zion. The SPLA instructed Kelei to ensure that the church at Pakeo was built as Kon required. Kelei offered opposition at first, citing the ongoing insecurity of the area, but when the SPLA promised to protect him, he consented to their demand.[22] In a short span of time, the usual order of things had been overturned. John Kelei was now working with Kon Ajith, the SPLA was furthering Kon's goals, and construction on the church at Pakeo had begun.

It is particularly noteworthy that Kon continued to insist on the four doors of the Zion church at Pakeo even after the Bor Massacre. The 1991 SPLA split and its aftermath was a moment of significant interethnic tension in southern Sudan. It is unclear what Kon's intent was in insisting on four doors. Informants remember it positively. One said, "He was not saying this church belonged to [the people of] Bor alone. But it was an icon of the unity of the people."[23] But given his other preaching about how the destruction of the *jak* would lead to protection from all attackers, including other groups on the east bank, it is not convincing that Kon was articulating a new moral community that included anyone other than Dinka. The four entrances at Pakeo are best seen primarily as means of egress, not as a place of in-gathering for the peoples of the east bank.

Whatever its purpose, the actual building of Zion is important in revealing Kon as a religious leader and a prophet. As noted, other

---

[20] Nikkel, "Notes on Zion."

[21] Paul Majer Mac, interview by Zink. Juba, South Sudan, 18 April 2013.

[22] John Kelei, interview by Zink. Bor, South Sudan, 16 April 2013.

[23] Stephen Mathiang Kuc, in-person interview by Zink. Bor, South Sudan, 9 April 2013.

Nilotic prophets have maintained a connection to a particular site, such as Ngundeng's mound. Zion could have functioned as a similar site for Kon. But not only was Zion a sacred site, it was also a covered structure akin to a *luak*. The periodic rebuilding of such structures has historically been invested with religious significance by Dinka. One well-documented case among the Agar Dinka in the early 1980s involved two religious leaders struggling for supremacy in the reconstruction of a new *luak*. By involving the entire community, the task of building the new *luak*, "involved a self-conscious recreation of the community."[24] In building Zion, Kon was doing at least two things. He was creating a single "holy" site at which the divinity who inspired him—the Christian God—could be accessed by his followers. But he was also involving people in a task that recreated them as a community at a time of great stress. Significantly, this recreation was understood in Christian terms. By standing firmly within Dinka cultural forms as a recognizable prophet while also imparting a Christian message, Kon Ajith was presiding over a process of renewal that was intelligible within the context of Dinka society but also made clear the extent of the religious change that was taking place.[25]

By the end of 1992, the Zion church was substantially completed. When Nikkel visited in 1994, he described the church as an astonishing sight:

> Certainly the church is the largest and most impressive building of local construction I have seen in Sudan. . . . Beautifully thatched, it rises to perhaps thirty feet at is center. Amid a forest of supporting poles, like a primitive cathedral, the congregation (numbering some four thousand on our visit) fills the arms of the cross, all facing toward a central octagonal dais.[26]

The construction of Zion brought forth a new prediction from Kon, that of his own imminent death. In Dinka tradition, when a *luak* was

---

[24] A. N. M. Mawson, "'Bringing What People Want': Shrine Politics among the Agar Dinka," *Africa: Journal of the International African Institute* 61, no. 3 (1991): 365.

[25] Maxwell documents a similar way in which traditional patterns of renewal were taken over by Christian converts in Zimbabwe. David Maxwell, *Christians and Chiefs in Zimbabwe: A Social History of the Hwesa People, c. 1870s–1990s* (London: Edinburgh University Press for the International African Institute, 1999), 220.

[26] Marc Nikkel, letter to supporters, 9 June 1994, collected in *Why Haven't You Left? Letters from Sudan*, ed. Grant LeMarquand (New York: Church Publishing, 2006), 117.

FIGURE 7.2
Zion church at Pakeo, c. 1994. Collection of Marc Nikkel.
Used by permission of Durham University Library.

completed, a goat is sacrificed in thanksgiving.[27] Kon said that he would be the goat sacrificed at the completion of the church. At Christmas, many people gathered at Pakeo to hear Kon preach. Yet Kon had also drawn the attention of the SAF, who had once again retaken Bor. On 26 December 1992, a large detachment of SAF soldiers left Bor, went to Pakeo, captured Kon, and killed him.[28] It is not difficult to see why

[27] A. N. M. Mawson, "The Triumph of Life: Political Dispute and Religious Ceremonial among the Agar Dinka" (Ph.D. dissertation, Cambridge University, March 1989), 307.

[28] Deborah Scroggins asserts that Kuol Manyang ordered the killing of Kon Ajith (*Emma's War: Love, Betrayal and Death in the Sudan* [London: HarperCollins, 2003], 305). The sources she cites in her footnote do not bear out this claim. She also cites Nuer pastors as a possible source, though has also written, "If your sources are Dinka who were close to Kon, you are probably right and I am wrong, sad to say." (Personal communication, 22 June 2013.) My informants universally attribute the death to the SAF. However, as Dinka leaders, they would be unlikely to implicitly criticize an SPLA leader (and governor of Jonglei at the time of my research) by attributing the death to him, so I cannot be entirely certain that the SAF was responsible for the death. But if Kuol Manyang was working closely with Kon Ajith, it is unclear why he would later order his death.

the SAF wanted Kon dead. Not only was he making predictions about the capture of Bor, he was gathering large crowds around him. He was also working closely with the SPLA, and potentially giving them hope and encouragement for the future at a time when their prospects seemed particularly bleak.

John Kelei was not present for the Christmas service, but after the death of Kon Ajith, he gathered with a small group at Pakeo.[29] By that time, the vast majority of religious material that remained among the Dinka Bor had been gathered at Pakeo. On 6 February 1993, Kelei presided over a mass burning of these religious items. There was some urgency to the task, brought about by the fear of what might happen if they waited any longer. Kelei told the crowd that had gathered: "We shall not wait for the fire from heaven. Let us put our fire on these symbols here. But the real *jak*, God will send fire on them and will burn them there [i.e., heaven]."[30] The deep desire of Kon Ajith—the destruction of the *jak*—had at last come to pass.

Although the events of 6 February 1993 seem a fitting conclusion to Kon's life and ministry, his legacy troubled ECS leaders. During Kon's ministry, particularly in the aftermath of the Bor Massacre, he had gathered around him a group of followers who were more committed to him than to ECS. They began to develop a set of practices that were unusual even for Christians, although it is difficult to separate their practices from the rumors spread about them. What seems most clear is that they separated themselves from Dinka culture and denounced those who did things such as wearing necklaces, ivory jewelry, or other traditional items.[31] Other claims, particularly relating to their sexual practices, are

---

[29] Nikkel asserts that there were 30,000 gathered at Zion for the burning of the *jak* ("'Children of Our Fathers' Divinities' or 'Children of Red Foreigners'? Themes in Missionary History and the Rise of an Indigenous Church among the Jieng Bor of Southern Sudan," *Land of Promise: Church Growth in a Sudan at War*, ed. Andrew C. Wheeler [Nairobi: Paulines Publications Africa, 1997], 72), but this must certainly be incorrect. A crowd that large at such an unsafe and uncertain time seems highly unlikely. Kelei himself only remembers a few hundred, much smaller than was reported at Kon's Christmas Day sermon prior to his death.

[30] John Kelei, interview by Zink. Bor, South Sudan, 16 April 2013.

[31] African Rights, *Great Expectations: The Civil Roles of the Churches in Southern Sudan, Discussion Paper no. 6* (London: African Rights, April 1995), 16. Nathaniel Athian Deng Mayen, *Christian Faith among the Jieeng: The Shift in Values, the Stages of Faith, and the Cultural and Religious Experiences of Jieeng Believers in the Episcopal Diocese of Bor* (Denver: Outskirts, 2015), 92.

more difficult to ascertain as fact. During Kon's life, he was able to stay connected both to ECS and to his followers. After his death, however, these connections ruptured. In a series of events that is very difficult to reconstruct in retrospect, ECS leaders sought to suppress Kon's followers as an independent movement and integrate them into the body of the church.[32] Some clergy who had been close to Kon were expelled from ECS.[33] The teachings of the group became "more idiosyncratic and sometimes violent" until it "dwindled in integrity and number."[34] What remains clear is that in the period following Kon's death, the vast majority of Dinka who became Christian as a result of Kon Ajith's preaching became members of ECS while a minority group resisted and gradually faded. For all the energy and effort church leaders had invested in educating clergy, organizing evangelistic tours, and starting new congregations, the most effective evangelist among east-bank Dinka was a man who had spent his childhood in a cattle camp and never attended school.

Nilotic Prophecy and Christianity

If the primary significance of Nilotic prophets is the way in which they speak to a particular moral community, then the primary significance of Kon Ajith is the way in which he embodied the changing nature of the east-bank Dinka moral community in the 1980s and 1990s. In the years immediately following his baptism, he appears to have had little success in communicating his message. Religious change was taking place, but it is not always clear that it was happening because of what he said. After the Bor Massacre of 1991, however, Kon Ajith's message was heard anew. His message at last matched events: the Bor Massacre proved the worthlessness of the *jak* and was God's punishment on the Dinka for worshipping them in the first place. God—*Nhialic*—still needed to be worshipped, but this could be done without the aid of

---

[32] Andrew C. Wheeler, "Church Growth in Southern Sudan 1983–1996: A Survey of Present Understanding," *Land of Promise: Church Growth in a Sudan at War*, ed. Andrew C. Wheeler (Nairobi: Paulines Publications Africa, 1997), 23.

[33] Nikkel, "Notes on Zion." This included Isaiah Malek Garang, who had been among the people closest to Kon and who was also an Anglican cleric. Malek Garang is now a member of the Seventh-Day Adventist Church and, though he received me with great hospitality, declined to speak with me about his memories of Kon.

[34] Nikkel, "Christian Conversion among the Jieng Bor," 167. Given Nikkel's strong sympathies with ECS and particularly with Nathaniel Garang, this statement must be read with caution.

the *jak*. That this message was coming not from an educated Christian leader but a prophet demonstrates the extent of the religious change among the Dinka. The Christian idiom had found its home in a form that was intimately rooted in Dinka cultural traditions.

Unlike other Nilotic prophets, Kon Ajith has not left a strong legacy. His church at Pakeo has been rebuilt in cinder block to give it permanence. But his legacy is otherwise insubstantial among many east-bank Dinka Anglicans today. What has endured, however, is the significance of the prophetic tradition. Isaiah 18, as the previous chapter demonstrated, maintains a crucial role in the self-understanding of Dinka Anglicans. With this in mind, Kon Ajith is best seen as a carrier of a larger message, working to articulate a particular understanding of moral community at a time of stress and change. But the underlying strata of the message remain that of the Christian gospel.

If Kon Ajith is an indication of the enduring relevance of Nilotic prophecy even at a time of religious change, he is also an example of the weakness of the prophetic tradition in the face of the militarization of Nilotic life during the civil war. Kon's prominence came at a time of SPLA weakness, that is, at the only moment when the social space was less monopolized by men with guns. By the end of his life, Kon's message was framed almost entirely in terms that the SPLA could understand—the military defeat of the SAF, the occupation of Bor, and an unclear message in relation to Nuer and other Nilotic peoples. There is a striking contrast here in relation to descriptions of Ngundeng's work among the Nuer a century prior, or with Ariandhit, the Dinka prophet active on the west bank in the early 1920s. Such military action as these prophets engaged in came much more as a response to external aggression and was not the sole feature of their prophetic leadership. These men were prophets of peace for whom violence was not central to their message.[35] Kon Ajith stands in a tradition that was apparently weakened, as many aspects of Nilotic society were, by decades of civil war. For Kon after 1991, there was much overlap and little distinction between the fields of religion, politics, and violence.

While Kon Ajith is clearly a Nilotic prophet, he is also reminiscent of other charismatic individuals in the history of the African church.

---

[35] Sharon Hutchinson challenges Johnson's argument that prophets are primarily concerned with peace: "Prophecy brings brutalities and horrors as well as—sometimes—peace." Sharon Hutchinson, "Prophecies of War and Peace," *The Times Literary Supplement*, 2 June 1995 (4809): 8.

Figures such as Simon Kimbangu in Congo or William Wadé Harris in West Africa were often named "prophets" after the biblical model of the itinerant preacher. These figures and others like them generated immense enthusiasm for Christianity but also encountered opposition and suspicion both from secular authorities and from missionary-led churches. Harris and Kimbangu were edged out of mission denominations or worked independently of them, often with the result that new churches were founded. Kon Ajith is in a similar mold, but the results were substantially different because of his postcolonial context. Rather than starting his own church, the primary legacy of Kon Ajith was the strengthening of the Episcopal Church of the Sudan, one of the major mission denominations in southern Sudan. In part, this is the result of canny leadership in ECS. Nathaniel Garang was repeatedly willing to stretch and change the traditions he had inherited to accommodate the new converts flooding into his churches. His openness to Kon Ajith was part of this flexibility. Because there was no significant involvement or leadership from European missionaries during the period of Kon's ministry, there was little for him to react against and no pressure for conformity. The grassroots energy generated by Kon was channeled into a mission denomination that was itself, at its core, a movement of popular Christianity.

To recall the photograph at the beginning of this chapter, a close study of Kon Ajith shows that it was not, perhaps, unusual for the Christian prophet and the educated pastor to pose together. Rather, it was the natural result of the kind of religious change then taking place among the Dinka. Kon embodied the existing cultural traditions that were shaping the emerging Christianity while also embodying the growing prominence of the church in society. The popular Christian movement was a totalizing phenomenon, encompassing all aspects of Dinka society. Dinka cultural forms and the legacy of Christian mission involvement had now become one.

The Creation of Sacred Place

Kon Ajith represents the narrowing of the distance between existing Dinka cultural forms and Christianity that took place during the second civil war. But in order for Christianity to truly take root among the Dinka, a further narrowing was necessary: landscape. Prior to the war, Christianity was associated with towns and urban centers and largely absent from villages and cattle camps. Previous chapters have demonstrated the way in which this division was transcended, including evangelism campaigns undertaken in cattle camps and the flight of educated Dinka in urban areas to rural villages at the beginning of the civil war. But the most complete melding of Christianity with Dinka rural landscape occurred at a place called Dhiaukuei, a community established by west-bank church leaders in the early 1990s. As with Kon Ajith, studying Dhiaukuei reveals how the beliefs and practices of Christianity came to be combined with the traditions and customs of the Dinka, this time at the level of the sacred landscape of a people.

Dhiaukuei originated in the severe shortage of educated leaders created by the rapid growth of the church. In 1988, Benjamin Mangar Mamur ended his itinerant ministry on the west bank when he was ordained bishop in Khartoum as part of a schism in ECS. Knowing of the need for clergy on the west bank, he returned briefly to Wau to ordain two of his close associates. One, Petro Marial Thon, was a young man who had spent most of his youth in a cattle camp. He represented the younger generation that was then entering the church. The other, Stephen Dongrin Thokriel, represented the inheritance of the CMS faith; his father had been educated at Akot, and the family had lived around the mission station for many years. The two newly ordained clergy had only the barest literacy skills and little knowledge of the Bible beyond the newly popular hymns, some of which Marial Thon himself had written. Mangar Mamur recalled giving the two priests a "crash program for 45 days" before ordination, but they remained ill-prepared for their ministry.[36]

At the instruction of Mangar Mamur, the two new priests returned to the area around Rumbek and Yirol and presented themselves to Reuben Maciir Makoi, the remaining senior priest on the west bank. Maciir had been invited to be consecrated bishop in 1988 but had declined, preferring to remain on the west bank and not take the chance that the war would prevent his return. Maciir embodied continuity with the traditions of CMS, in particular the tradition of only ordaining those who had been educated. Maciir himself had been trained as a teacher in the 1950s before his ordination. That Mangar Mamur had ordained two barely literate people offended Maciir's sensibilities. But he also

---

[36] Bengamin Mangar Mamur, in-person interview by Jesse Zink. Rumbek, South Sudan, 11 September 2013.

understood the validity of their ordination. Maciir called a meeting of Christians in the area and reminded them of the need for clergy to be able to read. Clergy could not lead the people simply with songs and prayers. They needed to be able to read the Bible as well. Beyond the two new priests, the need for education in the growing church remained enormous. Hymns and healing prayers alone would not sustain church growth, Maciir believed. To consolidate its growth, the church needed educated lay people who understood the Christian faith and could read the Bible and preach.

Maciir's appeal led to the establishment of Dhiaukuei, a Christian training center and community. Dhiaukuei was significant first for its location at the center of the traditional Dinka landscape. It was on the banks of the River Naam, a major river in the west-bank region, that served as an obvious year-round source of water. The Naam bisected the region, meaning people did not have to travel too far to reach it. But Dhiaukuei was also isolated. It was not in or near Rumbek, Yirol, or Akot, the major centers on the west bank, control of which changed hands several times during the war. Instead, the community was deliberately remote, unable to be reached by vehicle, and so safe from attack. It was heavily forested, which meant it was not targeted during the frequent aerial bombardments of the SAF. Across the river from Dhiaukuei was an open stretch of *toc*, the kind of seasonal grazing land that was central to Dinka cattle culture. Finally, by creating a new community rather than adopting an existing one, Maciir ensured that the church was not associated with a particular lineage or subset of the Dinka. Rather than making everyone come to his own home community, for instance, and potentially engendering conflict and resentment, Maciir used a neutral location. Everyone approached it equally.

Religious change in other parts of Africa has often involved Christian communities taking over existing sacred sites and making them holy in new ways.[37] In that context, creating a new community seems an innovation. But while Dhiaukuei was new, it also drew some of its significance from its proximity to a seasonal pool of water with historic importance. In March 1921, the pool appeared and was believed to be associated with Kejok, an early-eighteenth-century Dinka figure. Kejok was believed to have been born without human agency, able to

---

[37] Terence Ranger, "Taking Hold of the Land: Holy Places and Pilgrimage in Twentieth-Century Zimbabwe," *Past & Present* 117 (1987).

perform miracles, and promised his return at a future time. When the pool appeared in 1921, it quickly generated attention from many Dinka who believed it was a sign of Kejok's imminent return. As one colonial official wrote, "Pilgrims flocked to the spot, sacrifices were offered and there was much talk of signs and wonders and a general feeling that the miracle boded good to the Dinka and ill to the 'Foreigners.'"[38] Dinka in the area had risen against the British in 1917, and the pool apparently offered another opportunity for opposition. Indeed, a handful of Dinka leaders attempted to organize a rebellion against the Condominium based on the events at the pool. Led by a man who claimed to be speaking for the divinity in the pool, as well as another man who had been involved in an earlier uprising against the government, the incipient rebellion brought together religious fervor and political opposition to the government. The leaders claimed the events at the pool foretold the expulsion of foreign rulers. The rebellion was defused by a district commissioner who offered a sacrifice at the pool and ordered the arrest of the leaders.[39]

Nonetheless, the memory of the pool's appearance and its associations with Kejok remained strong. Abraham Mayom Athiaan, the church leader who returned from the Ethiopian refugee camps to the west bank in the early 1990s and later installed himself as a leader in Dhiaukuei, made a personal mission of recording stories about Kejok. For him, Kejok has clear parallels with Jesus Christ. Mayom called him a "black Messiah" and noted his promise to return after eight generations: "[H]e will come and the world will change. And I compare it with what Jesus said, his second coming."[40] Mayom is somewhat of an outlier among church leaders in his willingness to speak openly about Kejok. Others tend to downplay his significance out of fear of according too much importance to a pre-Christian figure. But it is not unreasonable to suppose that the well-known history of resistance and promise of change associated with the region gave credence to Dhiaukuei's location.

---

[38] V. H. Fergusson, "The Holy Lake of the Dinka," *Sudan Notes and Records* 5 (1922): 163.

[39] Fergusson, "The Holy Lake of the Dinka," 163; Lazarus Leek Mawut, *Dinka Resistance to Condominium Rule 1902–1932* (Graduate College Publications, monograph 3, University of Khartoum, 1983), 31–33.

[40] Abraham Mayom Athiaan Deng, in-person interview by Marc Nikkel. Location uncertain, September 1991 (transcript in NSCCA). I have also interviewed Mayom about Kejok and sought, without success, to obtain his writings on Kejok.

Change was coming—in the war and in Dinka religious life—only this time the change that was coming was clearly and closely associated with Christianity.

In the late 1980s and early 1990s when Dhiaukuei was founded, the church in the SPLA–controlled areas was almost completely isolated from the outside world and the ECS hierarchy. Few reports of church life emerged from the west-bank communities during this period. But Maciir remained in place and continued to emphasize his CMS heritage. As its missionaries had once built mission stations, Maciir would now do the same with the materials he had available. He gathered some Christians around him and began work: "At that time we were completely cut off. There is nobody, an agency or even the church leaders. Nobody. There was nothing at Dhiaukuei but bush. So they accepted, a group of people went [and] started cutting trees."[41] The isolation meant that there were few educational resources on which the nascent school could rely. The teachers were those few people who had had some kind of education before the war began. Because of the close connection of education and Christianity, this mostly meant people who were in some way associated with the church and the history of CMS. Two of the first teachers were Paul Manyuon Gaak and John Malith. Each had finished senior secondary school and been part of the CMS school system. Maciir called them "learned people and devoted Christians," something that in the rapidly growing church of the SPLA–controlled areas was in short supply.[42] The displacement of the war had brought educated Dinka such as Manyuon and Malith from towns into rural areas. Their proximity with rural, non-Christian Dinka led to an exchange of ideas that had previously not been possible. Dhiaukuei amounted to the formalization of this new model of town-village relations that ensured the transfer of this knowledge.

There were few resources with which to teach. Maciir recalled that at the beginning, after they had cleared the bush and built shelters in which to hold lessons, he told the people: "I am going to use cow hides for black board, I'm going to use cassava for chalk or charcoal. Your exercise book is the sand; your pen is your finger or a stick. If you all

---

[41] Reuben Maciir Makoi, in-person interview by Marc Nikkel. Thiika, Kenya, 10 February 1994 (transcript in personal files of Marc Nikkel).

[42] Reuben Maciir Makoi, interview by Nikkel. Thiika, Kenya, 10 February 1994. Also Paul Manyuon Gaak, in-person interview by Michael Medley. Dhiaukuei, South Sudan, 4 January 1995 (transcript provided by Michael Medley).

FIGURE 7.3
Dhiaukuei Bible School, 1994. Collection of Marc Nikkel.
Used by permission of Durham University Library.

co-operate with this, you'll be able to read and write."[43] There were also very few Bibles, prayer books, or books of any kind. In 1991 it was reported Dhiaukuei had a total of 10 Dinka hymn books and five Dinka New Testaments.[44] As a result, much of the teaching was oral. Marial Thon called the education at Dhiaukuei "a kind of a Bible study group. Even those who do not know how to read, they had to cram [memorize] what people were talking about. . . . When they go to different churches, they go and quote such things."[45] Dhiaukuei is yet another reminder in the history of religious change among the Dinka that although literacy was emphasized in the church and became a key part of the church's appeal, even the best efforts toward literacy education were undermined by the lack of resources. The primary means of knowledge transmission remained oral.

[43] Reuben Maciir Makoi, interview by Nikkel. Thiika, Kenya, 10 February 1994.
[44] Andrew C. Wheeler, "Report on a Visit to the Episcopal Church of the Sudan in the SPLA-Administered Areas of Southern Sudan, 12th–18th April, 1991" (NSCCA).
[45] Petro Marial Thon, in-person interview by Jesse Zink. Pacong, South Sudan, 18 September 2013.

The students at Dhiaukuei came from across the growing Dinka church, though primarily from the west-bank communities that were within a few days' journey of Dhiaukuei. The first class of students gathered in 1990 and consisted of about 90 students, not just the two newly ordained clergy who had provided the initial impetus for the founding of Dhiaukuei but lay leaders from other new congregations as well. Congregations were told to select someone to be sent for training. They were also to be sent with food to last for the several months of the training. Training happened during the dry season when travel was relatively easy and people were not needed at home for cultivation. By 1993 there were 160 students training at Dhiaukuei, half of whom were women.[46] At times, the food for students ran out and training had to be curtailed. At other times, the food was provided by church communities around Dhiaukuei. The idea of sharing one's produce for the common good reminded people of the early Christian community described in the Acts of the Apostles in that "all who believed were together and had all things in common" (Acts 2:44). In Dhiaukuei, 2,000 years later, God was believed to be recreating the experience of the early church.

Given the emphasis on literacy, it is not surprising that the primary focus of the curriculum was the Bible. But there were other aspects of the Dhiaukuei curriculum as well. By 1994 Enoch Marial, a former student at Bishop Gwynne College, was teaching classes in evangelism, history, and administration from notes that survived from his years at BGC.[47] The goal was to train students to return to their home congregations as educators in a variety of subjects. Still, the lack of resources continually hindered the education on offer. Literacy and study of the Bible remained the primary aspects of the education. Maciir described the reasons for this emphasis in words that almost perfectly echoed the reasons CMS gave for its own emphasis on biblical education and literacy: "If you read [the Bible], you can find the lessons, what it means for a human being to become a Christian or become a follower of Jesus. That is how I taught them at Dhiaukuei. And they are converted and they learn how to read. If they want to talk to somebody or teach people, they can open the Bible and read this message from God. Not [from] me, it is not

---

[46] Roland Werner, William Anderson, and Andrew Wheeler, *Day of Devastation, Day of Contentment: The History of the Sudanese Church across 2000 Years* (Nairobi: Paulines Publications Africa, 2000), 549.

[47] Marc Nikkel, "Notes on Akot, November 1994" (personal papers of Marc Nikkel).

my word, it is God who is saying this to you: 'Follow me.'"⁴⁸ Maciir acknowledged that the students were not learning "to the standards of those of the towns. . . . But [compared] to the village level, they are doing wonders."⁴⁹ From Dhiaukuei, students went back to their home communities, as Abraham Mayom recalled: "Everyone who is trained here, he has gone under a tree to train other people. So people now are able to read the Bible in their own language, whether an old woman or old man, whether a young girl or young boy . . . they are able now to read."⁵⁰ While Mayom's claim may have been hyperbolic, thanks to Dhiaukuei the church was—always in a limited fashion—raising the profile of literacy and hence Christianity through many parts of the west bank. Dhiaukuei was becoming a center of the church's work.

The constraints of the war frequently hindered the education available at Dhiaukuei. But the community retained great significance as a central gathering place for Christians. This was most clear at the end of the year and the Christian celebration of Christmas. Across the Dinka church, Christmas (and New Year's) was one of the most important celebrations. Even before the war, churches in the Rumbek area had been meeting in late December for an annual conference.⁵¹ This paralleled end-of-year public marches and demonstrations that took place among Christians in Khartoum, where Maciir had previously served. Christmas celebrations were also a central part of religious life in the refugee camps in Ethiopia.⁵² There is good reason for the emphasis on these celebrations. Christmas and New Year's come at the end of the growing season for many Dinka. It is the time of year, therefore, when the most food (and sorghum-based beer) is available. Traditionally, it was a time of celebration and a far cry from the period of hunger that awaited at the end of the dry season.⁵³ One young man who converted during the war remembered that in his youth, the end of the growing season was a time when people would kill animals like "cattle and chickens and make local

---

⁴⁸ Reuben Maciir Makoi, in-person interview by Jesse Zink. Juba, South Sudan, 22 September 2013.
⁴⁹ Reuben Maciir Makoi, interview by Nikkel. Thiika, Kenya, 10 February 1994.
⁵⁰ Abraham Mayom Athiaan, interview by Medley. Dhiaukuei, South Sudan, 26 December 1994 (transcript provided by Michael Medley).
⁵¹ Reuben Maciir Makoi, interview by Nikkel. Thiika, Kenya, 10 February 1994.
⁵² Abraham Mayom Athiaan, letter to Robert Runcie, 27 December 1989 (NSCCA).
⁵³ Lienhardt, *Divinity and Experience*, 6–7.

beer. And then the whole community will come and throw these things like offerings."[54]

In Dhiaukuei, these year-end celebrations reached a new pitch and did so in explicitly Christian terms. Marial Thon, who attended several of these celebrations, recalled, "It was a kind of fellowship. [But] it was also a sort of evangelization. People from the cattle camp could come and see, 'Why are all these people gathering together?' So they would come and see for themselves."[55] One visitor filed a lengthy report on the 1994 celebration:

> The Christmas Midnight Service is held under the trees. . . . The singing and drumming which has been going on all day has settled into a steady pattern, but now driven forward by the beating of handbells, sounding like anvils. . . . At midnight, [Abraham Mayom] stands, steps forward and, as usual, begins the event by punching the air . . . and shouting: "Alleluia!" . . .
>
> Companies of Christians from many parishes have come and camped at Dhiaukuei. On Christmas morning, each one forms up with its drums and its standards (of tall wooden crosses and even taller banners). . . . The morning service of worship is held under the trees. . . . There would be sitting room for about 400 people, but the number assembled is greater than that. . . . The service lasts more than three hours.[56]

Christmas celebrations allowed the Christian community to show itself off to the non-Christians in its midst. In the middle of a war, the celebration and the mood of the community became a testimony that this Christian God was worth paying attention to. Seen in the larger context of Dinka religious practice, the Christian emphasis on Christmas is a clear echo of non-Christian events, a traditional gathering time now interpreted in Christian terms. It is noteworthy that there are no memories or stories of events on a similar scale at Dhiaukuei or elsewhere at Easter, a holy day that is as significant, if not more so, to Christians as Christmas, but one that falls in the midst of the dry season and so at a time when far fewer resources are available.

As the Christmas celebrations indicate, Dhiaukuei represents the entry of Christian ideas and discourse into the landscape of the Dinka in a way not previously seen in Dinka Christianity. The west-bank church

---

[54] Abraham Yel Nhial, interview by Zink. Aweil, South Sudan, 19 July 2011.

[55] Petro Marial Thon, interview by Zink. Pacong, South Sudan, 18 September 2013.

[56] Field notes of Michael Medley, at Dhiaukuei, South Sudan, 25 December 1994.

had established a community that combined elements of a cattle camp and village in that it was a place to which groups of people came for a short period of time and one in which traditional ways of living sustained the community. But these groups of people gathered for explicitly Christian purposes. Rather than having to travel to a town for education and Christian community, Dinka could now find those same things in the very kind of community with which they were most familiar. What Maciir had done in establishing Dhiaukuei was offer a new reference point for Dinka Christians that was both rural and Christian. Dhiaukuei therefore parallels the creation of other sacred spaces by African Christian leaders, who offered a common social experience to their followers and "resituate[d]" the mental and material spaces of their followers in Christian terms.[57] In the midst of the displacement of the civil war, Dhiaukuei did something similar for Dinka Anglicans. By 1993, almost all of the 250 or so congregations on the west bank were led by someone who had been trained at Dhiaukuei.[58] That training may have been minimal, but it gave the church leadership on the west bank a common set of experiences to which they could point and which they could aspire to replicate in their work. It also meant that in their training they had not been removed from the rural context in which they had been raised. Christianity was not foreign but familiar.

The work at Dhiaukuei lasted only a few years before being felled by conflict between church leaders. On his return from the Ethiopian refugee camps in 1991, Abraham Mayom Athiaan succeeded in appealing to ethnic sentiment and his own familial connections to the SPLA to sideline Reuben Maciir. The SPLA, understanding the significance of the community and the strategic importance of the location, placed its regional headquarters nearby. For a time, Mayom used Dhiaukuei as a location to increase his own status through the distribution of international aid. As a resource for the church, Dhiaukuei began to fade in significance. But in its few years of existence, it demonstrated how Christian faith was becoming part of Dinka culture. The previous separation between town-based Christians and village-based non-Christians was dissolving. Now, in Dhiaukuei, Christianity had entered the social and sacred landscape of the Dinka.

---

[57] Elizabeth Gunner, *The Man of Heaven and the Beautiful Ones of God: Writings from Ibandla lamaNazaretha, a South African Church* (Leiden: Brill 2002), 24.

[58] Werner, Anderson, and Wheeler, *Day of Devastation, Day of Contentment*, 550.

Continuity and Change in a Civil War

The first two chapters of this book demonstrated the great distance—social and physical—that converts had to travel to become Christian in the generations before Sudan's second civil war. Becoming Christian during the Condominium meant leaving behind the landscape of villages and cattle camps in which one had been raised, rejecting existing religious beliefs, and being prepared for positions in the new political dispensation. Even after the missionaries were expelled, conversion still involved distance, whether in a move to Khartoum or to one of the urban centers of the south for education. Conversion to Christianity was understood as a moment of rupture with existing practice and belief.

The extent to which Christian conversion is continuous with previous cultural practices and the extent to which it is a rupture has been a key question in the scholarship on religious change.[59] An essential insight of scholars of religious change is that the value of the new religion must be understood in terms internal to the culture, an implicit argument for some form of continuity. Previous chapters demonstrated how Dinka converts during the civil war came to understand Christianity as a new and important resource in a changing world. Yet these earlier chapters have also revealed key moments of apparent rupture: the necessity of destroying items of the religion of the *jak* or the segmentation that took place in Dinka society as Christian and non-Christian separated from each other. Some converts continued to understand religious change as a moment and process of rupture with existing practice.

But there were also strong elements of continuity, whether at the level of landscape and social practice, as demonstrated in this chapter, or in the use of prophetic material, as in the prior one. The distance that had once existed between Christianity and Dinka culture narrowed considerably. Dinka cultural practices such as prophecy and the centrality of cattle camps became key features of the emerging popular Christianity in the emphasis accorded to both Isaiah 18 and Archibald Shaw as well as the influence of a place such as Dhiaukuei. The act of seeing oneself in biblical and Christian history made conversion seem an implicit statement of continuity. The *jak* remained central actors in the religious drama underway in the war. The war forced educated Dinka to return

---

[59] Robbins and his respondents offer the outlines of this debate. Joel Robbins, "Continuity Thinking and the Problem of Christian Culture: Belief, Time, and the Anthropology of Christianity," *Current Anthropology* 48, no. 1 (2007): 5–38.

to rural areas, which meant new converts could learn about Christianity in a setting that was most familiar to them. Where there were no true continuities, new interpretations were offered that appeared to create them: the reinterpretation of existing Dinka beliefs to include life after death and a particular, proto-Christian understanding of sacrifice. The distance between the religion of the *jak* and Christianity came to seem very narrow. Conversion from one to another came to seem a natural step. Christianity, a transnational faith that has existed in countless contexts around the world was, during the second civil war, made local to the Dinka. Its legitimation and usefulness made sense to Dinka only in the local terms of *jak*, prophets, and cattle camps.[60]

The need for that legitimation came from a dramatic moment of rupture: the *riäk* of the war, highlighted on the east bank by the cataclysm of the Bor Massacre and widespread displacement, was a definitive break with the past. The death, capture of cattle, and forced departures made it clear that Dinka life had to change. Indeed, with the existing cultural resources largely wiped out, it could not but change. In the midst of this catastrophe, Christian leaders—whether John Kelei and Kon Ajith at Pakeo, Reuben Maciir Makoi at Dhiaukuei, or those who pointed to Isaiah 18 and Archibald Shaw—were effective in presenting Christianity as an expression of both continuity with the past and hope for the future. With rupture all around, many Dinka embraced this message of continuity.

The embrace of Christianity as an expression of continuity was helped by the relative length of time that Christianity had been present among, if not embraced by, the Dinka. Unlike earlier, much-studied movements of African religious change that occurred in the colonial period not long after the introduction of a Christian missionary presence, many wartime Dinka converts did not know of a time in which Christianity had not been a religious option. Christianity may have had few adherents among the Dinka before the war but they had a certain visibility. Particularly during the Addis Ababa period, as Christians began returning in greater though still limited numbers to rural areas, the profile of Christianity was raised on the religious landscape. During the war, Christianity did not suddenly appear from nowhere, forcing potential converts to make a decision about something entirely new. Instead, it was embraced as something that had been around for some

---

[60] Cf. Maxwell, *Christians and Chiefs in Zimbabwe*, 218.

time and was now demonstrating its worth. New converts could turn to the Christian God and pray *jo wo liec*: turn back on us and remember us, too, who are now ready to join your church.

This suggests an important variable in understanding religious change, namely the length of time that Christianity is known among a people. Scholarship on rupture and continuity has tended to highlight how first-generation converts may tend toward rupture, while later generations of Christians assert greater continuity with their cultural traditions and religious practices.[61] The Dinka and other pastoralist peoples stand somewhat apart from these trends, in part because their initial encounter with Christianity consisted of making note of the new faith and then largely dismissing it for several generations. While the converts of the 1980s and 1990s were, by and large, first-generation converts, they were not the first generation of Dinka to know about Christianity. This lengthy encounter-but-not-embrace with Christianity meant that it was possible to see Christian conversion as an expression of continuity. Christianity had long been known to the Dinka; with the barriers to conversion lowered and the social distance to travel shorter, conversion became a much more attractive option.

From an outside perspective, Christianity can often look like a foreign importation in African communities. Particularly in mission denominations, the language of bishops, an obsession with proper dress, and the singing of translated hymns can heighten this perception. Yet Dinka adopted Christianity in ways that made sense in terms of the cultural frameworks of meaning that already existed. Christianity makes universal claims, but it only exists through a set of local, context-specific beliefs and practices. The key variable in understanding the Dinka experience of religious change is the catastrophic damage of the war. In need of new resources, many Dinka, urged on by figures like Isaiah, Archibald Shaw, and Kon Ajith, turned to a familiar-if-rejected faith and embraced it anew.

---

[61] David Maxwell, "Comments," in Robbins, "Continuity Thinking and the Problem of Christian Culture," 25–26.

Conclusion
Christianity and Catastrophe

In the conclusion to their study of education, religion, and politics in southern Sudan during the Condominium, the historians Lilian and Neville Sanderson wrote, "The problem with CMS is to explain how a Mission so half-heartedly launched, so distracted by fantasies of proselytisation in the Northern Sudan, so starved of men and money, so lacking in control over its own strategy of expansion, so closely linked to the colonial Government, could ever have given birth to a viable Church at all."[1] The Sandersons wrote prior to the outbreak of the second civil war and their question is primarily in reference to the church in Equatoria. But the task of this book has been to pose a similar question in regard to the Dinka in the former sphere of the Church Missionary Society (CMS): given the weakness of the missionary effort, the indifference of many Dinka, and the weak penetration of modernity among the Dinka, how does one explain the rapid growth in Christian adherence in the 1980s and 1990s?

The answer lies in the nature and varied impacts of Sudan's second civil war. First, the civil war created new patterns of movement and migration among Dinka. Dinka in towns and cities were displaced to rural villages and cattle camps. Dinka in both urban and rural areas were displaced across international borders to refugee camps. This migration created new interactions between Christian and non-Christian Dinka as

---

[1] Lilian Passmore Sanderson and Neville Sanderson, *Education, Religion and Politics in Southern Sudan, 1899–1964* (London: Ithaca, 1981), 407–8.

well as between Dinka and a larger world, interactions that were conducive to the spread of Christianity.

Second, one effect of the civil war and its migration was to make many Dinka realize that they needed new resources to assert themselves in a world that was something other than that which had historically shaped Dinka experience. The skills of cattle keeping that had been a path to survival and success for many Dinka men no longer worked in an environment in which cattle were seized and rural areas were laid waste by warfare. Instead, assets like education, international connections, and a sense of community, all uniquely to be found in the church, took on new importance and so led many Dinka toward Christianity.

Third, the war challenged the cosmological underpinnings of Dinka society. Questions were raised about the efficacy of the *jak* and how to survive in the middle of a war zone. Through Christian ideas, stories, and histories, many Dinka were able to construct new narratives and theologies that helped make sense of the destruction of the war in terms that were political, military, and religious. Dinka songs, prophecy, and places came to be infused with Christianity.

The result was widespread religious conversion in which many Dinka in the former CMS mission sphere came to understand themselves as Christians. They acted on this self-understanding by writing new hymns, creating new social groupings with Christian basis, establishing Christian institutions and places in new areas of Dinka landscape, and adapting the institution of prophecy to the Christian message. Although it is difficult to attach numbers to this growth, the widespread nature of religious change among the Dinka is evident from the changing way in which Dinka themselves came to understand their religious identity.

This study has made reference to the work of Robin Horton and his thought experiment concerning African religious change. Many of the predictions that Horton made are borne out in the case of the Dinka. By the end of the civil war, Anglicanism was for many Dinka an "instrument of explanation-prediction-control" in the way that the previous religious beliefs had once been.[2] Yet Anglicanism was more than that. The content of the new religion mattered. The civil war served as a catalyst for religious change. In the midst of devastation, Christianity offered new prophetic material, theological ideas, and communal life that appealed to many converts. It was this that generated the passion

---

[2] Robin Horton, "African Conversion," *Africa* 41, no. 2 (1971), 102.

and enthusiasm that is so characteristic of Dinka Anglicanism and that remains central to the study of religious change. The critique of Horton stands: new concepts and ideas introduced to African religion by world religions must be studied in careful detail.[3] The intellectualist approach to religious change provides a useful framework for considering conversion. But it is only by the careful study of religious interaction that the full picture of religious change becomes clear.

The example of the Dinka also broadens a common understanding of migration. While much study of migration in Africa has for good reason focused on urbanization, the movement induced by warfare takes many forms. There was wartime urbanization among the Dinka, particularly to informal settlements in and around Khartoum, an area of Dinka social life beyond the scope of this book. But much Dinka migration during the civil war was away from urban areas and toward rural communities. Other Dinka fled to large refugee camps in remote areas. In Horton's terms, the macrocosm returned to the microcosm. The migration set in motion by war is multidirectional. Heeding the unique and particular nature of wartime migration is crucial to understanding how religious change takes place.

A key part of this book has been to expand the history of an African Anglican church and challenge typologies of African Christianity. The Christian faith that emerged in Dinka communities during the civil war saw itself as self-consciously Anglican and part of a larger communion of such churches around the world. Refugees in Ethiopia appealed to Archbishop of Canterbury Robert Runcie on no grounds other than that he was seen as the leader of Anglicans worldwide. CMS' history in southern Sudan offered the grounds for claims on its resources during the war.

On one level, this is no surprise. The central figures of the Dinka church—Nathaniel Garang Anyieth, Reuben Maciir Makoi, and Benjamin Mangar Mamur—all had some personal connection to the CMS period. Female converts and female leaders of the church may not have been similarly connected to CMS but were aware of the past work of British missionaries through the stories that were told about them. Nor is Anglican identity merely for ecclesial elites. In the early 2000s, a group led by Abraham Mayom Athiaan broke away from the Episcopal Church of the Sudan (ECS), the official province of the Anglican Communion,

---

[3] Richard Gray, *Black Christians and White Missionaries* (New Haven: Yale University Press, 1990), 67.

and called their new church the Anglican Church of South Sudan. They made a key part of their appeal the claim that they were more Anglican than ECS because the word "Anglican" was in their title.[4] The sign outside their main gathering place in Rumbek says simply "Anglican Church." That this group has had success in attracting members and sustaining its existence shows the enduring appeal of Anglican identities. It was once thought that missionary Christianity would fade away in independent Africa. Yet as numerous studies have shown, these apparently foreign identities have been adopted and internalized by many African Christians, gaining energy and vibrancy.

Yet from another perspective the continued emphasis on Anglican identity is puzzling. Dinka Anglicanism has much in common with movements of Christian independency. With little control from external hierarchies during the war, and its own charismatic leaders, there was little to prevent it from emerging as a popular Christian movement unconnected to any mission denomination. Yet the church retained its mission heritage. Not only was Anglican identity important during the civil war, that emphasis continues today. Worship according to a translated version of the 1662 Book of Common Prayer continues in Dinka communities. The ECS archbishop has been a member of the standing committee of the Anglican Communion and is involved in leadership of African Anglican organizations. Dinka Anglicans are eager to share opinions on controversial issues before the Anglican Communion.

The apparent conundrum of Dinka religious identity, rooted in both Anglicanism and independency, can be resolved by challenging the dichotomy. At a grassroots level in particular, distinctions between various kinds of Christianities in Africa begin to dissolve. Dinka Anglicanism is both rooted in mission practice and responsive to local, cultural realities. It is both aware of the history it inherits and able to articulate new practices and new content. It proudly identifies itself with external church organizations and creates its own institutions and patterns of leadership. The key to understanding the complexity of the situation is more studies of Christianity at the grassroots level. A crucial historical fact about southern Sudan, for instance, was the almost complete lack of overlap in missionary spheres during the Condominium period. For Dinka in the east- and west-bank communities, to be Christian was to be

---

[4] Abraham Mayom Athiaan Deng, in-person interview by Jesse Zink. Rumbek, South Sudan, 19 September 2013.

Anglican. But the weakness of the Anglican missionary presence meant that there was little pressure to form an independent denomination.

The study of Dinka Anglicanism also raises questions about the importance of Christianity as a vehicle for a transnational religious identity. Such debates in African Christianity have primarily focused on Pentecostalism and the global links generated by that movement. But a key part of the appeal of Anglican identity for the Dinka was precisely its transnational links. Particularly after the 1991 split in the Sudan People's Liberation Army, when access to east- and west-bank communities became modestly easier, an Anglican identity proved a productive route for securing external assistance. The study of Anglican transnationalism, if it even exists, often focuses on elite institutions such as the Lambeth Conference.[5] Yet Nathaniel Garang Anyieth was forced to miss the 1988 Lambeth Conference because of the war and still managed to create a transnational Anglican identity among east-bank Dinka.

An Anglican grassroots transnationalism raises further questions about the study of Anglicanism. Rather than offer a history of global Anglicanism that is, at root, a chronological expansion of particular forms of English Christianity, Anglicanism needs more studies of particular churches in their context. Such studies reveal the clear and decisive role of local agency in shaping Anglicanism, over and above the Englishness of Anglicanism.[6] Yet there is a contradiction: Anglicanism is seen as important by Dinka because it has historically had no competitors and because it offers transnational connections that no other organization can. The first reason is an historical accident. The second reason is closely tied to the Englishness, internationalism, and general foreignness of Anglicanism that connected Dinka with a larger world. More local studies of Anglicanism are the best way to illuminate its reality across the world, yet at the same time the enduring importance of Anglicanism may best be explained by its original Englishness, the very aspect that recent studies have sought to move away from.

In addition to expanding the history of African Anglicanism, this book is also a rare study of religious change among an agropastoralist people. For the Dinka, religious change began when some young men

---

[5] A notable exception is Emma Wild-Wood, "Attending to Translocal Identities: How Congolese Anglicans Talk about Their Church," *Journal of Anglican Studies* 9, no. 1 (2011): 80–99.

[6] Kevin Ward, *A History of Global Anglicanism* (Cambridge: Cambridge University Press, 2006), 16.

sought a means of production other than cattle. As they moved to urban areas for wage labor or education, they were introduced to Christianity. But the greatest momentum toward religious change was found when the civil war devastated the historic means of production in Dinka society. The change is most clearly seen by comparing east-bank communities in the early years of the civil war with the years after the 1991 Bor Massacre. In the 1980s, religious change found its greatest strength among socially marginal constituencies. After 1991, however, the devastation of the war was inescapable. As it became clear that it was no longer possible to survive as a cattle-keeper, the pace of religious change increased enormously. As Dinka social life became increasingly dependent on international aid, which required education to exploit most fully, more and more Dinka turned to Christianity. In the absence of civil war, Dinka society likely would have continued on a trajectory toward a gradual and greater but still minority embrace of Christianity. The civil war, however, sped up this process and made it far more widespread.

The study of agropastoralist Christianity raises important questions about generational engagement with Christianity. Across Africa, many more settled and agrarian people took quickly to Christianity. The Zande in southern Sudan, for instance, are an example of a people among whom the church grew rapidly. Yet even though the same CMS missionaries who worked among the Zande had little success among the Dinka, it is clear in retrospect that their work created an awareness, if not an acceptance, of Christianity that laid the groundwork for future religious change. When the need for change became apparent, as it did for the Dinka during the war, many Dinka turned to a new set of religious beliefs and practices that did not actually appear all that new. Although the religious change that took place among Dinka during the civil war appears sudden and dramatic, it can in fact only be understood within the generations-long history of Dinka engagement and disengagement with the forces of colonial and Western modernity.

The difficulties of research in southern Sudan mean that its social history has only recently begun to receive renewed attention. As the social history of southern Sudan is written, it must include its religious history as well. The Christian theology that many Dinka Anglicans developed was not for a quiescent, private faith but provided the grounds for assertive and engaged interpretations that shaped how Dinka responded to the war. More broadly, there is a need for further research into religious change that takes place during times of civil war. The religious life of refugees, the patterns of migration set in motion by civil war, and the development of theologies of war are all fruitful fields of further research in African religious history.

A Future Agenda

At the end of any project, no matter how extensive, one is still left with the thought of how much remains unknown. One area that needs further study is the practices surrounding social organization for young men in Dinka society. There are apparent parallels between groups like *Jo Wo Liec* that young refugees created for themselves as unaccompanied minors and the age sets they might have known had they remained in cattle camps. These issues were broached with informants, but their responses were shaped by decades of Christian practice that make it difficult to construct an adequate picture of earlier practice. To pursue such themes would require more extensive anthropological and historical work that, for the Dinka, has largely not been done.

Dinka Anglicanism is situated on the boundary between literacy and orality. During the civil war, Dinka Christianity evolved a series of ways to transmit the faith that did not depend on literacy: hymns, oral versions of Isaiah 18, places like Dhiaukuei. Studies of religious change in Africa have emphasized how literacy contributed to conversion and the connections between writing and religious change. Yet the Dinka are a reminder that orality and literacy are on a continuum. Christianity may have shifted the balance toward literacy, but orality retained its foundational importance as it evolved ways of transmitting a new religious message. The difficulty of collecting this oral material means that there are further theological themes that went unexplored in this book. Given its roots in the societal collapse of civil war, further study could, for instance, illuminate the extent to which Dinka Anglicanism draws on apocalyptic and millenarian imagery.[7]

The segmentary lineage system has long given precedence to local, familial relations, a reality that has always challenged efforts to speak of a truly pan-Dinka identity. Dinka Anglicanism embodies similar lines of division. From the initial 4 dioceses in ECS in 1976, there are

---

[7] On this see, for instance, Arrtu Ahava, "No Going Back: Christian Conversion among the Twic Dinka of South Sudan" (M.Phil. dissertation, Oxford University, 2008), 32–33.

now at least 43. A plurality of dioceses and almost all of the newly created ones are in Dinka areas. In part, this is a reflection of the growth of Dinka Anglicanism. But it is also clear that part of the impetus for these new dioceses are existing lineage divisions. Newly created dioceses tend to be ever more homogeneous and particular to individual lineage groups. There is an increasing desire for ever-smaller groups to have their own bishop and diocese.[8] The result has been the creation of dioceses that cannot financially support the necessary ecclesiastical institutions and the elevation to the episcopate of clerics who are unprepared for such ministry. Another result has been debilitating ecclesiastical conflict in episcopal elections that reflects existing lineage divisions. To use Hutchinson's phrase, this could be called "segmentary Christianity."[9] Such a situation could be an opportunity to rethink the nature of African episcopal ministry and lead to a form of ministry that is more local and less "prince-like." But the more likely impact is on the unity of Dinka—and southern Sudanese—Anglicanism. The church is in danger of becoming one more site in Dinka society in which social conflict is played out. It raises further questions about the Christian identity created by Dinka communities. It is an identity that is at once transnational but also local and tied to existing kinship patterns.

* * *

Sudan's civil war officially came to an end in 2005 with the signing of the Comprehensive Peace Agreement (CPA). In January 2011, southern Sudanese voted for independence and, on 9 July of that year, officially became the world's newest nation. Yet the euphoria with which many southerners and their friends greeted that day was short lived. The political leaders of the country had not truly reconciled with one another. Rebellion against the central government, whether in Khartoum or in Juba, is still seen as a way to secure one's own position. In December 2013, the sporadic violence of the post-CPA years turned into full-fledged civil war within South Sudan. Fitful efforts to resolve the violence have not been successful, and there are now new refugee

---

[8] Such trends have been evident in other African Anglican churches. See Kevin Ward, "The Church of Uganda amidst Conflict: The Interplay between Church and Politics in Uganda since 1962," in *Religion and Politics in East Africa: The Period Since Independence*, ed. Holger Bernt Hansen and Michael Twaddle (London: James Currey, 1995), 94.

[9] Sharon Hutchinson, personal conversation, May 2014.

populations displaced within South Sudan and in countries like Uganda, Kenya, and Ethiopia. Communities in which research for this book was conducted—Malakal, Bor—have been devastated by interethnic violence that parallels divisions in the civil war of the 1980s and 1990s. Longtime students of Sudan report that they have never felt more depressed or less hopeful about the country's future than they do now.

In the midst of all this, this book has looked to the recent past to tell a story of the role of religion in the midst of societal collapse. It is a role expressed in one of the most popular wartime hymn compositions of Mary Alueel Garang, a leading shaper of the theology of Dinka Anglicanism. In it, she urges Dinka to praise God in the day of devastation (*riäk*) and the day of contentment. This book has been a study of how it was that Dinka came to praise God in the midst of the *riäk* of civil war. It is a rich history that has not always been connected with other scholarship on African Christianity. By investigating the emergence of Christianity among some Dinka, this book has sought to broaden conversations about religious change, violence, and identity across sub-Saharan Africa. And, as recent events tragically remind us, it is a history that is not all that far in the past.

Appendix
A Note on Methodology and Sources

My interest in Dinka Christianity originates in my training as an Anglican priest. While still a theological student, I first traveled to southern Sudan in 2010 and spent several weeks as a student at Bishop Gwynne College, an Anglican theological college in Juba. In 2011, I made a subsequent visit to what was then the newly independent country of South Sudan and visited several students in their home regions to learn more about their experience of civil war, church, and ministry. I also began working with the Dinka diaspora in the United States. I spent the summer of 2012, by then ordained as a priest, working with a Sudanese congregation in Phoenix, Arizona. In 2013, I made two further visits to South Sudan, one in which I was based in the communities on the east bank of the Nile, and the second in which I was based in west-bank communities. During this time, I stayed in and around church communities and so became a participant-observer of religious life.

This six months of fieldwork in Dinka communities produced approximately 65 semi-structured, open-ended, oral history interviews. My informants included bishops, priests, male and female church leaders, and lay people who offered a variety of perspectives on Dinka Christianity. I conducted interviews either in English, which because of the close connection between education and Christianity many church leaders speak, or Dinka, through a translator, who was generally a young, educated male priest from the area. These translators helped me locate informants, arranged logistics, and made introductions, while also shaping and responding to the stories that were elicited in the interviews. In some instances, they also told me that it was not safe to travel to particular places and interview individuals, which constrained my list of interviewees.

My research received ethics approval from the Cambridge University Faculty of Divinity. I began each interview by explaining I was interested in learning about the church during the war so that I could share these stories with other people outside South Sudan and that I would make a recording to help me do that. Each time I made clear that no informant had to answer any question and could end the interview at any time, whether because the memories of the war were too difficult to bring to mind or for any other reason. In general I found my informants were eager to speak with me. In part, I attribute this to the pride that many Dinka Anglicans take in the growth of their church during the war. It was also clear that some people regarded me as a useful tool to advance their particular understanding of past events. As I became more aware of this and broadened my understanding of the church, I was able to use these moments to bring out more detail about what had happened. The eagerness to speak with me is also due to the strong sense among many South Sudanese that they are not paid sufficient heed by the world. As one elderly female informant told me at the close of a lengthy interview, "Thank you for coming and listening to me. I now feel like something will live on beyond me." It did not seem to matter that her story was well known by other Dinka. Only once I had heard it—a non-Sudanese and a Westerner—could it be considered recorded.

My research was limited by who I am: white, male, and a priest. My gender made it difficult at times to conduct interviews with women. I was repeatedly frustrated in my efforts to find a female translator. As an ordinand and then priest, I was concerned that informants might shape their memories into the kind of narrative they thought a priest would want to hear. But the longer I spent in communities and the more I made myself known, the less I found this to be a problem. What it does mean, however, is that this is a book shaped by the church and particularly by the Episcopal Church of the Sudan. This weakens aspects of the work. The section on the prophet Kon Ajith would benefit from more non-church and non-ECS sources. An associate of Kon's who is now a member of the Seventh Day Adventist Church declined to speak with me (the only time I was denied an interview) because I had been introduced to him by a member of ECS. More generally, the challenges of fieldwork in South Sudan remain immense. Logistical and security challenges make it extraordinarily difficult to be an independent researcher. At this point in South Sudan's history, virtually all research is mediated, whether through the church, an international nongovernmental organization, a local government official, or someone else. The challenge is to be conscious of the mediation and aware of how it shapes one's sources.

The student of South Sudanese church history is blessed with the work of earlier generations of missionary-scholars. In the late 1990s and early 2000s, Paulines Publications in Nairobi published the multi-volume *Faith in Sudan* series, a fantastic wealth of historical detail. The student of Dinka Christianity also benefits from the work of Marc Nikkel, an American Episcopal priest who taught in southern Sudan in the 1980s, wrote a doctoral dissertation on Dinka Christianity in the early 1990s, and then worked with Sudanese refugees in Kenya until his untimely death in 2000. It is impossible to write about the Dinka church without reference to these works. Yet this book also benefits from the time that has elapsed, especially since Nikkel's work. People and places that merit a paragraph in earlier work, such as Dhiaukuei or Kon Ajith, are in this book more fully researched and set in historical, social, and religious context.

I also conducted archival work in three countries. The archives of church and international organizations that have worked in southern Sudan proved helpful to my research. The nascent South Sudan National Archive in Juba offered a wild cornucopia of material, a smattering of which relates to this book. In an indication of the challenges of research in a post–civil war context, however, no material survives in that archive from the Bahr el Ghazal region, including the west-bank communities that are a key focus of this book. The most helpful archive was also the most difficult to locate. During the war, the New Sudan Council of Churches (now South Sudan Council of Churches) began an archive at its offices in Nairobi. This material was then moved to Kampala before being brought to Juba after the Comprehensive Peace Agreement. I located this archive in a warehouse on the edge of a market in Juba. The description of its condition was best provided by the staff member who first took me to see it: "I think you have been misled if you think this is going to be a library with books on shelves." Instead, we found approximately 20 cubic meter cardboard boxes in varying states of weather-related disrepair, overflowing with letters, binders, reports, and more, all covered in a generous helping of dust. It had clearly been neglected for some time. I spent nearly two weeks sorting through this material and photographing as much of it as possible. I retain a photograph of every document from that archive cited in this book.

Finally, there are personal papers that also shed light on Dinka religious change. The family of Marc Nikkel generously offered me much of the material he left behind, including much of his personal correspondence as well as approximately 500 of his photographs, one of which appears on the cover of this book. In 2016, I donated all this material to the Sudan Archive at Durham University in England. In addition, I found more of Nikkel's personal papers and notes in the NSCC archive in Juba, to which he had donated them in the hopes they would one day be found useful. As the precarious state of the NSCC archive makes clear, preserving documents in the middle of a civil war is difficult. For the most part, records of the Dinka church created during the war no longer exist. I listened in horror, for instance, as a retired Dinka bishop related how he had carefully tracked each baptism, confirmation, and service he performed during the war and then in the next breath describe how it had all been destroyed when his home was attacked and burned to the ground. That means that there are many moments in which the existing historical record is insufficient, and I have been able to speak only in general terms.

It is vitally important that we understand the recent history of the African church. Given the traumatic events that have shaped the church and the challenges of collecting research material, it is only possible to study this history with a combination of sensitive interviews, mediated access, and the cobbling together of written sources.

Bibliography

Archives

Anglican Communion Office Archives, London, UK
References in footnotes are to ACOA and give citation information following the conventions of the archive.

Cambridge Centre for Christianity Worldwide Archive, Cambridge, UK
References in footnotes are to CCCWA and give citation information following the conventions of the archive.

Church Missionary Society Archive, Birmingham University
References in footnotes are to CMSA and give citation information following the conventions of the archive.

New Sudan Council of Churches Archive, Juba, South Sudan
The disorganization of this resource makes citation information almost impossible to give. When I consulted the archive, it was stacks of paper and files in crumbling boxes with no apparent organization. In footnotes, therefore, I am able to refer only to this archive as NSCCA with no further citation information. I retain a photograph of every document I cite.

South Sudan National Archive, Juba, South Sudan
References in footnotes are to SSNA and then the citation information as it was at the time I consulted the archive (April and September 2013). At that time, however, the archive was in the process of reorganization and possible move, meaning that my citation information may no longer be up-to-date. I retain a photograph of every document I cite.

Sudan Archive, University of Durham
References in footnotes are to SAD and give citation information following the conventions of the archive.

United Nations High Commission on Refugees, Geneva, Switzerland
References in footnotes are to UNHCRA. Report authors, titles, and classification system (if any) are given.

Documents Privately Held

Timothy Biles
A priest in the Diocese of Salisbury in the Church of England, who visited Ethiopian refugee camps in late 1990 and early 1991. He generously shared pictures of his trip with me and gave me permission to reproduce them.

John Chol Daau
A Dinka priest from the east bank of the Nile River and a former refugee in Ethiopia, Kenya, and Uganda. He has begun but not fully completed a study of the ministry of Nathaniel Garang Anyieth and allowed me to consult and quote from that work.

Nancy Frank
Former executive director of the American Friends of the Episcopal Church of Sudan, who shared papers and videos with me from both her trips to Sudanese refugee camps beginning in 1998 and other advocacy work in the United States.

Nathaniel Garang Anyieth
Retired bishop of the Diocese of Bor in the Episcopal Church of the Sudan, who allowed me to consult the private pictures and papers that survive from his lengthy ministry, at his home in Nakuru, Kenya.

Hilary Garang Deng
Bishop of Malakal in the Episcopal Church of South Sudan, as well as former principal of Bishop Gwynne College in Juba. He spent a sabbatical term in Cambridge, UK, in 2016 and shared with me a draft of the paper he produced but did not publish. This is listed in the footnotes as "The Second Revival among the Dinka Anglicans in South Sudan, 1970–2010."

Michael Medley
Former researcher for the NGO African Rights, and lead researcher of the report *Great Expectations* (see below). He shared with me field notes from that trip as well as transcripts of the interviews he conducted.

Marc Nikkel
In addition to the papers he deposited in the New Sudan Council of Churches archive before his death, his sister and brother-in-law, Marvis and Sam Bergen, in Reedley, California, shared with me additional papers, correspondence, and photographs they had preserved. These have now been donated to the Sudan Archive in Durham, UK, where they await cataloguing.

Interviews Conducted by Jesse Zink

interviews marked with a * were conducted with the assistance of a translator

*Gordon Aboi Ajith, Bor, South Sudan, 13 April 2013
*Mary Achol Deng, Juba, South Sudan, 28 April 2013
Phillip Adwong Thiong, Juba, South Sudan, 9 September 2013
Thomas Agau Kur, Bor, South Sudan, 8 April 2013
*Joseph Akol Gak, Malek, South Sudan, 14 April 2013
Ruben Akurdit Ngong Akurdit, Bor, South Sudan, 12 April 2013
Mark Ajak Arok, Malakal, South Sudan, 4 September 2013
Mary Alueel Garang Nongdit, Bor, South Sudan, 14 April 2013
*Mary Aruay Majak, Rumbek, South Sudan, 13 September 2013
Amos Awan de Gak, Juba, South Sudan, 4 April 2013 and 25 April 2013
Emmanuel Ayel, Juba, South Sudan, 4 April 2013
Santino Bol, Nakura, Kenya, 26 September 2013
John Chol Daau, Juba, South Sudan, 23 September 2013
Gabriel Chol Kuany, Phoenix, Arizona, 27 June 2012
Daniel Deng Bul Yak, Juba, Sudan, 10 September 2010
Isaac Dhieu Ater, Rumbek, South Sudan, 12 September 2013
Ezekiel Diing, Bor, South Sudan, 5 April 2013
Nancy Frank, telephonically, 16 February 2013
Samuel Galuak Marial, Juba, South Sudan, 20 April 2013 and 23 September 2013
Nathaniel Garang Anyieth, Bor, South Sudan, 8 April 2013
Hilary Garang Deng, Malakal, South Sudan, 3 September 2013
Gabriel Garang Machot, Bor, South Sudan, 7 April 2013
Rhys Hall, telephonically, 22 September 2013
Richard Jones, telephonically, 29 January 2013
John Jurkuc Wal, Rumbek, South Sudan, 11 September 2013
*John Kelei, Bor, South Sudan, 16 April 2013
Daniel Kon Malwal, Bor, South Sudan, 5 April 2013
*Martha Kuei Marier, Rumbek, South Sudan, 19 September 2013
*Samuel Kuir Deng Kuir, Malakal, South Sudan, 4 September 2013
Jacob Kunyuat Jany, 13 September 2010, Juba, Sudan
Andreaj Lual Arok, Phoenix, Arizona, 26 July 2012
Reuben Maciir Makoi, Juba, South Sudan, 22 September 2013
David Magot Ngong, Bor, South Sudan, 11 April 2013
*Michael Maikol Lang, Malakal, South Sudan, 4 September 2013
Paul Majer Mac, Juba, South Sudan, 18 April 2013
*Johnson Majok Joseph Luel, Akot, South Sudan, 15 September 2013
George Maliet Dut, Juba, South Sudan, 18 April 2013
Abraham Mamer Kur, Bor, South Sudan, 16 April 2013

Benjamin Mangar Mamur, Rumbek, South Sudan, 11 September 2013
*Peter Manyak Mangok, Rumbek, South Sudan, 12 September 2013
Alapayo Manyang Kuctiel, Rumbek, South Sudan, 12 September 2013
*Petro Marial Thon, Pacong, South Sudan, 18 September 2013
Stephen Mathiang Kuc, Bor, South Sudan, 5 April 2013 and 9 April 2013
*James Matiop Malwal, Rumbek, South Sudan, 13 September 2013
Meshach Mayom Bol Achuk, Bor, South Sudan, 15 April 2013
Andrew Mayol Ajak, Juba, South Sudan, 4 April 2013 and 25 April 2013
Mark Mayol Malek, Juba, South Sudan, 22 April 2013
Abraham Mayom Athiaan Deng, Rumbek, South Sudan, 19 September 2013
*Joseph Meen Kuotwel, Nemthok, South Sudan, 14 September 2013
Cimbir Alkaatib Ngalu, 14 September 2010, Juba, Sudan
James Nhial Maler, Bor, South Sudan, 6 April 2013
Abraham Noon Jiel, Bor, South Sudan, 7 April 2013 and 14 April 2013
Bernard Oringa, Juba, South Sudan, 26 April 2013
*Anderia Osman Okelo, Rumbek, South Sudan, 18 September 2013
Richard Parkins, telephonically, 25 January 2013
Andrew and Janet Persson, Kidlington, England, 22 February 2013
Nicolas Lo Polito, Birmingham, England, 5 December 2012
Daniel Ewot Roman, Juba, Sudan, 14 September 2010
Stefan Sävenstedt, telephonically, 28 January 2013
Roger Sharland, Nairobi, Kenya, 2 May 2013
Changkuth Wal Leul, Juba, Sudan, 16 September 2010
Andrew Wheeler, Guildford, England, 13 December 2010 and 22 November 2012
*Martha Yar Mawut, Akot, South Sudan, 15 September 2013
Abraham Yel Nhial, Aweil, South Sudan, 19 July 2011

Primary Documents

African Rights. *Components of a Lasting Peace in Sudan: First Thoughts*. London: African Rights, 1993.
———. *Great Expectations: The Civil Roles of the Churches in Southern Sudan*. London: African Rights, 1995.
———. *Sudan's Invisible Citizens: The Policy of Abuse against Displaced People in the North*. London: African Rights, 1995.
———. *Food and Power in Sudan: A Critique of Humanitarianism*. London: African Rights, 1997.
Alier, Abel. *Southern Sudan: Too Many Agreements Dishonoured*. 2nd ed. Reading, UK: Ithaca, 1992/1990.
Allison, Oliver. *A Pilgrim Church's Progress*. London: Highway, 1966.
———. *Through Fire and Water*. London: Church Missionary Society, 1976.

Biles, Timothy. *Windows on the Sudan: A Story of Pain and Pride*. 3rd ed. Dorset, UK: self-published, 1994/1991.
Bung de Diɛt ke Duɔ̈ɔ̈r (Book of Songs for Worship). Nairobi: Sudan Literature Centre for the Episcopal Church of Sudan, 1999. 8th printing, 2007.
Church Missionary Society. *Missions of the Church Missionary Society: The Egypt and Soudan Missions*. London: Church Missionary Society, 1910.
———. *Among the Pagans of the Southern Sudan*. London: Church Missionary Society, 1922.
Dau, John Bul, with Michael S. Sweeney. *God Grew Tired of Us*. Washington, D.C.: National Geographic, 2007.
Dempsey, James. *Mission on the Nile*. London: Burns & Oates, 1955.
Deng, Ayuel Leek, Beny Ngor Chol, and Barbara Youree. *Courageous Journey: Walking the Lost Boys' Path from the Sudan to America*. Far Hills, N.J.: New Horizon, 2008.
Deng, Benson, Alephonsion Deng, and Benjamin Ajak with Judy A. Bernstein. *They Poured Fire on Us from the Sky: The True Story of Three Lost Boys from Sudan*. New York: Public Affairs, 2005.
Diocese of Egypt and Sudan. *Our Church's Work for the People of the Sudan*. Khartoum, Sudan: n.p., 1925.
Diocese of Rumbek [Roman Catholic]. *The Church in Sudan: Journeying towards Justice and Peace*. Nairobi: Paulines Publications Africa, 2001.
Eggers, Dave, with Valentino Achak Deng. *What Is the What: The Autobiography of Valentino Achak Deng: A Novel*. London: Vintage, 2006.
Haumann, Mathew. *The Long Road to Peace: Encounters with the People of Southern Sudan*. Leominster, UK: Gracewing, 2000.
———. *Travelling with Soldiers and Bishops: Stories of Struggling People in Sudan*. Nairobi: Paulines Publications Africa, 2004.
Kitching, A. L. *From Darkness to Light: A Study of the Pioneer Missionary Work in the Diocese of the Upper Nile*. London: SPCK, 1935.
Lek Jot de Bɛnydiitda ku Duluɛngda Yecu Kritho (The New Testament in Dinka Bor). Juba: The Bible Society in South Sudan, 1959/1941.
Maker, Joseph Akol. *From Africa to America: The Journey of a Lost Boy of Sudan*. Mustang, Okla.: Tate, 2007.
Nhial, Abraham, and DiAnn Mills. *Lost Boy No More: A True Story of Survival and Salvation*. Nashville, Tenn.: B&H, 2004.
Nikkel, Marc, with Grant LeMarquand, eds. *Why Haven't You Left? Letters from the Sudan*. New York: Church Publishing, 2006.
Nyaba, Peter Adwok. *Politics of Liberation in South Sudan: An Insider's View*. Kampala, Uganda: Fountain, 1997.
Oostland, Rolanda, and Ronald Berkvens. *Sudanese Life Stories: Voices from Kakuma Refugee Camp*. Utrecht: Churches in Action & Pax Christi, 1998.
Pengko Pilot Project, Technical Note no. 9. *The Social and Economic Setting of Rural Bor Dinka*. Arnhem, the Netherlands: ILACO, December 1979.

Pengko Pilot Project, Technical Note no. 20. *Bor Dinka: Prospects for Development*. Arnhem, the Netherlands: ILACO, November 1981.

Piööc de Lëk Theer (Në Wël Cï Ke Kueny Bei Në Baibolic): Lessons from the Old Testament, in the Words of the Bible, in Dinka, Bor Dialect. London: SPCK, 1996/1950/1935.

Sharland, Leonard W. C. "Memories of Archibald Shaw: Sometime Archdeacon in the Southern Sudan." 1977. Private collection of Roger W. Sharland.

Southern Development Investigation Team. *Natural Resources and Development Potential in the Southern Provinces of the Sudan: A Preliminary Report by the Southern Development Investigation Team 1954*. London: Sudan Government, 1955.

Toniolo, Elias, and Richard Hill, eds. *The Opening of the Nile Basin: Writings by Members of the Catholic Mission to Central Africa on the Geography and Ethnography of the Sudan, 1842–1881*. London: Hurst, 1974.

Witts, Diana. *Springs of Hope*. Stanhope, UK: The Memoir Club, 2005.

Zutt, Johannes. *Les enfants de la guerre: seuls dans la vie au sud du Soudan*. New York: UNICEF, 1994.

Secondary Sources

Ahava, Arrtu. "No Going Back: Christian Conversion among the Twic Dinka of South Sudan." M.Phil. dissertation, Oxford University, 2008.

Ahmed, Abdel Ghaffar M., and Mustafa Abdel Rahman. "Small Urban Centres: Vanguards of Exploitation: Two Cases from Sudan." *Africa* 49, no. 3 (1979): 258–71.

Akol, Joshua O. "A Crisis of Expectations: Returning to Southern Sudan in the 1970s." In *When Refugees Go Home: African Experiences*, ed. Tim Allen and Hubert Morsink, 78–95. Trenton, N.J.: Africa World Press, 1994.

Anderson, William B. "The Role of Religion in the Sudan's Search for Unity." In *African Initiatives in Religion*, ed. David B. Barrett, 73–90. Nairobi: East African Publishing House, 1971.

Ashworth, John, ed. *One Church from Every Tribe, Tongue and People: Symposium on the Role of the Church in the Independence of South Sudan: Papers Presented at a Symposium Held at Nyakuron Cultural Centre and St. Theresa's Cathedral Juba, South Sudan, 13th–16th October 2011*. Nairobi: Paulines Publications Africa, 2012.

Ashworth, John, and Maura Ryan. "'One Nation from Every Tribe, Tongue, and People': The Church and Strategic Peacebuilding in South Sudan." *Journal of Catholic Social Thought* 10, no. 1 (2013): 47–67.

Ashworth, John, Haruun Lual Ruun, Emmanuel LoWilla, and Maura Ryan. *The Voice of the Voiceless: The Role of the Church in the Sudanese Civil War, 1983–2005*. Nairobi: Paulines Publications Africa, 2014.

Bartolomei, Linda, Eileen Pittaway, and Elizabeth Pittaway. "Who Am I? Identity and Citizenship in Kakuma Refugee Camp in Northern Kenya." *Development* 46, no. 3 (2003): 87–93.

Beidelman, Thomas O. *Colonial Evangelism: A Socio-Historical Study of an East African Mission at the Grassroots.* Bloomington: Indiana University Press, 1982.

Berger, Carol. "Southern Sudan's Red Army: The Role of Social Process and Routinised Violence in the Deployment of Underaged Soldiers." D.Phil. dissertation, Oxford University, 2010.

Biowel, Philip Chol. "The Christian Church in the Southern Sudan before 1900." In *Southern Sudan: Regionalism and Religion*, ed. Mohamed Omer Beshir, 205–23. Khartoum, Sudan: Graduate College Publications, 1984.

Bixler, Mark. *The Lost Boys of Sudan: An American Story of the Refugee Experience.* Athens: University of Georgia Press, 2005.

Blenkinsopp, Joseph. *Isaiah 1–39: A New Translation with Introduction and Commentary.* New Haven: Yale University Press, 2000.

Bol Deng, Bartholomayo. "Different Routes, but One God: Dialogue Between Muslims and Christians in Sudan in the Postwar Era." M.T.S. thesis, Virginia Theological Seminary, 2006.

Brown, Elijah M. "The Road to Peace: The Role of the Southern Sudanese Church in Communal Stabilisation and National Resolution." Ph.D. dissertation, University of Edinburgh, 2008.

Brueggemann, Walter. *Isaiah 1–39.* Louisville: Westminster John Knox, 1998.

Burr, J. Millard, and Robert O. Collins. *Requiem for the Sudan: War, Drought, and Disaster Relief on the Nile.* Oxford: Westview, 1995.

Burton, John W. "Christians, Colonists, and Conversion: A View from the Nilotic Sudan." *The Journal of Modern African Studies* 23, no. 2 (1985): 349–69.

———. "When the North Winds Blow: A Note on Small Towns and Social Transformation in the Nilotic Sudan." *African Studies Review* 31, no. 3 (1988): 49–60.

Cabrita, Joel. *Text and Authority in the South African Nazaretha Church.* Cambridge: Cambridge University Press, 2014.

Campbell, James T. *Songs of Zion: The African Methodist Episcopal Church in the United States and in South Africa.* New York: Oxford University Press, 1995.

Collins, Robert O. *The Southern Sudan, 1883–1898: A Struggle for Control.* New Haven: Yale University Press, 1962.

———. *Land beyond the Rivers: The Southern Sudan, 1898–1918.* New Haven: Yale University Press, 1971.

———. *Shadows in the Grass: Britain in the Southern Sudan, 1918–1956.* New Haven: Yale University Press, 1983.

———. *The Southern Sudan in Historical Perspective*. London: Transaction, 2006 [1975].
Copnall, James. *A Poisonous Thorn in Our Hearts: Sudan and South Sudan's Bitter and Incomplete Divorce*. London: Hurst, 2014.
Cormack, Don. *Killing Fields, Living Fields: An Unfinished Portrait of the Cambodian Church—the Church That Would Not Die*. Crowborough, UK: OMF International, 1997.
Cormack, Zoe. "The Making and Remaking of Gogrial: Landscape, History and Memory in South Sudan." Ph.D. dissertation, Durham University, 2014.
Crisp, Jeff. "A State of Insecurity: The Political Economy of Violence in Kenya's Refugee Camps." *African Affairs* 99 (2000): 601–32.
Daly, M. W. *Empire on the Nile: The Anglo-Eyptian Sudan, 1898–1934*. Cambridge: Cambridge University Press, 1986.
Dau, Isaiah Majok. *Suffering and God: A Theological Reflection on the War in Sudan*. Nairobi: Paulines Publications Africa, 2002.
———. *Free at Last: South Sudan Independence and the Role of the Church*. Kijabe, Kenya: Kijabe, 2011.
de Saram, Brian. *Nile Harvest: The Anglican Church in Egypt and the Sudan*. Bournemouth, UK: Bourne, 1992.
Dellagiacoma, V. *History of the Catholic Church in Southern Sudan 1900–1995*. Khartoum, Sudan: n.p., 1996.
Deng, Francis Mading. *The Dinka of the Sudan*. Long Grove, Ill.: Waveland, 1984/1972.
———. *The Dinka and Their Songs*. Oxford: Clarendon, 1973.
———. *Dinka Folktales: African Stories from the Sudan*. New York: African Publishing Company, 1974.
———. "Dinka Response to Christianity: The Pursuit of Well-Being in a Developing Society." In *Vernacular Christianity: Essays in the Social Anthropology of Religion Presented to Godfrey Lienhardt*, ed. Wendy James and Douglas H. Johnson, 157–69. Oxford: JASO, 1988.
———. "Scramble for Souls: Religious Intervention among the Dinka in Sudan." In *Proselytization and Communal Self-Determination in Africa*, ed. Abdullahi Ahmed An-Na'im, 191–227. Maryknoll, N.Y.: Orbis, 1999.
———. "The World of the Dinka: A Portrait of a Threatened Culture." In *Traditions, Values, and Humanitarian Action*, ed. Kevin M. Cahill, 53–82. New York: Fordham University Press and the Center for International Health and Cooperation, 2003.
Donovan, Vincent J. *Christianity Rediscovered*. Maryknoll, N.Y.: Orbis, 2003/1978.
Drønen, Tomas Sundnes. *Communication and Conversion in Northern Cameroon: The Dii People and Norwegian Missionaries, 1934–1960*. Leiden: Brill, 2009.

Duncan, Julianne. "Sudanese 'Lost Boys in the United States: Adjustment after Six Months." Washington, D.C.: United States Catholic Conference/Migration and Refugee Services, 2001. http://www.brycs.org/documents/upload/lostboys.pdf. Accessed 27 November 2017.
Eshete, Tibebe. *The Evangelical Movement in Ethiopia: Resistance and Resilience*. Waco, Tex.: Baylor University Press, 2009.
Etherington, Norman. "Outward and Visible Signs of Conversion in Nineteenth-Century KwaZulu-Natal." *Journal of Religion in Africa* 32, no. 4 (2002): 422–39.
Evans-Pritchard, E. E. *The Nuer: A Description of the Modes of Livelihood and Political Institutions of a Nilotic People*. Oxford: Clarendon, 1940.
———. *Nuer Religion*. New York: Oxford University Press, 1956.
Falge, Christiane. "Countering Rupture: Young Nuer in New Religious Movements." *Sociologus* 58, no. 2 (2008): 169–95.
Fea, John. *The Bible Cause: A History of the American Bible Society*. Oxford: Oxford University Press, 2016.
Fergusson, V. H. "The Holy Lake of the Dinka." *Sudan Notes and Records* 5, no. 2 (1922): 163–66.
Fisher, Humphrey J. "Conversion Reconsidered: Some Historical Aspects of Religious Conversion in Black Africa." *Africa* 43, no. 1 (1973): 27–40.
Fortes, M., and E. E. Evans-Pritchard. "Introduction." In *African Political Systems*, ed. M. Fortes and E. E. Evans-Pritchard, 1–23. London: International African Institute by Oxford University Press, 1940.
Garrard-Burnett, Virginia. *Protestantism in Guatemala: Living in the New Jerusalem*. Austin: University of Texas Press, 1998.
Good News Bible: Today's English Version. First British usage edition. The Bible Societies, 1976.
Goździak, Elżbieta M., and Dianna J. Shandy. "Editorial Introduction: Religion and Spiritual in Forced Migration." *Journal of Refugee Studies* 15, no. 2 (2002): 129–35.
Gray, Richard. *A History of the Southern Sudan, 1839–1889*. Oxford: Oxford University Press, 1961.
———. *Black Christians and White Missionaries*. New Haven: Yale University Press, 1990.
Gunner, Elizabeth. *The Man of Heaven and the Beautiful Ones of God: Writings from Ibandla lamaNazaretha, a South African Church*. Leiden: Brill, 2002.
Harris, Lillian Craig. *In Joy and in Sorrow: Travels among Sudanese Christians*. Nairobi, Kenya: Paulines Publications Africa, 1999.
———. *Keeping the Faith: Travels with Sudanese Women*. Nairobi: Paulines Publications Africa, 1999.
Hastings, Adrian. *African Christianity: An Essay in Interpretation*. London: Geoffrey Chapman, 1976.

———. *The Church in Africa, 1450–1950*. Oxford: Clarendon, 1994.
Hecht, Joan. *The Journey of the Lost Boys*. Jacksonville, Fla.: Allswell, 2005.
Hefner, Robert W., ed. *Conversion to Christianity: Historical and Anthropological Perspectives on a Great Transformation*. Berkeley: University of California Press, 1993.
Hewitt, Gordon. *The Problems of Success: A History of the Church Missionary Society, 1910–1942*. London: SCM, 1971.
Hill, Richard. "The Gordon Literature." *The Durham University Journal* 47, no. 3 (June 1955): 97–103.
Hodgson, Dorothy L. "Pastoralism, Patriarchy and History: Changing Gender Relations among Maasai in Tanganyika, 1890–1940." *The Journal of African History* 40, no. 1 (1999): 41–65.
———. *The Church of Women: Gendered Encounters between Maasai and Missionaries*. Bloomington: Indiana University Press, 2005.
Holton, M. Jan. *Building the Resilient Community: Lessons from the Lost Boys of Sudan*. Eugene, Ore.: Cascade, 2011.
Horton, Robin. "A Hundred Years of Change in Kalabari Religion." In *Black Africa: Its People and Their Cultures Today*, ed. John Middleton, 192–211. London: Macmillan, 1970.
———. "African Conversion." *Africa* 41, no. 2 (1971): 85–108.
———. "On the Rationality of Conversion." *Africa* 45, no. 3 (1975): 219–35.
Horton, Robin, and J. D. Y. Peel. "Conversion and Confusion: A Rejoinder on Christianity in Eastern Nigeria." *Canadian Journal of African Studies* 10, no. 3 (1976): 481–98.
Howell, Paul, and Andrew Mawson. "Society and Rural Economy in the Jonglei Area." In *The Jonglei Canal: Impact and Opportunity*, ed. Paul Howell, Michael Lock, and Stephen Cobb, 225–50. Cambridge: Cambridge University Press, 1988.
Howell, Paul, Andrew Mawson, and Sjöerd Zanen. "Recent Change among the Nuer and Dinka Peoples of the Jonglei Area." In *The Jonglei Canal: Impact and Opportunity*, ed. Paul Howell, Michael Lock, and Stephen Cobb, 251–76. Cambridge: Cambridge University Press, 1988.
Human Rights Watch. *Behind the Red Line: Political Repression in Sudan*. London: Human Rights Watch, 1996.
Human Rights Watch / Africa. *Civilian Devastation: Abuses by All Parties in the War in Southern Sudan*. New York: Human Rights Watch, 1994.
———. "The Lost Boys: Child Soldiers and Unaccompanied Boys in Southern Sudan." New York: Human Rights Watch, 1994.
Hutchinson, Sharon E. "Prophecies of War and Peace." *The Times Literary Supplement*, 2 June 1995 (4809): 8.
———. *Nuer Dilemmas: Coping with Money, War, and the State*. Berkeley: University of California Press, 1996.

———. "Nuer Ethnicity Militarized." *Anthropology Today* 16, no. 3 (2000): 6–13.

———. "A Curse from God? Religious and Political Dimensions of the Post-1991 Rise of Ethnic Violence in South Sudan." *The Journal of Modern African Studies* 39, no. 2 (2001): 307–31.

———. "Spiritual Fragments of an Unfinished War." In *Religion and African Civil Wars*, ed. Niels Kastfelt, 28–53. London: Hurst, 2005.

———. "'Food Itself Is Fighting with Us': A Comparative Analysis of the Impact of Sudan's Civil War on South Sudanese Civilian Populations Located in the North and the South." In *Violence and Belonging: The Quest for Identity in Post-colonial Africa*, ed. Vigdis Broch-Due, 131–52. London: Routledge, 2005.

———. "Uncertain Ethics: Researching Civil War in Sudan." In *Researching Violence in Africa: Ethical and Methodological Challenges*, ed. Christopher Cramer, Laura Hammond, and Johan Potter, 79–94. Leiden: Brill, 2011.

Hutchinson, Sharon E., and Naomi R. Pendle. "Violence, Legitimacy, and Prophecy: Nuer Struggles with Uncertainty in South Sudan," *American Ethnologist* 42, no. 3 (2015): 415–30.

Ifeka-Moller. "White Power: Social-Structural Factors in Conversion to Christianity, Eastern Nigeria, 1921–1966." *Canadian Journal of African Studies* 8, no. 1 (1974): 55–72.

Iliffe, John. *Africans: The History of a Continent*. 2nd ed. Cambridge: Cambridge University Press, 2007/1995.

Jackson, H. C. *Pastor on the Nile: Being Some Account of the Life and Letters of Llewellyn H. Gwynne, C.M.G., C.B.E., D.D., LL.D., Formerly Bishop in Egypt and the Sudan and Deputy Chaplain-General in France in the First World War*. London: SPCK, 1960.

James, Wendy. *'Kwanim Pa: The Making of the Uduk People*. Oxford: Clarendon, 1979.

———. "Uduk Faith in a Five-note Scale: Mission Music and the Spread of the Gospel." In *Vernacular Christianity: Essays in the Social Anthropology of Religion Presented to Godfrey Lienhardt*, ed. Wendy James and Douglas H. Johnson, 131–45. Oxford: JASO, 1988.

———. *War and Survival in Sudan's Frontierlands: Voices from the Blue Nile*. Oxford: Oxford University Press, 2007.

Johnson, Douglas H. "Divinity Abroad: Dinka Missionaries in Foreign Lands." In *Vernacular Christianity: Essays in the Social Anthropology of Religion Presented to Godfrey Lienhardt*, ed. Wendy James and Douglas H. Johnson, 170–82. Oxford: JASO, 1988.

———. "Enforcing Separate Identities in the Southern Sudan: The Case of the Nilotes of the Upper Nile." In *Les ethnies ont une histoire*, ed. Jean-Pierre Chrétien and Gérard Prunier, 235–45. Paris: Karthala, 1989.

———. *Nuer Prophets: A History of Prophecy from the Upper Nile in the Nineteenth and Twentieth Centuries.* Oxford: Clarendon, 1994.

———. "Increasing the Trauma of Return: An Assessment of the UN's Emergency Response to the Evacuation of the Sudanese Refugee Camps in Ethiopia, 1991." In *In Search of Cool Ground: War, Flight and Homecoming in Northeast Africa*, ed. Tim Allen, 171–81. London: UNRISD/James Currey, 1996.

———. *The Root Causes of Sudan's Civil Wars.* Rev. ed. Oxford: James Currey, 2011/2003.

Johnson, Douglas H., and David M. Anderson. "Revealing Prophets." In *Revealing Prophets: Prophecy in Eastern African History*, ed. David M. Anderson and Douglas H. Johnson, 1–26. London: James Currey, 1995.

Johnson, Douglas H., and Gerard Prunier. "The Foundation and Expansion of the Sudan People's Liberation Army." In *Civil War in the Sudan*, ed. M. W. Daly and Ahmad Alawad Sikainga, 117–41. London: British Academic Press, 1993.

Jok, Jok Madut. *Militarization, Gender and Reproductive Health in South Sudan.* Lampeter, UK: Edwin Mellen, 1998.

Jok, Jok Madut, and Sharon Elaine Hutchinson. "Sudan's Prolonged Civil War and the Militarization of Nuer and Dinka Ethnic Identities." *African Studies Review* 42, no. 2 (1999): 125–45.

Kayanga, Samuel E., and Andrew Wheeler, ed. *"But God Is Not Defeated!" Celebrating the Centenary of The Episcopal Church of the Sudan.* Nairobi: Paulines Publications Africa, 1999.

Kelly, Raymond C. *The Nuer Conquest: The Structure and Development of an Expansionist System.* Ann Arbor: University of Michigan Press, 1985.

Lako, George Tombe. "The Impact of the Jonglei Scheme on the Economy of the Dinka." *African Affairs* 84, no. 334 (1985): 15–38.

LeMarquand, Grant. "'Faith in Sudan': Recent Work on the History and Theology of Christianity in the Sudan." *Anglican and Episcopal History* 71, no. 2 (2002): 247–60.

LeRiche, Matthew, and Matthew Arnold. *South Sudan: From Revolution to Independence.* New York: Columbia University Press, 2012.

Leonardi, Cherry. *Dealing with Government in South Sudan: Histories of Chiefship, Community and State.* Woodbridge, UK: James Currey, 2013.

Lienhardt, Godfrey. "The Western Dinka." In *Tribes Without Rulers: Studies in African Segmentary Systems*, ed. John Middleton and David Tait, 97–135. London: Routledge and Kegan Paul, 1958.

———. *Divinity and Experience: The Religion of the Dinka.* Oxford: Clarendon, 1961.

———. "Morality and Happiness among the Dinka." In *Religion and Morality: A Collection of Essays*, ed. Gene Outka and John P. Reeder Jr., 108–22. New York: Anchor, 1973.

———. "The Dinka and Catholicism." In *Religious Organization and Religious Experience*, ed. J. Davis, 81–95. New York: Academic Press, 1982.

Lo Polito, Nicola. "The Verona Fathers in Southern Sudan from 1899 to 1964: A Contribution to the Understanding of the Historical and Religious Roots of the Conflict between North and South in the Sudan, and the Role Played in It by the Verona Fathers and Brothers," M.A. dissertation, Catholic Theological Union at Chicago, 1986.

Lubkemann, Stephen. *Culture in Chaos: An Anthropology of the Social Condition in War*. London: University of Chicago Press, 2008.

Maglad, Nour El-Din Ahmed. "An Empirical Analysis of Rural-Urban Migration in the Sudan," *Sudan Notes and Records* 64 (1983): 53–61.

Majok, Damazo Dutt. "British Religious and Educational Policy: The Case of Bahr el-Ghazal." In *Southern Sudan: Regionalism and Religion*, ed. Mohamed Omer Beshir, 224–40. Khartoum, Sudan: Graduate College Publications, 1984.

Malou, Job. *Dinka Vowel System*. Dallas: Summer Institute of Linguistics, 1988.

Malou Ater, John. "The Dinka Priesthood: A Study against the Background of Native Religious Belief and Cult, Leading to a Comparison with Biblical Concepts of Priesthood, and an Evaluation of Missionary Strategies." M.A. dissertation, Near East School of Theology, 1976.

Mawson, Andrew Nicholas Mirehouse. "The Triumph of Life: Political Dispute and Religious Ceremonial among the Agar Dinka of Southern Sudan." Ph.D. dissertation, Cambridge University, 1989.

———. "'Bringing What People Want': Shrine Politics among the Agar Dinka." *Africa* 61, no. 3 (1991): 354–69.

Mawut, Lazarus Leek. *Dinka Resistance to Condominium Rule 1902–1932*. Khartoum, Sudan: University of Khartoum Graduate College Publications, 1983.

Maxwell, David. *Christians and Chiefs in Zimbabwe: A Social History of the Hwesa People c. 1870s–1990s*. London: Edinburgh University Press, 1999.

———. "Historicizing Christian Independency: The Southern African Pentecostal Movement c. 1908–60." *Journal of African History* 40 (1999): 243–64.

———. "Christianity." In *The Oxford Handbook of Modern African History*, ed. John Parker and Richard Reid, 263–80. Oxford: Oxford University Press, 2013.

Mayen, Nathaniel Athian Deng. *Christian Faith among the Jieeng: The Shift in Values, the Stages of Faith, and the Cultural and Religious Experiences of Jieeng Believers in the Episcopal Diocese of Bor*. Denver: Outskirts, 2015.

Metzger, Bruce M., and Michael D. Coogan, ed. *The Oxford Companion to the Bible*. Oxford: Oxford University Press, 1993.

Meyer, Birgit. *Translating the Devil: Religion and Modernity among the Ewe in Ghana*. Edinburgh: Edinburgh University Press for the International African Institute, 1999.

Muhindi, Martin Masumbuko, and Kiganzi Nyakato. "Integration of the Sudanese 'Lost Boys' in Boston, Massachusetts, USA, 2002." https://cis.mit.edu/sites/default/files/documents/IntegrationOfTheSudaneseLostBoys.pdf. Accessed 29 January 2018.

Newcomer, Peter J. "The Nuer Are Dinka: An Essay on Origins and Environmental Determinism." *Man* 7, no. 1 (1972): 5–11.

Nikkel, Marc. "The Outcast, the Stranger, and the Enemy in Dinka Tradition Contrasted with Attitudes of Contemporary Dinka Christians." S.T.M. thesis, The General Theological Seminary, 1988.

———. "Aspects of Contemporary Religious Change among the Dinka." *Journal of Religion in Africa* 22, no. 1 (February 1992): 78–94.

———. "The Cross of Bor Dinka Christians: A Working Christology in Face of Displacement and Death." *Studies in World Christianity* 1, no. 2 (1996): 160–85.

———. "The Cross as a Symbol of Regeneration in Jieng Bor Society." In *Land of Promise: Church Growth in a Sudan at War*, ed. Andrew C. Wheeler, 86–114. Nairobi: Paulines Publications Africa, 1997.

———. "'Children of Our Fathers' Divinities' or 'Children of Red Foreigners'? Themes in Missionary History and the Rise of an Indigenous Church among the Jieng Bor of Southern Sudan." In *Land of Promise: Church Growth in a Sudan at War*, ed. Andrew C. Wheeler, 61–78. Nairobi: Paulines Publications Africa, 1997.

———. "Songs of Hope and Lamentation from Sudan's 'Unaccompanied Minors.'" *Sewanee Theological Review* 40, no. 4 (1997): 486–98.

———. "Archibald Shaw 'Machuor': 'The Only White Man with the Heart of the Jieng.'" In *Gateway to the Heart of Africa: Missionary Pioneers in Sudan*, ed. Francesco Pierli, Maria Teresa Ratti, and Andrew C. Wheeler, 102–25. Nairobi: Paulines Publications Africa, 1998.

———. "Death Has Come to Reveal the Faith: Spirituality in the Episcopal Church of the Sudan amidst Civil Conflict." In *Anglicanism: A Global Communion*, ed. Andrew Wingate, Kevin Ward, Carrie Pemberton, and Wilson Sitshebo, 73–78. London: Mowbray, 1998.

———. "ECS Worship and Music: Isolation and Innovation." In *"But God Is Not Defeated!" Celebrating the Centenary of the Episcopal Church of the Sudan 1899–1999*, ed. Samuel E. Kayanga and Andrew C. Wheeler, 137–48. Nairobi: Paulines Publications Africa, 1999.

———. *Dinka Christianity: The Origins and Development of Christianity among the Dinka of Sudan, with Special Reference to the Songs of Dinka Christians*. Nairobi: Paulines Publications Africa, 2001.

———. "Jieng 'Songs of Suffering' and the Nature of God." *Anglican and Episcopal History* 71, no. 2 (2002): 223–40.

———. "Christian Conversion among the Jieng Bor." In *Religion and Conflict in Sudan: Papers from an International Conference at Yale, May 1999*, ed. Yusuf Fadl Hasan and Richard Gray, 162–68. Nairobi: Paulines Publications Africa, 2002.

Ossome, Marilyn. "Abduction, Confinement and Sexual Violence against South Sudanese Women and Girls in Kakuma Refugee Camp, Kenya." In *After the Comprehensive Peace Agreement in Sudan*, ed. Elke Grawert, 158–75. Woodbridge, UK: James Currey, 2010.

Peel, J. D. Y. *Aladura: A Religious Movement among the Yoruba*. Oxford: Oxford University Press for the International African Institute, 1968.

———. "Syncretism and Religious Change." *Comparative Studies in Society and History* 10, no. 2 (1968): 121–41.

———. "Conversion and Tradition in Two African Societies: Ijebu and Buganda." *Past & Present* 77 (1977): 108–41.

———. "The Christianization of African Society: Some Possible Models." In *Christianity in Independent Africa*, ed. Edward Fasholé-Luke, Richard Gray, Adrian Hastings, and Godwin Tasle, 443–54. London: Rex Collings, 1978.

———. "For Who Hath Despised the Day of Small Things? Missionary Narratives and Historical Anthropology." *Comparative Studies in Society and History* 37, no. 3 (1995): 581–607.

———. *Religious Encounter and the Making of the Yoruba*. Bloomington: Indiana University Press, 2000.

———. "Postsocialism, Postcolonialism, Pentecostalism." In *Conversion after Socialism: Disruptions, Modernisms and Technologies of Faith in the Former Soviet Union*, ed. Mathijs Pelkmans, 183–200. Oxford: Berghahn, 2009.

Perlez, Jane. "Children Recruited as Manpower Pool." *New York Times*. 14 August 1991.

Peterson, Derek. *Ethnic Patriotism and the East African Revival: A History of Dissent, c. 1935–1972*. Cambridge: Cambridge University Press, 2012.

Pitya, Philip Legge. "History of Western Christian Evangelism in the Sudan, 1898–1964." Ph.D. dissertation, Boston University, 1996.

Pobee, John. "Let Ethiopia Hasten to Stretch Out Its Hands to God." *Ecumenical Review* 49, no. 4 (1997): 416–26.

Ranger, Terence. "Christian Independency in Tanzania." In *African Initiatives in Religion*, ed. David R. Barrett, 122–45. Nairobi: East African Publishing House, 1971.

———. "Religious Movements and Politics in Sub-Saharan Africa." *African Studies Review* 29, no 2 (1986): 1–69.

———. "Religion, Development and African Christian Identity." In *Religion, Development and African Identity*, ed. Kirsten Holst Petersen. Uppsala, Sweden: Scandinavian Institute of African Studies, 1987.

———. "Taking Hold of the Land: Holy Places and Pilgrimage in Twentieth-Century Zimbabwe." *Past & Present* 117 (1987): 158–94.

———. "The Local and the Global in Southern African Religious History." In *Conversion to Christianity: Historical and Anthropological Perspectives on a Great Transformation*, ed. Robert W. Hefner, 65–98. Berkeley: University of California Press, 1993.

———. "New Approaches to the History of Mission Christianity." In *African Historiography: Essays in Honour of Jacob Ade Ajayi*, ed. Toyin Falola, 180–94. Harlow, UK: Longman, 1993.

Rigby, Peter. "Pastors and Pastoralists: The Differential Penetration of Christianity among East African Cattle Herders." *Comparative Studies in Society and History* 23, no 1 (1981): 96–129.

———. *Persistent Pastoralists: Nomadic Societies in Transition*. London: Zed, 1985.

Robbins, Joel. *Becoming Sinners: Christianity and Moral Torment in a Papua New Guinea Society*. Berkeley: University of California Press, 2004.

———. "Continuity Thinking and the Problem of Christian Culture: Belief, Time, and the Anthropology of Christianity." *Current Anthropology* 48, no. 1 (2007): 5–38.

Rolandsen, Øystein H. *Guerrilla Government: Political Changes in the Southern Sudan during the 1990s*. Sweden: Nordiska Afrikainstitutet, 2005.

Ruler, Sheila. "Refugees from Sudan Strain Ethiopia Camps." *New York Times*. 1 May 1988.

Sanderson, Lilian Passmore, and Neville Sanderson. *Education, Religion and Politics in Southern Sudan 1899–1964*. London: Ithaca, 1981.

Shandy, Dianna J. "Nuer Christians in America." *Journal of Refugee Studies* 15, no. 2 (2002): 213–21.

Schoffeleers, Matthew. "Ritual Healing and Political Acquiescence: The Case of the Zionist Churches in South Africa." *Africa* 60, no. 1 (1991): 1–25.

Scott-Villiers, Alastair and Patta, and Cole P. Dodge. "Repatriation of Sudanese Refugees from Ethiopia: A Case Study in the Manipulation of Civilians during Civil Conflict." *Refuge* 14, no. 1 (1994): 19–25.

Scroggins, Deborah. *Emma's War: Love, Betrayal and Death in the Sudan*. London: HarperCollins, 2003.

Seligman, C. G., and Brenda Z. Seligman. *Pagan Tribes of the Nilotic Sudan*. London: Routledge, 1932.

Stearns, Jason K. *Dancing in the Glory of Monsters: The Collapse of the Congo and the Great War of Africa*. New York: Public Affairs, 2011.

Stone, Lydia. "'We Were All Soldiers': Female Combatants in South Sudan's Civil War." In *Hope, Pain and Patience: The Lives of Women in South*

Sudan, ed. Friederike Bubenzer and Orly Stern, 25–52. Johannesburg: Fanele, 2011.

Sundkler, Bengt G. M. *Bantu Prophets in South Africa*. 2nd ed. Oxford: Oxford University Press, 1961.

———. "African Church History in a New Key." In *Religion, Development and African Identity*, ed. Kirsten Holst Petersen, 73–84. Uppsala, Sweden: Scandinavian Institute of African Studies, 1987.

Thomas, Edward. *South Sudan: A Slow Liberation*. London: Zed, 2015.

Titherington, G. W. "The Raik Dinka of Bahr El Ghazal Province." *Sudan Notes and Records* 10 (1927): 159–210.

Tvedt, Terje. "The Collapse of the State in Southern Sudan after the Addis Ababa Agreement: A Study of Internal Causes and the Role of the NGOs." In *Short-Cut to Decay: The Case of the Sudan*, ed. Sharif Harir and Terje Tvedt, 69–104. Uppsala, Sweden: Nordiska Afrikainstitutet, 1994.

Twose, Nigel, and Benjamin Pogrund, eds. *War Wounds: Development Costs of Conflict in Southern Sudan*. London: The Panos Institute, 1988.

Tuttle, Brendan R. "Life Is Prickly: Narrating History, Belonging, and Common Place in Bor, South Sudan." Ph.D. dissertation, Temple University, 2013.

Ubbens, Lilly R. Sanders. "Chasing after the Cross: The Early Life of Rev. John Chol Daau." M.A. thesis, Trinity School for Ministry, 2011.

Verdirame, Guglielmo. "Human Rights and Refugees: The Case of Kenya." *Journal of Refugee Studies* 12, no. 1 (1999): 54–77.

Waller, Richard. "They Do the Dictating and We Must Submit: The Africa Inland Mission in Maasailand." In *East African Expressions of Christianity*, ed. Thomas Spear and Isaria N. Kimambo, 83–126. Oxford: James Currey, 1999.

Ward, Kevin. "Africa." In *A World History of Christianity*, ed. Adrian Hastings, 192–237. London: Cassell, 1999.

———. *A History of Global Anglicanism*. Cambridge: Cambridge University Press, 2006.

———. "The Church of Uganda amidst Conflict: The Interplay between Church and Politics in Uganda since 1962." In *Religion and Politics in East Africa: The Period Since Independence*, ed. Holger Bernt Hansen and Michael Twaddle, 72–105. London: James Currey, 1995.

Werner, Roland, William Anderson, and Andrew Wheeler, eds. *Day of Devastation, Day of Contentment: The History of the Sudanese Church across 2000 Years*. Nairobi, Kenya: Paulines Publications Africa, 2000.

Wheeler, Andrew C. "Church Growth in Southern Sudan, 1983–1996: A Survey of Present Understanding." In *Land of Promise: Church Growth in a Sudan at War*, ed. Andrew C. Wheeler, 11–38. Nairobi: Paulines Publications Africa, 1997.

———. "'Can You Announce the Darkness after You Have Seen the Light?' Catholic Catechists' Achievement in Upper Nile 1970–1996." In *Announcing the Light: Sudanese Witnesses to the Gospel*, ed. Andrew C. Wheeler, 161–79. Nairobi: Paulines Publications Africa, 1998.

———. "From Mission to Church in an Islamizing State: The Case of Sudan, 1946–64." In *Christian Missions and the State in the Third World*, ed. Holger Bernt Hansen and Michael Twaddlem, 284–95. Oxford: James Currey, 2002.

———. "Richard Jones and the Sudan Revival of 1938." *Anglican and Episcopal History* 71, no. 2 (2002): 168–86.

———. "Finding Meaning amid the Chaos: Narratives of Significance in the Sudanese Church." In *Religion and African Civil Wars*, ed. Niels Kastfelt, 54–81. London: Hurst, 2005.

Wild-Wood, Emma. *Migration and Christian Identity in Congo (DRC)*. Leiden: Brill, 2008.

———. "Attending to Translocal Identities: How Congolese Anglicans Talk about Their Church." *Journal of Anglican Studies* 9, no. 1 (2011): 80–99.

———. "Powerful Words: Reading the Diary of a Ganda Priest." *Studies in World Christianity* 18, no. 2 (2012): 134–53.

Willis, Justin. "Who Put the 'Y' in the BYDA? Youth in Sudan's Civil Wars." In *Africa's Young Majority*, ed. Barbara Trudell et al., 91–111. Edinburgh: Centre of African Studies, University of Edinburgh, 2002.

Wilson, K. B. "Refugees and Returnees as Social Agents: The Case of the Jehovah's Witnesses from Milange." In *When Refugees Go Home: African Experiences*, ed. Tim Allen and Hubert Morsink, 237–50. Trenton, N.J.: Africa World Press, 1994.

Wooldridge, Mike. "Why They Fled." In *War Wounds: Development Costs of Conflict in Southern Sudan*, ed. Nigel Twose and Benjamin Pogrund, 139–42. London: Panos Institute, 1988.

Wycliffe Bible Translators. *Ethnologue: Languages of the World*. 17th ed. http://www.ethnologue.com/. Accessed 27 November 2017.

Zetter, Roger. "Labelling Refugees: Forming and Transforming a Bureaucratic Identity." *Journal of Refugee Studies* 4, no. 1 (1991): 39–62.

Journals Consulted in Entirety

Our African Missions: A Magazine of the Congregation of the Sons of the Sacred Heart
Sudan Diocesan Review (later *Sudan Church Review*)
Sudan Monthly Record
Sudan Notes and Records
Southern Sudan Mail Bag

Index

Aboi Ajith, Gordon, 191
Abyei, 13, 66
Achol Deng, Mary, xiii, 135, 136, 138, 141, 144, 145, 158, 193n8
Acts of the Apostles, 196, 210
Addis Ababa Agreement, 47–48, 60–61
Adhar Arop, Victoria, 141
age sets, 74, 108, 182, 223
Akol Gak, Joseph, 53
Akot, 22, 26, 37, 41, 44, 140, 146, 177, 205, 206
Akot revival, 30–33, 38, 80, 135
Akuek Makuac, Doruka, 148–49
Akurdit Ngong, Rueben, xiv, 147, 187, 188, 194, 195, 196
Alier, Abel, 25
Allison, Oliver, 42
Alueel Garang Nongdit, Mary, 54, 62, 135, 148–52, 155, 225
Anglican church, 9, 12, 28, 35, 43, 45, 55–56, 65, 68, 73, 87, 98, 109, 126, 130, 134, 146, 147, 150, 183, 185, 219–20, 224n8; *see also* Episcopal Church of the Sudan

Anglican Church of South Sudan, 220
Anglican Communion, 2, 55, 219–20
Anglican identity, 176, 178, 185, 219–21; as basis for appeals for assistance, 109, 178, 221; importance in church conflict, 183, 219–20
Anglican mission, 8, 22, 23, 29, 41, 221; *see also* Church Missionary Society
Anglicanism, 9, 78, 85–87, 183, 220–21; *see also* Dinka Anglicanism
Anglo-Egyptian Condominium, 25, 30, 37, 71, 97, 130, 207, 214, 217, 220; missionary sphere system, 23–24; pacification campaigns, 21–22; subsidies to missionary organizations, 26, 29, 36
Anyidi, 49
Ariandhit, 22, 165, 180n53, 203
Aruay Majak, Mary, 67n17, 68n22, 88, 139–40, 150, 152

Aruor, Jon, 28
Awan de Gak, Amos, 40
Aweil, 13, 23, 63, 66, 125–30, 163
Awerial, 48
Ayup, Daniel, 31, 146, 149

Babylon, 169
Bai, Ater, 31, 146
Baidit, 37, 192, 197
baptism, 32, 38, 39, 48, 60, 67–68, 74, 75, 92, 109–10, 113, 119, 126, 130, 133, 137, 180, 187–88, 191, 196–97, 202, 230; difficulty women confronted in preparing for, 28, 54–55, 135; dispute over in west bank church, 78–79, 183; prompted by dreams, 78, 191; as protection from *jak*, 77, 154, 191–92; requirements for, 6, 28, 32, 52, 54–55, 78–81, 86, 129, 137, 184
Barac Mabior, Khedekia, 52–53, 55, 63, 64, 78, 80–81, 135, 187
bëny bith, 18, 82
Bible, 9, 24, 28, 55, 64, 67, 68, 71–72, 76, 107–8, 115, 118, 121, 122, 153, 157, 163, 166–75, 195–96, 205, 209; teaching of, 43–45, 55, 104, 205–6, 210–11
Bishop Gwynne College, 38, 44, 52–53, 64, 87, 104, 147, 187, 210, 227, 232
Bol, Alier, 181
Bol, Santino, 126
Bol Arok, Peter, 109–10
Bor, Dinka dialect, 32, 53, 147, 166, 166n8
Bor, Diocese of, xxiv, 1, 63, 84, 84n67, 85n68, 120, 129, 140, 147, 177, 232
"Bor Massacre," 92–94, 113, 197–98, 201–2, 215, 222

Bor, town of, 1, 3, 12, 23, 40–41, 45–47, 50, 55, 57, 60–63, 78, 92, 99, 115, 150, 162, 168, 177, 183, 187–89, 194, 197–98, 200–203, 225; Anglican congregation in, 46, 53–55, 61, 187–88; in colonial period, 21, 25, 29, 36; in second civil war, 1, 61, 65, 187, 194, 197, 200
Bullen, Guy, 48, 176
Bung de Diɛt ke Duɔ̈ɔ̈r, 122, 128, 134, 145–48, 151

Carey, George, 90, 120
cattle camps, 11, 12, 15, 17, 26, 32, 35, 38–39, 42–43, 46, 49–50, 54, 56–57, 61–62, 66, 75, 88, 94, 108, 111, 120, 131, 135, 140, 145–46, 179–80, 189, 205, 214–15, 217, 223; *see also wut*
chiefs (community leaders), 37, 59, 70, 199, 215
Christianity, 2, 5–12, 21, 27–29, 31–33, 40, 45–47, 51, 55, 57, 64, 65, 104, 108, 111–13, 119, 123–25, 127, 130–34, 136–37, 139–42, 145–46, 149–51, 154–55, 157, 161–64, 166, 169–70, 178, 180n53, 181, 182–84, 188–89, 197, 204–5, 218–22, 223–24, 225, 229, 230; and education, 40, 43, 49, 54, 55, 70, 72, 73, 107, 120, 122, 184, 211; opposition to, 56, 81–83, 113, 185; and religious change, 59–60, 62, 68–70, 74, 75–80, 88, 90–94, 172, 174, 187, 197, 205, 208, 212–16; as religious movement, 2, 8, 45, 51, 54, 59, 65, 73, 80, 84–87, 95, 129, 134, 161, 174, 176, 196, 204, 220

Christmas, 70, 74, 105, 200–201, 211–12
Church, Joe, 30
Church Missionary Society (CMS), 9, 11, 22, 23, 25, 27–29, 30–33, 38, 41, 45–46, 48, 52–53, 66, 69, 75, 93, 94, 146, 147, 152–54, 166, 167, 170, 178, 181, 205, 208, 217–19, 222; and baptism, 28, 52, 78–79; and education/literacy, 24, 26, 32–33, 37–39, 43, 44, 64, 72, 184–85, 210; view of by Dinka, 29–30, 176–79, 182
civil war, 1, 3–5, 6–7, 162, 223, 229–30; *see also* Sudan's second civil war
clergy, 38, 41, 44, 45, 55, 57, 66–67, 84–85, 103–4, 119, 127–29, 140, 170, 176, 187–88, 195, 202, 205–6, 210
Collison, John, 30
Comprehensive Peace Agreement (CPA), xxiv, 3, 224, 229
confirmation (church rite), 42, 80, 119, 230
conversion (to Christianity), 3–6, 8, 12, 28, 29, 40, 51, 54, 60, 72–74, 77–78, 86–88, 91–94, 97, 104, 107, 109, 112–13, 124–25, 130–32, 134–37, 139, 153, 157, 160–62, 166, 174, 176, 183, 187–88, 191, 194, 197, 218–19, 223; connection to existing religious beliefs, 27, 81, 111, 131, 154–55, 164, 169, 184, 214–16; connection to music, 107, 118, 130, 149–50; eternal life as reason for, 90, 111; *see also* religious change
cross, 2, 77, 115, 117, 144, 193; as instruments of worship, 76, 85, 143, 162, 212; role in theology, 159–60
Crowther, Samuel Ajayi, 6
Cush, 169, 170, 174–75, 194

Deng, Rudolph, 125
Deng Atong, Daniel, 29–32, 38–39, 41, 46, 52
Deng Bul, Daniel, 43–45
Der, 190–91
Dhiaukuei, 189, 205–15, 223, 229
Diing, Ezekiel, 97–98, 127
Dinka, 1, 2, 6, 9, 51, 54–55, 59–61, 78–79, 82, 84, 92–94, 116, 134, 140, 149, 151, 167, 180–81, 184, 189, 198, 202, 212, 215, 222–23, 227, 229; Agar, xiii, 9, 21, 97, 199; Aliab, 9, 21, 36, 191; belief in life-after-death, 5, 167, 215; Bor (sub-tribe and dialect), xiii, 26, 32, 41, 50, 92, 105, 113, 142, 149–50, 153, 161; and cattle, 14, 15, 18, 19, 20, 25, 36, 49, 50, 51, 54, 136, 168, 187–88, 197, 206, 218, 222; and cattle camps, 11–12, 13n5, 15, 17, 26, 31–32, 35, 38–40, 42–43, 45–46, 49–50, 54, 56–57, 61–62, 66, 75, 77, 88, 94, 100, 108, 111, 120, 131, 135, 145, 146, 179, 180, 187, 189, 202, 205, 212, 213–15, 217; Cic, 9; on east bank of White Nile, 1–2, 9, 17, 20, 23, 32, 36–38, 39, 42, 47, 49, 51, 53–55, 63, 66, 73, 75, 78, 79, 81, 84–85, 92–94, 101, 104, 112, 114, 119, 122, 135, 138, 140–41, 147, 175, 177, 181, 187, 189–90, 192–98, 202–3, 215, 221–22; generational relations, 18, 50, 57, 76, 81, 83,

93, 109, 111, 131, 138; Ghol, 9, 42, 53; governance, 19, 33, 36, 40, 50, 55, 57; importance of birth order, 19, 25 37, 45, 74; migration to north, 42–47; and modernity, 26, 36, 49–50, 57, 90–91, 217, 222; Nyarweng, 9, 42, 53; Padang, xiii, 28, 166n8; Rek, xiii, 97, 125; response to Christian missionaries, 2, 6, 25–27, 29–30, 40, 152–54, 176–85; ritual experts, 18, 25, 57, 82–83, 136; sacrificial practices, 14–15, 17–18 27, 40, 47, 68, 81, 145, 157–61, 199–200, 207; social landscape, 12, 15, 17, 47, 49; traditional religion, 2, 89, 128, 183, 207; Twic, 9, 32, 42, 61, 97; on west bank of White Nile, 2, 9, 15, 17–23, 26, 29, 37, 44, 47n40, 48, 51, 54–55, 57, 59, 63–64, 66, 69–71, 74, 78, 79–80, 85–91, 93–94, 104, 111, 115, 131, 133, 138–41, 149–50, 152, 176–77, 181, 183, 189, 191n4, 194, 203, 205–8, 210–13, 220–21

Dinka Anglicanism, 9, 12, 28, 35, 48, 53, 55, 56, 59, 73, 85–88, 98, 105, 125, 130, 134–35, 150, 166, 185, 187, 192, 218–21, 223–25, 228; distance from church hierarchy, 65, 80, 109, 120; and evangelicalism, 27, 158; ministry in urban areas in north, 43–45, 52; relations with Roman Catholicism, 125–30, 175

Dimma refugee camp, 99, 141

Diocese of Bor: *see* Bor, Diocese of

displacement, 72, 89, 125–26, 145, 197, 213; connection with war and violence, 1–2, 7, 61–62, 64, 72, 84, 88, 94, 98, 100–101, 109, 113–14, 126, 131–32, 208, 215; across international borders, 8, 45–46, 66, 92, 95, 97, 98, 104, 124, 161, 225; parallels seen with biblical experience, 118, 168; within southern Sudan, 46, 61–62, 115, 131n101, 161, 208, 217; *see also* migration

Dit Makok, Stephen, 147, 149

Dongrin Thokriel, Stephen, 205

dreams, 78, 191, 193

Duk Fadiet, 42, 48

Duk Faiwil, 37, 42, 140

East African Revival, 30, 39

Easter, 212

education, 24, 26–28, 36–38, 40, 44, 47–49, 51, 64, 68, 72, 74, 78–79, 82, 94, 98, 101–2, 122, 131, 132, 139, 184–85, 187–88, 206, 214, 217, 218; association with the church, 12, 43, 45, 48, 54–57, 59, 70–73, 80, 93, 107, 111, 112, 124, 208–11, 213, 227; relationship to Christian conversion, 28, 46, 70–73, 91, 95, 105–8, 121, 130, 161, 222; views by Dinka, 25–26, 30, 32, 36–37, 43, 49, 56, 82, 120–21, 123; *see also* Church Missionary Society; literacy; schools

Episcopal Church of the Sudan, xxiv, 55, 63–64, 97, 105, 178, 183, 188, 195–96, 201–2, 204–5, 208, 219–20, 222

Equatoria, 30, 38, 41, 45, 63, 217

Ethiopia, xxiii, 3, 61, 64, 66, 79,

97–105, 107–9, 111–15, 118–21, 124–26, 128, 130, 132, 138, 141–42, 152, 157, 169, 170, 173, 180, 211, 219, 225
Eucharist, 68, 107, 119
evangelism, 24, 37, 68–69, 88, 107–8, 122–23, 132, 143, 163, 192, 196, 210; strategies pursued by young Dinka, 40, 45, 53, 66, 104–5, 123, 205
Evans-Pritchard, E. E., 13n4, 164–65, 183
exile, 132, 166, 168, 178

flooding, 10, 15, 42, 174, 194
foreign aid, 89; *see also* international aid
Fugnido Refugee Camp; *see* Pinyudu Refugee Camp

Garang, John, 61, 92, 99, 102, 155, 174, 175
Garang, Wilson, 126–27, 163
Garang Anyieth, Nathaniel, xiv, 45–46, 59, 67, 73, 75, 81, 90, 119–20, 137, 147, 177–78, 181, 197, 202n34, 204, 219, 221, 232; ministry in east-bank communities, 1–4, 53–54, 63–65, 83, 84n67, 85–86, 109; ministry in west-bank communities, 126–27, 129; Pentecostal background, 53, 78–79, 86–87; relationship to Kon Ajith, 187, 191–92, 195–96, 204; theological views of, 153, 157, 172–73
gender, 4, 12, 56, 133–35, 140, 149, 228,
generational relations, 4, 7, 18–19, 29, 50, 73, 93, 109, 133, 154, 164–165, 182, 216, 222,
God, 1, 2, 30, 40, 45, 62, 76, 82, 93, 107–8, 137–38, 142–46, 154–56, 158, 161, 177, 180–81, 183, 193–94, 196–97, 199, 210–12, 216, 225; Dinka views of, 70, 74, 92, 94, 111, 133, 122–24, 151–52, 155, 167–69, 171–72, 174–75; role in civil war, 88, 145, 149, 152, 157, 163, 173, 201–2; *see also* Nhialic
Good News Bible, 171–73
Gordon, Charles, 22
Gordon Memorial Sudan Mission, 22, 37
Gulu, Uganda, 147

Hastings, Adrian, 56
healing prayer, 81, 136–37
Holy Cross, 19
Horton, Robin, 4, 5, 57, 100, 153, 218–19
Hosea (biblical prophet), 151
Hutchinson, Sharon, 76, 77, 203n35
hymnal, 122, 128, 134, 145–50, 161, 209; *see also Bung de Diɛt ke Duɔ̈ɔ̈r*
hymns, 7, 31, 60, 85, 115, 117, 121, 128, 142, 144, 146–48, 168, 191, 205–6, 216, 218, 223, 225; composition by women, 134–35, 144, 146, 148–50, 161; as expressions of Dinka theology, 134–35, 151–58, 173, 181, 184, 223; relation to Christian conversion, 107–8, 118–19, 130, 137; *see also* hymnal; music

illiteracy, 108, 184; *see also* orality
independency, Christian, 60, 85–88, 220
international aid/assistance, 89, 98, 114, 178, 213, 222

Isaiah (biblical prophet), 164, 166, 171–74, 181, 189, 196, 216; chapter 18 as prophetic text, 163, 169n17, 170–75, 184, 194, 203, 214–15, 223
Islam, 12, 91, 156, 169
Israelites, 114, 118, 167, 168, 175
Itang Refugee Camp (Ethiopia), 99, 103, 104, 105, 106, 109, 110, 132

Jeremiah, 169n17, 196
Jiech amer, 102, 125
Jieng, 13, 28, 133, 179–80; see also Dinka
Jo Wo Liec, 122–23, 128, 134, 141–42, 147, 156, 216, 223
jɔk (pl. *jak*), 40, 42, 60, 68–69, 71, 74, 82–83, 91–93, 98, 111, 122, 131, 138–39, 145, 151, 161–63, 167, 190, 214–15, 218; Christian conversion providing protection from, 77, 109, 112; destruction of by Christian converts, 75–77, 92, 126, 191–93, 196–98, 201; repudiation of as part of Christian conversion, 27, 73, 78–79, 93, 148–49, 151–52, 157, 160, 194–95; role in causing the civil war, 88, 152, 154, 172; role in traditional religion, 17, 30, 68, 81, 30, 94, 136; seen as undermining Dinka welfare, 77, 202–3; understand as agents of evil, 153, 154–57
Jones, Richard, 30
Jonglei Canal, 36
Juba, xxiv, 26, 33, 35, 51–54, 60–62, 64, 78, 98, 107, 146, 169, 187, 191, 224
Juba Conference, 35
jur, 167–68

Kakuma Refugee Camp, 114–17, 121, 125, 132, 150, 156, 168; church in, 114–15, 117–24, 128, 130, 142–45, 147, 158–60
Kejok, 206–7
Kelei, John, 92, 195, 197–98, 201, 215
Kenya, xxiii, 3, 46, 53, 87, 92, 97–99, 113–14, 116–19, 121, 124, 130, 132, 142, 159–60, 173, 180, 181, 225, 229
Khartoum, 1, 3, 22–23, 41–45, 51–54, 61, 64, 66, 72–73, 79, 91, 97–100, 105, 115, 131n101, 135, 139, 155, 175, 205, 211, 214, 219, 224
Khartoum North congregation, 44, 52
Kimbangu, Simon, 204
Kitchener, Lord, 21
Kon Ajith, Paul, 92, 187–92, 195–99, 201–4, 200n28, 205, 215–16, 228
Kongor, 32, 38–40, 42–43, 47, 97, 135
Kuei Marier, Martha, 133, 137

Lambeth Conference, 170n20, 221
Lau, 181–82
Leopold, King of Belgium, 21
Lienhardt, Godfrey, 13n4, 15–18, 145, 167, 191n4
Lierpiɔu, 17, 23, 40–41, 47, 57, 92, 153
literacy, 5, 72, 122, 135, 172, 185, 205, 223; connection to Christian conversion, 28, 32, 52, 78–79, 137, 147, 184, 209–11; see also education
Loka, 30
"Lost Boys of Sudan," xxiii, 98–99,

114; *see also* unaccompanied minors
Lui, 24

Maasai, 56, 137
Maciir Makoi, Reuben, 36–38, 52, 64–67, 72, 77, 90, 139, 181, 215, 219; and healing prayer, 69, 86; ministry at Dhiaukuei, 205–6, 208–13; ministry in Khartoum, 44, 54, 78; views on baptism, 78, 80, 183
Mading Deng, Francis, 16, 146
Mahdi, the (Muhammad Ahmad bin Abd Allah), 19, 21, 22
Majok Deng, Samuel, 53
Majok Dau, Isaiah, 175
Majok Tuil, John, 142–43
Malakal, 54, 60–61, 135, 225
Malek, 23–29, 32–33, 38, 40–41, 45–46, 57, 93, 177–79
Malith, John, 208
Malou Ater, John, 44, 97, 167
Mandari, 29, 194, 197
Mangar Mamur, Benjamin, xiv, 64–65, 67, 79–80, 86–87, 137, 181, 183, 205, 219
Manyang, Kuol, 101, 174, 192, 197–98, 200n28
Manyang Jok, 82
Manyuon Gaak, Paul, 208
Maper, 139–40
Marial, Enoch, 210
Marial Thon, Petro, 74–75, 205, 209, 212
Mathiang Kuc, Stephen, 190
Matong, Dominic, 105, 142
Mayol Ajak, Andrew, 108–9
Mayom Athiaan, Abraham, 59, 62, 64, 67, 69, 72, 77, 104, 109, 126, 138, 173, 177–78, 183, 207, 211–12; involvement in church conflict, 79–80, 183, 213, 219; relationship to SPLA, 90, 177, 213
Melut, 13, 28
Mengistu Haile Mariam, 99, 113
Meyer, Birgit, 154
Midian, 169
migration, 4, 6–8, 10, 35, 60, 125, 128, 130, 162, 218, 223; to northern Sudan, 42–46; rural to urban, 12, 35, 42, 46–47, 50–51, 55, 57; urban to rural, 60–61, 217, 219; *see also* displacement
miracles, 69, 207
missionaries, 2, 6, 11–12, 19–20, 22–29, 33, 35, 38–41, 45, 56, 66, 79–80, 86, 129, 146–47, 152–54, 164, 166, 170, 185, 189, 204, 208, 214–15, 217, 219, 222, 229; and education, 24–26, 29, 32, 38, 43–44, 79, 107, 121, 133–34, 184; views of by Dinka, 176–83, 208; views of Dinka religious change, 27–28, 30–31; *see also* Church Missionary Society
modernity, 26, 36, 49–50, 57, 90–91, 217, 222
Moru, 11, 24, 30, 42, 55
Mou, Stephen, 128, 147
Mount Zion, 172, 194
Mundri, 44, 55, 63
Murle, 194, 197
music, 38, 133, 145–46, 148, 150; role in Christian evangelism, 97, 107–8, 137, 147; *see also* hymns

Naam River, 206
Nairobi Pentecostal Bible College, 46, 53

New Sudan Council of Churches (NSCC), 84n67, 90, 105, 120, 139, 147, 175, 229–30
New Testament, 32, 53, 166, 167, 209
Ngalamu, Elinana, 55, 64
Ngundeng Bong, 165–66, 184, 189, 194
Nhialic, 16, 18, 94, 142–45, 149–50, 156, 161–62, 164, 202; *see also* God
Nhomlau, Paul, 53, 78
Nikkel, Marc, 117, 143–44, 187, 190n1, 199, 201n29, 202n34, 229–30, 232
Nile River, 1–2, 9, 12, 15, 19, 21, 24, 39, 59, 114, 189, 191
Nilotic peoples, 9, 12, 13n4, 38, 41, 61, 99, 112, 164, 166, 183, 203
Nimeiri, Gaafar, 47, 60
Nimule, 114–15, 120, 142, 145
Nubia, 169
Nuer, 13, 19, 20, 56, 61, 76–77, 92, 104–5, 115–116, 142, 156, 164–65, 183, 194, 197, 200n28, 203
Nyanroor Duoot Chol, Mary, 135

Old Testament, 151, 164–69, 170, 172, 174; belief that Sudan appears in, 166, 168–70; translation of, 32, 166, 166n8
orality, 148, 172, 175, 180, 183–85, 209, 223
ordination, 31–32, 44, 52, 64, 68, 87, 127, 128, 205, 206
Ottoman Empire, 19

Pacong, 48–49, 70
Pakeo, 198, 200, 201, 203, 215
Pal Mut, Joseph, 104

Peel, J. D. Y., 131, 160
Pentecostalism, 79, 86, 221
Pinyudu (alt. Fugnido, Panyido) Refugee Camp, 99–101, 103, 105–6, 108–9, 132
Port Sudan, 45
prayers, 31, 74, 75, 142–45, 206; in relation to healing, 69–70, 144, 206
praying, 67–68, 70, 75, 126, 142, 144
preaching centers, 67–68, 70, 84–85, 91, 104, 130, 136, 138, 140, 161
prophecy, 9, 163–66, 173, 175, 178, 180–82, 183–85, 197, 202–3, 214, 218
prophet(s), 6, 9, 18, 82, 86, 92, 163–66, 171–73, 176, 178–79, 180n53, 181–83, 187, 189–90, 192–96, 198–99, 202–4, 215, 228

ran Nhialic, 164; *see also* prophet
refugee camps, 45–46, 64, 79, 98–99, 113, 115, 130–34, 141, 145, 152, 161, 207, 213, 217, 219, 224–25; abrupt closure of camps in Ethiopia in 1991, 113, 142; church life in, 104, 108–10, 122–24, 134, 173, 180, 211; connection with SPLA training camps, 101–3, 138; education in, 105–6; *see also* Kakuma Refugee Camp; Pinyudu Refugee Camp
refugees, 2, 98, 102–3, 105, 115, 125–26, 132, 144, 223; Christianity among, 103, 111–15, 123–25, 128, 132, 155–57; in Ethiopia, 98–100, 111, 113, 141, 173, 219; in Kenya, 99, 114, 116–18,

120–21, 123, 144, 159–60, 229; in Uganda, 99, 114
religious change, 9–10, 11–12, 30, 33, 35, 51, 56, 59–60, 86, 95, 97–98, 104, 109, 111, 113, 141, 145, 162, 164, 166, 176–85, 194, 199, 202–4, 209, 221, 225, 230; connection to war, 88–94, 130–32, 133–35, 171, 189, 222; in first civil war, 46–47; theories of, 3–7, 131–32, 160–61, 206, 214–16, 218–19, 223; *see also* conversion
Renk, 13
riäk, 10, 20, 57, 82, 91, 95, 166, 215, 225
Roman Catholic church, 8, 87, 103–5, 123, 128–30, 142, 175, 180n53; and missionary sphere system, 23, 97, 125, 163
Roman Catholic mission, 9, 19, 20, 125, 130, 163
Rumbek, 23, 36–38, 44, 48, 52, 54–55, 60–61, 64, 66, 73, 84, 97, 139, 183, 193, 205, 206, 211, 220
Rumbek, Diocese of (Anglican), 52, 55, 63, 84, 142, 176
Rumbek, Diocese of (Roman Catholic), 96, 130n99
Rumbek Senior Secondary School, 36, 45, 64
Runcie, Robert, 2, 109, 178, 219

sacrifice, 18, 27, 40, 47, 68–69, 136, 161, 190, 207; of animals in worship, 14–15, 17, 81; as Christian theological concept, 159–60, 215; relation to Christian concept of sin, 157–58
schools, 31, 36–40, 47–49, 51, 178, 181; in refugee camps, 105–7, 114, 117, 121; part of CMS mission effort, 24–26, 29, 39, 64, 73, 184; part of Dinka church, 43–44, 71, 91; *see also* education
Scroggins, Deborah, 200n28
Sharland, Leonard, 31, 37–42, 134,
Shaw, Archibald, 24, 29, 32, 37, 134, 190, 214–16; seen as prophet, 163–64, 176–83, 185
sin, 27, 53, 151, 155–57
slave trading, 19
South Sudan (independent country), 8, 8n15, 87, 88, 162, 185, 224–25, 227–29; *see also* southern Sudan
Southern Policy, 26, 35
southern Sudan (region of Sudan), 1–3, 6–9, 11–12, 18–19, 21–24, 28–29, 32, 35–36, 57, 73, 87, 89, 91, 95, 98, 100, 102, 104–5, 107, 110–11, 113–15, 121, 125–26, 129–31, 133–34, 138, 141–42, 145, 161, 164, 165, 170, 172, 174, 176, 178–81, 198, 204, 217, 219–20, 222, 227
students, 24–26, 30–33, 37–38, 40–41, 43, 48, 51, 54, 60, 62, 73, 105–6, 121, 169, 210–11, 225
Sudan, 2, 4, 19, 21, 22, 25, 30, 35, 103, 108–9, 113, 115–17, 120, 147, 173, 176, 178, 199, 225; appearance in Bible, 163, 166, 169–71, 173–75; civil war in, 3, 41, 73, 133, 156; independence of, 3, 35, 41; "new Sudan," 61, 102; northern Sudan, 44–46, 217; *see also* southern Sudan; Sudan's second civil war
Sudan Armed Forces (SAF), 1, 61, 64, 66, 126, 156, 187, 192, 194, 197, 198, 200–201, 203, 206

Sudan Pentecostal Churches, 53, 175
Sudan People's Liberation Army (SPLA), 1, 61, 62, 65–66, 68, 70–72, 76, 84, 88–89, 91, 97, 99, 102–4, 107, 109–10, 113, 115–16, 124, 126, 130, 133, 136, 138–39, 147, 151, 172, 174, 177, 180, 187, 194, 196–98, 200n28, 201, 203, 208, 213; appearance in Christian hymns, 155–56; division in, 92–93, 113, 116, 198, 221; relationship with church, 64, 89–90, 112, 174, 192, 195; role in sending unaccompanied minors to Ethiopia, 101–2, 108
Sudan Relief and Rehabilitation Association, 71, 89
Sudan's first civil war, 12, 44–47, 51, 60–61, 92, 165
Sudan's second civil war, 1–3, 11–12, 35, 55, 57, 66, 84, 86, 98–99, 113, 137, 141, 146, 148–49, 155, 157, 165, 168, 170–73, 175, 177–80, 185, 189–90, 192, 217, 220, 223, 225, 227; beginning of, 3, 57, 61, 205; as conflict between Christians and Muslims, 91, 156; connection to religious change, 6–9, 35, 59–60, 88–91, 94n91, 130–31, 161, 163, 204, 213–15, 217–19, 222; end, 218, 224; impact on Dinka life, 60, 73–74, 133–34, 162, 203, 217–18; as *riäk*, 10, 91, 95, 166, 215, 225
Sudan United Mission, 28
Sudd, 13, 36

Taban, Paride, 175
theology, Christian, 31–32, 124, 149–51, 161, 163, 222, 225; as popular theology, 150, 152, 154, 156; political theology of war, 134, 150–56, 172
Thiec Nhialic, 134, 142–45, 150, 156, 161, 162; *see also* women in the church
tiet (*tit*), 18, 74, 181
toc, 15, 21, 57, 189, 206
Tonj, 23, 84
Torit, 3, 41, 175
translation, 146, 148, 153, 167–68, 184, 216; of Book of Common Prayer, 32, 52, 53, 220; of Bible, 53, 122, 166, 169, 170–71
Turkana, 56, 116, 142

Uganda, 3, 45–46, 92, 98–99, 114, 147, 154, 225
unaccompanied minors, 98, 99, 100, 104, 108, 114, 125, 131, 132, 141, 142, 223; *see also* "Lost Boys of Sudan"
United Nations, 99, 103, 143
United Nations High Commission on Refugees (UNHCR), 123, 232

Verona Fathers Mission, 22; *see also* Roman Catholic mission

Wadé Harris, William, 204
war; *see* civil war
Wau, xxiii, 23, 61, 97, 125–27, 180n53, 205
Wesley, Charles, 149
White Nile; *see* Nile River
Witts, Diana, 177–78
women in the church, 2, 8, 54–55, 69, 70, 83, 85, 127, 132, 133–150, 156, 158–59, 162, 184, 191, 228; during mission period

12, 28, 31, 134–35; role in evangelism and church leadership, 55, 76, 112, 133–34, 136–41, 161, 210; role in music composition, 145–50, 161–62; role in refugee camps, 112, 141–45, 158–59; *see also Thiec Nhialic*
World Council of Churches, 90
World War II, 12, 29, 33, 35, 37
worship, 5, 40, 52, 64, 67–69, 76, 84, 92, 104–5, 112, 117, 119, 133, 136, 138, 146, 147, 150, 152, 162–63, 172, 174, 180, 212, 220
wut, 13–14, 17; *see also* cattle camp

Yambio, 28, 30, 32

yath (pl. *yiëth*), 16, 94
Yirol, 36, 38, 61, 84, 168, 183, 205, 206
young people, 8, 12, 29, 36, 40, 45, 102, 108, 111–15, 131, 140, 142, 156, 161; leadership role in Christian conversion movement, 62, 73–76, 83, 97–100, 104–5, 118–19, 122–24, 127, 130; prophecy about, 179–81; *see also Jo Wo Liec*
Yugusuk, Benjamina, 63–64, 120, 170, 172, 176

Zande, 11, 28, 30, 32, 222
Zion, Mount; *see* Mount Zion
Zion Church, 194, 198–200, 201n29